Children in Secure Accommodation

of related interest

Children's Homes and School Exclusion
Redefining the Problem
Isabelle Brodie
ISBN 1 85302 943 2

The Child's World
Assessing Children in Need
Edited by Jan Horwath
ISBN 1 85302 957 2

Public Inquiries into Abuse of Children in Residential Care
Brian Corby, Alan Doig and Vicki Roberts
ISBN 1 85302 895 9

State Child Care
Looking After Children?
Carol Hayden, Jim Goddard, Sarah Gorin and Niki Van Der Spek
ISBN 1 85302 670 0

Issues in Foster Care
Policy, Practice and Research
Edited by Greg Kelly and Robbie Gilligan
ISBN 1 85302 465 1

Understanding Drug Issues
A Workbook of Photocopiable Resources Raising Issues for Young People
David Emmett and Graeme Nice
ISBN 1 85302 558 5

Young People Leaving Care
Life After the Children Act 1989
Bob Broad
ISBN 1 85302 412 0

Children in Secure Accommodation

A Gendered Exploration of Locked Institutional Care for Children in Trouble

Teresa O'Neill

Foreword by Allan Levy QC

Jessica Kingsley Publishers
London and Philadelphia

First published in the United Kingdom in 2001 by
Jessica Kingsley Publishers Ltd
116 Pentonville Road
London N1 9JB, England
and
325 Chestnut Street
Philadelphia, PA 19106, USA

www.jkp.com

Library of Congress Cataloging in Publication Data
A CIP catalog record for this book is available from the Library of Congress

British Library Cataloguing in Publication Data
A CIP catalogue record for this book is available from the British Library

ISBN 1 85302 933 5

Printed and Bound in Great Britain by
Athenaeum Press, Gateshead, Tyne and Wear

Contents

List of tables

Foreword

This novel study examines the use of local authority secure accommodation as a response to children in trouble. It examines comprehensively the circumstances and experiences of girls and boys who have been put in secure accommodation under welfare and criminal justice legislation. It focuses in particular on the generally neglected position of girls and gender differences in the treatment of young people. The voices of the young people are heard. The study is based on six secure units run by English local authorities.

In recent years there has been a real sense of unease in many quarters about the perceived enthusiasm for locking up young people and specifically in regard to the workings of the secure accommodation system. This important and timely book, with its in depth coverage of all the relevant aspects, provides the mature observations and conclusions that put secure accommodation in its proper perspective. It is especially useful now that young people can draw on the Human Rights Act 1998 and the U.N. Convention on the Rights of the Child in order to protect themselves when necessary and to try and ensure that their needs are appropriately met.

The book may also prompt the search for better practices and procedures for children in trouble. The study demonstrates that for many children, particularly girls, secure accommodation is not the right answer and may be counter-productive. The inside stories related in the book should prompt the authorities, both central and local, to search energetically for better alternatives.

Allan Levy QC
London, 2001

Acknowledgements

I am very grateful to the University of Bristol for support which enabled me to undertake this research, and especially to staff, colleagues and friends in the School for Policy Studies. Most of all I am indebted to Dr Elaine Farmer for her invaluable advice and encouragement throughout the research, to whom I would like to express my warmest thanks. I would also like to thank Professor David Berridge and Professor Hilary Land for their encouragement and advice on the manuscript.

I am indebted to the local authorities and the managers and staff in the secure units who allowed me access to this controversial area of service and practice and who shared their experiences and views, and to the young people's social workers who participated in the research. All of their contributions were invaluable. Most of all I am grateful to the courageous young people who shared with me their stories. For the purposes of confidentiality, their names must remain anonymous.

Introduction

This book is about children in trouble, and specifically the children who are incarcerated through the care and criminal justice systems in secure accommodation provided by local authority social services departments. The concept of 'troubled' and 'troublesome' children is broad and includes those who have committed serious crimes as well as minor misdemeanours, children 'at risk' as well as those whose behaviour, such as running away, constitutes an offence because of their status as children.

Children conceptualized as 'troubled' or 'troublesome' have become the focus of increasing political and media attention since the early 1990s in the re-politicization and prioritization of youth crime and the systematic demonization of all children in trouble.

Ironically, this backlash against children in trouble, who have been characterized as a threat to society, has occurred simultaneously with a new concern with the rights of children stimulated by the UN Convention on the Rights of the Child.

Policy and practice with children in trouble in the care and criminal justice systems have been significantly influenced by the competing ideological priorities of 'welfare' and 'justice'. Historically, the legal and professional systems have witnessed swings between these two polarized paradigms, but in recent years policy and practice towards children in trouble have increasingly been focused on control, punishment and retribution. The treatment of boys and girls is different within the care and criminal justice systems which makes this a gendered issue. Consistent with the swing toward control and punishment, since the early 1990s there has been substantial government investment in custodial facilities for children, in a political and social climate that has witnessed an increase in the use of custody and a widening of the net of those likely to be locked up, and changes in the criminal justice legislation which reflect the renewed commitment to incarceration as the solution for children in trouble. As well as investment in prison service provision such as young offender institutions and the three privately-run secure training centres, there has been an expansion of local authority secure accommodation through a joint-funded Department of Health/Home Office capital development programme. The increase in secure accommodation has taken place at the same time as the substantial reduction in the number of non-secure children's homes, and it seems that the supply-led nature of secure accommodation has resulted in the admission through both care and criminal justice systems of some children who would formerly have been accommodated in non-secure care.

Local authority secure accommodation is an ambiguous and controversial custodial facility provided under the Children Act 1989 by local authority social services departments. It accommodates children 'at risk' in the community admitted through the care system together with different categories of offender admitted through the criminal justice system. It seems an elusive concept, but is essentially a means of social control and it has been described as both 'incarceration' (for those who would otherwise be 'looked after' by their families or in community placements) and 'an alternative to incarceration' (for those in the criminal justice system who would otherwise be placed in secure training centres, young offender institutions or prison) (Harris and Timms 1993, p.4). It is the interface where the conflicting philosophies of welfare and justice represented by these two systems converge, resulting in a prevailing confusion about whether it provides care or punishment and constraining the opportunities for staff as well as young people to make the experience a positive one. As the majority of residents are admitted through criminal justice routes, and conceptualized as offenders rather than children in need, it functions and is now seen as a facility for offenders, with the emphasis on control and punishment rather than care and therapeutic intervention. This has serious implications for all the children inside, but particularly the non-offenders, the majority of whom are girls who have been largely invisible in the discourse about youth crime.

The research described in this book developed out of my interest with children in trouble who are at the margins of or excluded from their families, communities and mainstream society and my professional involvement with children placed in secure accommodation. The complexities and ideological confusion characterized by secure accommodation raised imperative issues for investigation. Of particular interest in this research is the position of girls, and gender differences in the treatment of young people in the care and criminal justice systems. In the secure unit population, between a quarter and a third are girls (DH 2000), and an examination of their experiences of secure accommodation, in girls' units and with boys in mixed-gender units, is overdue. Girls are more frequently policed and controlled through the welfare system, and those in the criminal justice system often find themselves subject to a double penalty. Most of the previous studies of secure provision for young people have focused exclusively or predominantly on the position of boys within the system, perhaps unsurprisingly, as secure accommodation has been regarded primarily as a facility for offenders, and so by definition for boys. With a few exceptions, research has neglected the position of girls in the wider residential care world as well as in secure provision (see Ackland 1982; Giallombardo 1974; Petrie 1986).

The main focus of this study was the children living in secure accommodation. However, the research also explored professional views on the roles of secure accommodation and on some of the key issues of debate, and these were important both in their own right and in providing a context for the children's stories. The research examined the purpose of secure accommodation, the regimes and practice in the units, the balance between care and control including the use of sanctions, the debate about specialization on the basis of legal status and gender, relationships in the units, contact between the units and other professionals, including social workers and other agencies involved in the wider child care world, the provision of specialist therapeutic services and the ability of secure unit staff to address the complex needs of the children and to evaluate the impact of placements in achieving positive outcomes.

The investigation of the professional perspectives of secure unit managers and staff and the young people's field social workers in the care and youth justice systems revealed some similarities but many more very significant and disturbing differences in attitudes, expectations and practice between members of staff in the units, between the six secure units and between the units and the field social workers involved in the provision of child care services.

Aims

The main purpose of my research is to investigate under-researched issues in the use of local authority secure accommodation as a response to children in trouble, through an examination of the circumstances and experiences of girls and boys admitted under welfare and criminal justice legislation. A key objective is to explore the young people's own constructions of their lives, as their voices are largely absent in the research literature. Becker (1967) contends that the 'official' definitions of problems by those in power are accepted too readily while 'lower participants' in services have no right to be heard, so those in power define both the problem and its solution. This is evident in the approach to young people held in secure conditions (Millham *et al.* 1978).

The primary aim of this book is to fill some of the gaps in the knowledge and understanding of the meaning and effect of placement in secure accommodation, from the standpoint of the young people and the professional staff most closely involved with them, that is their social workers and the managers and staff in the secure units, and to provoke thought and discussion on the part of those involved in the provision of secure accommodation and other services for children 'in need' in the care and criminal justice systems.

The research had a number of more specific aims to enable the investigation and analysis of similarities and differences between young people on the basis of their legal status and admission route, as well as their gender:

- To carry out an intensive study of a mixed-gender sample of young people admitted to secure accommodation through all the legal routes of entry, in order to:
  - (i) examine the characteristics and backgrounds of the children and the circumstances precipitating their placement in secure accommodation
  - (ii) examine the young people's experiences of the regimes in the units, the care and therapeutic interventions provided and their views on the value of these, and their perspectives on the mix within units of girls and boys and offenders and non-offenders
  - (iii) consider the impact of the young people's experiences on their views of themselves and to examine gender differences in their experiences, perspectives and levels of self-esteem.
- To examine the perspectives of social workers on the needs and reasons for young people's admission, the value of the placements and their general views on the role and function of secure accommodation, and to investigate the views of staff and managers in the secure units with regard to the practice in the units and the role and function of secure accommodation.

Finally, this study shares an important objective of research, that is to achieve change in policy and practice through the sharing of personal experiences which provide the foundation for the development of theoretical understanding, analysis and consciousness (MacKinnon 1987; Stanley and Wise 1993).

Design of the Research

Berridge and Brodie (1998, p.25) suggest that 'in-depth studies of children's homes must be among the most sensitive and potentially threatening areas of social inquiry'. The residential child-care world is characterized by defensiveness (Nunno and Motz 1988) and 'defence mechanisms' are particularly rigorously employed in secure accommodation. Littlewood (1996) contends that secure units operate in a climate of secrecy which can be attributed to the fear of adverse media publicity, and that restriction of information is the main defence mechanism employed (Blumenthal 1985). Research which is designed to illuminate processes in secure accommodation must therefore be regarded as 'socially sensitive' (Sieber and Stanley 1988, p.49). Moreover, Lee (1993) argues that research is likely to have implications for the researcher and the research participants where it meets one or more of three criteria: where it deals with private and stressful issues, where it studies social control and where the findings may be incriminating (Lee 1993). It is suggested that some researchers have avoided the problems of studying sensitive issues by opting out of such research completely (Sieber and Stanley 1988) but by not doing research with children on matters of concern to them, it is argued that social researchers may fail to prevent harm (Alderson 1995).

In view of the sensitive nature of this research, a high priority was accorded to ensuring confidentiality and privacy to participants and all the customary assurances were given. Confidentiality for children is a contentious issue and there have been many conflicting court rulings regarding their rights in this area. Young people in secure accommodation are normally afforded little confidentiality or privacy. The work with young people described here was undertaken privately and they were guaranteed confidentiality, with the essential exception if it emerged that they or someone they knew was at risk of harm. This reservation was included in the research agreement, and was discussed with young people before the work started.

The research was undertaken between September 1996 and June 1997 and focused on six secure units run by English local authorities which were selected to provide a combination of metropolitan and shire authorities, single- and mixed-gender units, older and newly developed units located in different geographical regions of England. There are 31 secure units in England and Wales accommodating almost 500 young people.

Selection of the Sample

The six secure units were invited to participate in the study through an initial written approach to the Directors of Social Services. The information provided to local authorities at this stage included the aims and design of the research study together with brief details of my professional experience with young people. Confidentiality and anonymity were assured to the local authorities and secure units. The negotiations in each local authority proceeded over varying periods of time and involved written and telephone communication and meetings with the secure unit managers and staff who were given information about the research aims and design and individual invitations to participate in focus discussion groups.

The young people who were accommodated in the units at that time were invited to group meetings about the research, and all those who attended were given individual written invitations to participate in the study. The aim was to engage a self-selecting mixed-gender sample of approximately 30 young people, representing all the legal admission routes, and to involve young people from minority ethnic groups where possible. As boys form the majority in secure accommodation, there were potentially more male participants, although it was anticipated that the research design, as well as my own gender, might have a positive influence on the participation of girls. As it turned out more girls than boys participated in the study. In addition to the above factors, the proportion of male/female participants was influenced by one unit which at the time of the study was in transition from single to mixed gender and accommodated only girls. Access to some young people required the agreement of their parents and written information about the research was sent to seven parents, followed up in several cases by a telephone discussion. Of the 50 young people who were invited, 35 expressed their wish to take part, although 3 of these did not proceed beyond the initial meeting.

With the young people's agreement, information about the research was sent to their social workers and followed up by telephone contact to discuss the research and to pre-arrange an interview. However, 13 young people were placed by 12 local authorities in 'out of area' secure units, so the agreement of these local authorities was also required. This was negotiated directly by written and telephone contact with the responsible social worker or their manager. Although none of them refused access to the young people, four of these local authorities were unwilling for social workers to participate in research interviews.

Theory and Concepts

This research was undertaken within the interpretive paradigm, complemented by feminist theories and a children's rights perspective (Fox Harding 1991). These analyses have particular relevance to this study, which involves children as research participants and has an especial interest in gender issues.

The interpretive paradigm is characterized by a commitment to the representation and interpretation of the multiple realities described by research participants in terms of the concepts, behaviours and accounts of the people it is about, and the use of qualitative research methodologies. Within this paradigm the researcher is seen as the primary research instrument and an active participant in the research process. In rejecting the value-free objectivist stance of the positivist approach, it emphasises the inevitably value-laden nature of research design, inquiry and interpretation (Denzin 1989). The personal involvement of the researcher is recognized as an important element in establishing trust with the participants. Participants' views of the researcher and the research itself influence the nature of their involvement and responses. Similarly, the experiences of the researcher are brought into the research and the inter-dependence and subjectivity of the researcher and the research participants, the influence they have on the process and the findings, are recognized as a natural and inevitable part of the social process of research.

The involvement of children in research studies about them is contentious. Although the UN Convention on the Rights of the Child includes principles which support the involvement of children in research, it continues to be the case that children are excluded from research about them, leaving them 'strangely silent' (Alderson 1995, p.1). The need to protect vulnerable children from possible exploitation by researchers has been used to justify a cautious attitude by adults and professionals to granting access to children. However, Jones and Myers (1997) suggest that children's silence is contrived to protect the interests of institutions and observe that research with children is generally regarded as a negative and complex process. New ways of thinking in research ethics with children have been advocated (Alderson 1995; NCH 1994). It is argued that while traditional ethics rightly stresses the importance of avoiding harm to research participants, little is said of the harm which can result from 'protecting' children to the extent that they are silenced and excluded from research. There is a danger that the protection of young people who are considered vulnerable may amount to no more than paternalism which denies them the opportunity to make choices on their own behalf and the support which they need to be able to do so.

The power of the researcher is multi-dimensional and there are two important aspects of the concept of power-sharing which are especially relevant here. The first concerns the complexities involved in working in an empowering way with participants in institutions where they experience unequal power relationships along a number of dimensions, including age and gender. In such situations the vulnerability of research participants can be increased by the information which they reveal. The second concerns the concept of power itself and the power held by the institutions being studied. Where research involves studying institutions, the researcher's concern shifts from power-sharing to limiting the power of the institutions to prevent the exploration of the issues of concern to the research questions, which may be hidden (Kelly *et al.* 1994). It is argued that where unequal power relationships are observed, oppressive attitudes and behaviour should be challenged through the process of the research and exposed.

Research Methods

A variety of complementary methods was used for data collection in the study, comprising narrative interviews, semi-structured telephone interviews and group interviews, with three different groups of research participants: the young people, their social workers and the managers and staff in the secure units. These complementary methods were chosen because they are traditionally associated with interpretive and feminist research and are seen as the way to achieve inter-subjectivity and non-hierarchical relationships between researcher and research participants (Kelly *et al.* 1994). In addition, to complete the work with the young people, a standardized questionnaire, the 'Self-Perception Profile for Adolescents' (Harter 1988) was used to measure the levels of their self-worth. The use of this measure enabled an exploration of differences between young people on the basis of gender and admission route, in comparison with the findings from other studies and with the young people's descriptions of themselves. Its use was consistent with the research approach in that it was administered to young people at the conclusion of the narrative interviews to encourage and facilitate continuing self-reflection.

Young People

The young people participated in a preliminary meeting and two interviews conducted privately approximately one week apart, that in total took an average of three hours. The approach to the interviews with the young people was through an examination of self narratives, that is the stories they tell about their lives and their interpretation of events. Narrative is described as 'a way of organising episodes, actions and accounts of actions … the narrative allows for the inclusion of actors' reasons for their acts, as well as the causes of happening' (Sarbin 1986, p.9). A self narrative is characterized by four features. First, it is told from the perspective of the author, relating the activity of telling the story to the self-concept. Second, self narratives relate elements of relevance to the self across time, so the story is about the past, the present and usually also includes a future prospect. Third, they are ordered, so that the elements of the story are organized sequentially. The final characteristic is conformity with the standards of rational explanation to ensure the story is understandable to the audience. The use of personal narratives as data, which gives prominence to human agency and imagination, is an approach particularly suited to feminist studies and studies of subjectivity and identity (Mishler 1986; Riessman 1993).

There were several factors which informed the choice of narrative as a main source of data. Self narrative is a primary way that people make sense of difficult life transitions and experiences, particularly those which have been defining or traumatic (Bruner 1990). Through self narrative the individual attempts to make connections and understand the relationship between life events (Gergen and Gergen 1988). Self narrative facilitates and supports young people in exploring their experiences, and allows their own construction and interpretation of the world and their problems to emerge. The exploration of personal narratives can be a means of empowering those who are unused to speaking and being heard, and thereby obtaining new insights into young people's experiences and a more complete understanding of their situations. Furthermore, self narrative is an important social skill which can be used as a means of creating and amending one's sense of self (Gergen and Gergen 1983). The importance attached to the development of identity in adolescence means that this approach is particularly appropriate for work with young people, especially those whose self-concept may have been adversely affected by the events in their lives.

One of the issues resulting from the use of this method is that it produces inconsistent data and therefore provides incomplete coverage of the research questions. This is because the interviews were structured as far as possible to allow young people control over the material they included in their narratives, while at the same time addressing the issues of interest to the research aims. While all the young people addressed all the issues of interest to the research questions, there were differences in their coverage of the issues. Although some comprehensiveness was sacrificed, the use of the method can be justified on the basis of the quality of the data it produced overall. It also met the objective that the research process should provide positive benefit for the participant young people.

Recording and Transcribing

The use of a portable computer was chosen as the method for recording the interviews with young people, to complement the use of self narrative in the attempt to redress the power imbalance inherent in the traditional interview situation (Apter 1990; Martin 1995). This method, which was chosen with awareness of the potential loss of the benefits of tape-recording (Millett 1971; Riessman 1993), involves the researcher typing the spoken word into a computer. In practice, as speakers see all their words transcribed the process slows encouraging self-reflection and authenticity, with speakers taking control of the written text by instructing amendments to be made. This self-reflection is supported by the space created when the speaker pauses to allow the researcher to catch up. The speaker has possession of all the material at the conclusion of the interview to encourage and support continuing reflection. Agreement was reached in advance with secure unit staff and social workers to ensure that the young people's ownership of the research material and confidentiality would be respected.

Secure Unit Managers and Staff

Managers and staff in the units were invited to participate in focus group interviews. Separate groups for staff and managers were arranged in recognition of disparities in power between them and to avoid potential constraints on the expression of their views. The purpose was to engage those working in the secure units in the research, to obtain their perspectives on the role and function of secure accommodation, and in the hope that they would provide a potential source of support for young people participating in the study. It was the intention to engage staff in reflecting on their own practice, and to identify differences between the stated philosophy and the realities of practice in the units. Group interviews were considered to be an appropriate method, as staff share the experience of working in secure units, and the issues to be addressed were not thought to be too sensitive to be shared in groups. However, this proved not to be the case in two units where some members of staff requested individual interviews, as they wanted to express their views confidentially and in another unit the group interview was postponed twice and then a smaller than expected proportion of the staff group attended. Eleven discussion groups, each of approximately an hour and a half duration, were attended by a total of 65 managers and staff. In addition, five individual semi-structured interviews were conducted. With the agreement of research participants, all the focus groups and the interviews were tape-recorded and subsequently transcribed verbatim.

Social Workers

The aim of the semi-structured telephone interviews conducted with the social workers was twofold: first, to obtain background information about the young people and the social workers' views of their placements in secure accommodation; and second, to seek the social workers' perspectives on the role and function of secure accommodation in the care and criminal justice systems. A total of 24 social workers participated in telephone interviews of approximately one and a half hours' duration which were recorded in note form. The interview with one social worker was conducted privately at the secure unit, at his request. Four social workers declined to take part on the basis of concerns about confidentiality, although one of these sent written comments about the secure unit and evaluated the young person's placement.

Structure of the Book

This book will start with a review of the research and practice literature, an examination of the legal framework for children in trouble in the care and criminal justice systems and analysis of policy and professional practice issues, to provide the broad social, legal, political and organizational context for the research. The remainder of the book will concentrate on the research study itself: Part II, Chapter 4, introduces the children who participated in the study, describing their characteristics and circumstances which provides the context for the examination of professional perspectives and the later chapters which explore the young people's experiences and views. The complexity and diversity of their needs and difficulties are compelling. Part III examines the professional context: Chapters 5–6 explore the perspectives of the secure units managers and staff on the roles of secure accommodation, the complexities of the task for staff within secure accommodation, and on the young people who are resident in secure units; Chapter 7 examines the perspectives of social workers on the young people and the roles of secure accommodation in the care and criminal justice systems. Part IV focuses on the young people's stories: Chapter 8 deals with their experiences and perspectives on their lives and circumstances before placement in secure accommodation; Chapter 9 examines their experiences in the secure units and their views on some of the important issues of debate about the use of secure accommodation; Chapter 10 examines the professional and therapeutic help offered to the young people; Chapter 11 deals with evaluation of the young people's placements and some of the short-term outcomes. Part V, Chapter 12, concludes the book with a summary of the research findings and the implications of these for policy-makers and practitioners. The findings address important themes and issues which must be taken seriously if so many already disadvantaged young people with complex needs and problems are to be helped to improve their life-chances and not to be further damaged by their placements in secure accommodation.

Terminology

The young people in this study were legally children under the Children Act 1989. They will be referred to interchangeably as children, young people, young men, young women, boys and girls. The names and some of the details of the individuals who are described have been changed to preserve confidentiality.

Part I

The Context: Research and Practice Literature

ONE

Children in Trouble

The Historical and Legal Context

Introduction

Children in contemporary society who are regarded as troubled or troublesome find themselves subject to a complex range of legal and professional measures, in a social and political climate that is hostile and punitive. Ideas about contemporary childhood are intensely political. Debates about children and young people who are seen as out of control and strategies for dealing with them have long preoccupied politicians. A recurring theme which has significantly influenced policy in the care and criminal justice systems is the relationship between the dichotomous ideologies of 'welfare' and 'justice'. The legal and professional systems have been characterized by swings between these two paradigms, reflecting changes in political philosophies and attitudes to children in trouble. Although attempts have been made to achieve a balance between welfare and justice, the basic principles of the two philosophies remain fundamentally irreconcilable (Walgrave 1996). The different and unequal treatment of girls and boys within these two paradigms in the care and criminal justice systems makes this a gendered issue.

This chapter will examine the concept of childhood, the social, legal and political context and theoretical approaches to children in trouble, from a feminist and children's rights perspective. It will establish a foundation from which to explore, in the next chapter, the nature of 'troubled' and 'troublesome' children and the professional responses to them.

Concepts and Conceptions of Childhood

The concept of childhood is socially constructed on the basis of 'culturally specific sets of ideas and philosophies, attitudes and practices' (James and Prout 1990, p.1). There are substantial areas of dispute about the nature and history of childhood. It has been argued that the significance of the historical study of childhood lies in challenging the view that it constitutes a fixed state and in providing a reminder that conceptions of childhood are constantly shifting (Frost and Stein 1989). Childhood is not a static, universal phenomenon determined by biological and psychological facts, but shifts with changing social, political and economic priorities and is experienced differently on the basis of a range of factors such as race, class, gender and economic status.

Contemporary childhood has been described as an artificial period, a separate state or stage which emphasizes inequality and the relative incompetence of children (Archard 1993; Farson 1974; Holt 1975). The UN Convention on the Rights of the Child defines a child as any person below the age of 18 years, and this wide age range spans an 'enormously varied range of needs, abilities and potentials' (Franklin 1986, p.7), although children are frequently regarded as a homogeneous group who lack the capacities, skills and powers to participate in adult activities. The division between the two states of childhood and adulthood is arbitrary as different 'adult' activities – sexual, criminal, political, medical, economic – have different qualifying ages, illustrating that the difference between childhood and adulthood reflects no more than the prevailing social priorities (Archard 1993). For example, a child is held criminally responsible at age 10 but is disenfranchised politically and economically until age 18. Furthermore, there are gender differences in where the boundaries are drawn.

The dominant conceptualization of childhood in Western culture is of an idealized 'golden age' (Holt 1975, p.22) of innocence, freedom and happiness. Because of their innocence and weakness, children are protected by adults from the 'harshness of the world outside' and the trials and tribulations of adult life to enjoy an asexual existence of freedom and pleasure within the family (Franklin 1986; Holt 1975; Kitzinger 1988). Childhood thus becomes a lost dreamworld, cut off from adult reality, but providing an escape into fantasy from the pressures of adulthood (Moore 1993; Morrison 1994). The second and related idealized perception of childhood and adult–child relationships suggests that adult treatment of children is benign, based on respect and protection of the best interests of the child (Goldson 1997a). However, a different analysis of these notions of dependence and protection reveals the social exclusion and control of children on the basis of paternalistic adult agendas and interests (Davis and Bourhill 1997; Goldson 1997a). Marginalized groups become 'objects' of state policy, and are excluded from participation in the construction of policies which are applied to them (Lea and Young 1984). In contemporary society, children are treated as 'objects' in almost all aspects of law, policy and debate affecting them.

These idealizations deny the realities of childhood and child–adult relationships experienced by many children, such as poverty and child abuse (Franklin 1986). It has been argued that such myths are impossible to sustain in the face of the increasing problems faced by children and a denial of human rights that in any other group would result in political action (Children's Rights Office 1995). Furthermore, it is argued that children form a silent, oppressed group in society who are unrepresented and denied basic civil rights and that the main differentiating factor between adults and children is power (Franklin 1986; Frost and Stein 1989). Power relations are structured so that one person or group of people benefit at the expense of another person or group of people (McNay 1992). The term 'child' indicates a specific power relationship of domination and subordination (Franklin 1986). Differentiation has been drawn between structural and personal concepts of power (Waldby 1989). Structural power is that which is accorded to individuals on the basis of factors such as age, class, gender and income. Personal power is power within the self which, when under-developed or distorted, may be harmful to others, particularly in a social environment such as the family or an institution for children, where that individual also exercises structural power.

Power relationships based on domination occur along a number of dimensions such as gender, race, sexual orientation, ability, class and economic status as well as age. Fundamental to any awareness of power relations is the acknowledgement of the interlocking nature of the different forms of domination and oppression. Black feminist writers have highlighted the interconnectedness of different forms of oppression and cautioned against the creation of a hierarchy, as 'a matrix of domination contains few pure victims or oppressors' (Collins 1990, p.229). The concept of powerlessness of children was first explored in relation to their experience of abuse (Finkelhor 1983) and the high risk of individual and systematic abuse of power in families and institutions for children has been repeatedly exposed. Jones (1993) developed a framework to analyse power relationships which illustrated the powerlessness of children, compounded when they are female, black, poor or disabled and experience stigmatization as a consequence of prevailing social attitudes, echoing others' concerns that a child's dependence is based as much on power relations as on biological immaturity (Ennew 1986; Newell 1991, 1995).

These mythical constructs of childhood partly explain the powerful adult reaction against children in trouble (Franklin 1995). During the 1990s children became the focus of a new moral panic with media portrayals of them as demons who constitute the new 'enemy within'. The killing of two-year-old James Bulger, by two ten-year-old boys in 1993 became the symbol of all that was wrong with children. Conflicting stereotypes and simplistic generalizations about children were presented, moral outrage prevailed and children were at the centre of a political agenda focused on 'law and order', designed to reverse the alleged decline in traditional values by means of discipline, punishment and control (Littlechild 1997). Pearson (1993) argues that crises about unprecedented childhood deviance and lawlessness have been a recurring feature throughout this century, revealing that the past is both forgotten and idealized by successive generations.

The language which is used to describe and define children in trouble serves further to distort the concept of childhood and alienate children. Some derogatory terms such as 'juvenile', 'delinquent', 'absconder' and 'persistent young offender', are institutionalized. Others such as 'joyrider', 'bail-bandit' and individually attributed names such as 'Ratboy' have been used by the media to construct damaging images in the process of the 'demonization' of children. There is an additional dimension to this for girls, who are subject to verbal abuse focusing on sexuality which serves as a powerful form of social control (Lees 1986,1989).

These images of children out of control have serious implications, as they determine and reflect the attitudes towards children, the policies that affect them and practices in the institutions that manage children (Stainton-Rogers and Stainton-Rogers 1992). The demonization of children has resulted in changes in policy and legislation, with a shift in emphasis away from the protection of children towards protection of the community from children and the threat they present (Franklin 1995).

The Legal Context

The recognition by the legal system of the status of childhood during the nineteenth century legitimated intervention in the lives of children and has resulted in a weight of legislation which applies to children, their relationships with their families and with the state. As children have traditionally been considered to be in need of both protection and control, they are subject to welfare and criminal justice legislation. A brief review of the legal context and theoretical concepts will provide a foundation from which to consider the political and professional responses to children in trouble.

Initially a distinction was drawn between delinquent and neglected children. Intervention in the life of the delinquent child was based on their conduct or behaviour, for which they were deemed to be responsible, while intervention in the life of the neglected child was on the basis of their status, a matter over which they were deemed to have no responsibility. However, the distinction became less clear as the emphasis on welfare 'served to consolidate children in trouble into a single conceptual category: the deprived and the depraved were one and the same' (Morris *et al.* 1980, p.7). The Children and Young Persons Act 1933 was the first legislation to require the court to have regard to the welfare of the child. The effect of this emphasis on 'welfare' was to make the child the object rather than the subject of concern, and the focus of increasing intervention as growing numbers of children were pulled into the system through assessments of their need for treatment (Thorpe *et al.* 1980).

The concepts of 'welfare' and 'justice' underpin legislation, policies and practice with children. Until recently they could be seen to be linked to the approaches characterized by the different political parties. The Conservatives used criminal justice to condemn and punish while the Labour Party emphasized a welfare approach to understanding and treating the underlying causes of behaviour. However, these political differences have become blurred since the 1990s as Labour has moved away from a 'socio-liberal' model of criminal justice (Rutherford 1997), although some differences in emphasis remain, particularly in the attitudes to poverty, unemployment and deprivation. These theoretical concepts of welfare and justice are informed by conflicting principles of care and control, treatment and punishment. The welfare model assumes that delinquency is a symptom of maladjustment resulting from adverse experiences; treatment is the preferred intervention and priority is given to the welfare of the child. In contrast, the justice model regards delinquency as a matter of choice, and as such society has the right to impose its standards through the use of controls (Rutter and Giller 1983). These dichotomous ideologies have each been subject to criticism and it is clear that they are both open to abuse, with infringements of the rights of children and the principles of natural justice (see Frost and Stein 1989; Morris *et al.* 1980; Taylor *et al.* 1980).

The ascendancy of the welfare model culminated with the Children and Young Persons Act 1969, which saw all children in trouble as 'in need', whatever the nature of their difficulties. It blurred the boundaries between offenders and non-offenders, seeking to decriminalize children's offending. It shifted the balance away from legal rights towards the 'needs' of the child as determined by the professionals and the courts. Social work practice was required to provide treatment interventions to meet welfare needs and to prevent offending. It has been argued that this was confusing and proved counter-productive (Pratt 1985) and that the unification of provision for children in need with that for offenders underestimated the significance of the differences between them (Harris and Timms 1993). It provoked widespread criticism, particularly in the legal system and resulted in an increase in the courts' use of institutional 'sentencing', interchangeably on treatment and punishment grounds.

Ideological confusion about the underlying causes of offending and the most appropriate approaches to children in trouble continued through the 1970s (see House of Commons Expenditure Committee 1975; Morris *et al.* 1980). The late 1970s and 1980s witnessed a shift from the welfare to the justice paradigm, with a revival of traditional criminal justice values, driven by political ideology and by concerns about the unanticipated consequences of the 1969 Act. The Conservative Party made crime a major election issue in 1979 and ideological differences between the political parties meant that significant sections of the 1969 Act were never implemented, for example raising the age of criminal responsibility from 10 to 14 years.

Academics and pressure groups for children promoted an alternative 'justice' or 'just deserts' perspective, the principles of which were seen as oppositional to those underlying a welfare perspective. The criticisms of the welfare model can be summarized as follows: treatment interventions which were presented as being in their best interests were experienced by children as stigmatizing and punitive and pathologized the individual, despite the rhetoric of care and welfare; indeterminate treatment interventions could result in longer periods of incarceration and intervention than determinate sentences; there was no evidence that treatment was effective; and the role of the court was confused since the treatment-orientation was seen to be at odds with the administration of justice. Finally the net-widening effect of the welfare approach brought more children 'at risk' into the system (Donzelot 1980; Morris *et al.*

1980). In the justice perspective the emphasis is on: the gravity of the offence rather than the underlying needs of the offender; responsibility and accountability; equality of sanction rather than individualised treatment; determinate sentences rather than indeterminate treatment programmes (Gelsthorpe and Morris 1994). A complex mix of these principles and the Conservative government's law and order ideology were reflected in subsequent legislation during the 1980s, which also incorporated some welfare provisions such as mandatory social enquiry reports.

Research findings that the criminal behaviour of the majority of young people was petty and transitory and that the application of criminal labels could increase the likelihood of further offending (Morris and Giller 1983; Pitts 1988; Rutherford 1986) resulted in two key policy objectives in the 1980s, diversion (from crime, court and custody) and decriminalization. The third objective, decarceration, was formulated on the basis of: evidence of the failure of custodial responses to young offenders (Pitts 1990); the increase in social problems for the offender following release; and higher levels of criminality in the longer term (Bottoms 1995; Howard League 1995). Decarceration was supported by government imperatives to reduce public spending on custodial provision. These three objectives were repeatedly affirmed in government documents and legislation through the 1980s and into the early 1990s (Criminal Justice Acts 1982, 1988 and 1991, 'Punishment, Custody and the Community' Green Paper 1988, Children Act 1989) and resulted in an increase in the use of cautioning, a decline in the number of criminal prosecutions and a decline in the use of custody for children (Gelsthorpe and Morris 1994; The Children's Society 1993).

The Criminal Justice Act 1991 (implemented in October 1992) continued this trend based on the conception of offending as a transient feature of adolescent behaviour or an anti-social response by young people to social or family pressures beyond their control. The Act, which introduced rules to govern criminal proceedings in the newly named youth court, was welcomed by some who suggested that it confirmed the move away from the dichotomy of welfare versus justice and combined the benefits of both approaches (Graham 1996). However, others warned that the separation from care and family proceedings could result in the loss of the welfare dimension required by the Children and Young Persons Act 1933 and the development of a punitive mentality similar to that which had been evident in relation to young-adult offenders (Ball 1992). Furthermore, the implementation of the 1989 Children Act provided for civil proceedings relating to children to be dealt with in a re-named family proceedings court. It removed the care order as an option available to the court in criminal proceedings as well as the offence condition in care proceedings symbolizing 'the separation of the "deprived" and the "delinquent"' (Gelsthorpe and Morris 1994, p.981). However, this new emphasis on 'justice' did nothing to remove the institutional injustices and structural inequalities which permeated the system and particularly affected black young people and girls. Racism was evident at every stage in the criminal justice process, from arrest through to the court proceedings and in decisions relating to remand and sentencing (Commission for Racial Equality 1992; NACRO 1992). The inequality suffered by girls will be examined in more detail.

Gender Issues in the Legal System

The dominant discourse in criminology has always been male-oriented and the invisibility of girls and women has been regarded by feminist writers as characteristic of their position in society and in the social sciences generally. Traditional theories about delinquency have virtually ignored girls and their problems and much of the academic literature equated female delinquency with sexual delinquency (Campbell 1981). However, recent feminist research has argued that the best way to understand women and crime is not through feminist criminology but by studying 'the role, position and social control of women which can be derived from other studies of women's oppression' (Heidensohn 1996, p.197).

Feminist research with girls has revealed that the role of the family is particularly important in policing girls' behaviour, time, labour and sexuality and that they are policed and sanctioned more in their families than boys (Nava 1984). They are policed by other girls and by boys, inside the family and outside in schools, youth clubs and on the streets using a language based on sexuality that functions 'as a form of generalised social control ... steering girls, in terms of both their actions and their aspirations, into the existing structures of gender relations' (Lees 1989, p.21). Girls have essentially been regarded as the property of the family and their rights to be elsewhere, including on the streets like their male counterparts, have been challenged. When outside the family, complaints have been made that they are beyond control, fuelling the anxiety and condemnation of girls' participation in 'girl gangs' (Carroll 1998; Chesney-Lind 1997; Lagree and Lew Fai 1989). The power relationships and inequalities between girls and members of their families, particularly their fathers, have been minimized or ignored in the collusion with the myth that the family is a safe place. This has prevailed even with the increased consciousness of the extent of sexual abuse, one of the most powerful mechanisms by which girls are kept in the family.

Carlen (1987) reviewed a number of studies and concluded that professional intervention with most girls results from concerns about their sexual behaviour or because they fail to conform to expectations of adolescent femininity. Hudson (1984) found that girls' behaviour which was regarded as 'gender-inappropriate' was interpreted as a sign of individual pathology or that a girl was out of control requiring intervention and resocialization into 'culturally defined femininity'. Adolescent girls face conflicting personal and political expectations: adolescence is about challenge, yet femininity is about conformity. While delinquent behaviour is regarded as 'normal' for adolescent boys it is interpreted as a transgression of the female role for girls. The sexualized behaviour of girls has been met with fear and rejection by professionals who have labelled the girls concerned as troublesome (Farmer and Pollock 1998; Hudson, A. 1989). The ideology of the girl as property is carried into the institutions which care for them where the objective is frequently concerned with social control and re-establishing the traditional female role (Hudson, B. 1989). The unequal power relationships which exist in many institutions between male and female staff as well as between children and staff and between boys and girls can result in cultures of abuse. This issue will be explored in subsequent chapters.

In the legal and criminal justice systems, girls experience discriminatory treatment (Bottoms and Pratt 1989; Cain 1989; Campbell 1981; Chesney-Lind 1997; Hudson, B. 1989; Howard League 1997; Smart 1976). Females appearing before criminal courts are subject to a double penalty, receiving punishment for both the offence and their contravention of the social expectations of their gender role (Heidensohn 1996; Smart 1976). The 'welfare' approach has continued to be adopted in respect of girls with more attention paid to their character and way of life than to the 'offence' which has been committed, resulting in a higher level of intervention and social policing than experienced by their male counterparts (Adams 1986; Heidensohn 1996). Furthermore, there is little evidence to support the so-called 'chivalry myth' which suggests that in court proceedings women receive more favourable treatment than men. On the contrary, females appear to be punished more severely than males where the degree of their criminality is similar and lighter sentences reflect the less serious nature of their offences (Farrington and Morris 1983).

Although there are increasing numbers of girls in the criminal justice system, girls are more frequently dealt with by the care system, which exercises powers exceeding those available to a criminal court, and are justified on the basis of what is in their best interests, concealing a complex pattern of control (Campbell 1981; Casburn 1979). This is illustrated by the power in the Children Act 1989 to detain in secure accommodation children who have committed no criminal offences or minor offences which would not warrant a custodial sentence in a criminal court. The majority of young people dealt with under this power are girls. Even though there are now almost equal numbers of boys and girls in the care system (DH 1999), little is known about the different needs of girls and the lack of gender differentiation results in a continuing absence of clear policies and strategies to respond to the needs of girls.

An important question is whether a 'justice' approach to girls would lead to less intervention or to a disproportionately serious view being taken of relatively minor offences. Hudson (1984) expresses concern that girls whose behaviour is interpreted as a failure to adapt to their female social role, rather than an adolescent phase, could be treated more harshly by a 'justice' approach which would judge them against the standards of adult femininity rather than adolescent immaturity. The justice approach would have little to offer girls if it led to them being sentenced to penal custody rather than placed in welfare institutions. This is particularly important in the context of the recent sensationalized media reporting of girls involved in violent crime which has given the impression that 'girl violence' is a major problem and may be influencing courts to give more girls custodial sentences (Howard League 1997).

The definitions of 'troublesome' girls have been challenged (Hudson, A. 1989) and an approach to girls advocated, which normalizes their behaviour from a perspective which recognizes the pressures which they face (Lees and Mellor 1986). Young women are accorded very little priority politically and largely remain invisible subjects in social policy discourses. The position of girls in the care and criminal justice systems is a key theme which will be examined further.

The 1990s

The principles and objectives pursued during the 1980s and early 1990s were dramatically abandoned in 1992/1993 with a major governmental shift to policies and legislation which promoted an overtly punitive response to children in trouble and particularly to very young offenders (Littlechild 1997). This agenda was driven by a renewed commitment to the incarceration of young people in trouble whose vulnerability was negated in the political reconstruction of detention as the only solution. A number of factors appear to have contributed to the changing mood.

Police and magistrates were unhappy about the limitations on the sentencing powers of the courts contained within the Criminal Justice Act 1991 and expressed a lack of confidence in the youth justice agencies which provided information and sentencing recommendations to the court (Ball 1995). Increasing police and media attention on young people who were regarded as being outside the law, gave the impression that crime committed by young people was out of control, although considerable doubt was cast on the reality of this public perception (Hagell and Newburn 1994). At the same time, the Conservative government was intent on re-establishing its waning popularity by restating its commitment to 'law and order' with explicit 'get tough' policies.

A reversal of the policies of the 1980s was already gaining momentum when James Bulger was killed in February 1993. As already noted, politicians and the media ignored the unusual nature of this case and it was presented as an example of the lawlessness and immorality of children. The resulting moral panic influenced policies and legislation through the 1990s and reinforced the new focus on discipline, punishment and retribution. It is interesting to note that if the section of the Children and Young Persons Act 1969 raising the age of criminal responsibility to 14 had been enacted, the boys would have been dealt with outside the criminal law, as would have been the case in most other European countries.

The Criminal Justice Act 1993 was drafted within months of the implementation of the 1991 Act and reversed several of its key provisions. It was rapidly followed by the Criminal Justice and Public Order Act 1994 which introduced a number of punitive measures for children, reflecting a complete reversal in the policies of diversion and decarceration. For example, it extended the powers of the courts to order children aged 10 to 13 to be detained under section 53[2] of the Children and Young Persons Act 1933 in line with 14- to 17-year-olds, it extended the powers of the courts to place a 'security requirement' on 12- to 14-year-olds as well as 15- to 17-year-olds, and it doubled the maximum length of detention in a young offender institution from 12 to 24 months for 15- to 17-year-olds. Furthermore, it provided for new, privately run Secure Training Centres for 12- to 14-year-old offenders, with a minimum sentence of six months and a maximum of two years. In addition, the Police and Criminal Evidence Act 1984 (section 38(6)) was amended reducing the age limit from 15 to authorize the police to detain 12-year-olds overnight in custody rather than in local authority care.

Many child-care charities and penal reform groups opposed the introduction of Secure Training Centres and orders (see for example, Crowley 1998; Penal Affairs Consortium 1994; The Children's Society

1993), although their views were outweighed by those expressed by the courts, the police and prison officer organizations (Card and Ward 1994). The orders, which became available to courts on 1 March 1998, were to be targeted on 'persistent young offenders', although there was little reliable information about the nature of 'persistent' offending or the most appropriate response to it (Hagell and Newburn 1994, p.22). Concerns were expressed about the increasingly punitive ethos of the youth court and the likelihood that Secure Training Orders would be used to supplement what the courts considered to be their inadequate sentencing powers, with damaging consequences for young offenders (Ball 1995). As it was the responsibility of the courts to determine who is a persistent offender, the likelihood of custodial sentences was thought to be increased (Russell 1998).

The contract for the first of five privately run Secure Training Centres was signed by the Conservative government just before the general election in 1997. Although the Labour Party originally opposed this strategy, in government it confirmed the contract and its commitment to the establishment of the further four centres which had been planned. The first centre opened in Medway, Kent in April 1998, followed by centres at Rainsbrook and Hassockfield. The Youth Justice Board for England and Wales (YJB), a new executive public body established by the Crime and Disorder Act 1998, has taken responsibility for the development work on the two additional centres promised by the government, as part of its role in commissioning and purchasing places for young offenders. The Government's decision to proceed with the establishment of the Secure Training Centres can be understood in the context of the increase in the use of custodial provisions for children and young people contained in the Crime and Disorder Act 1998 (Russell 1998).

The introduction of Secure Training Centres was just one of the Conservative strategies for dealing with 'troublesome' young people which was adopted by the Labour government in May 1997. It declared that 'youth crime is one of the most serious problems facing England and Wales today' (Home Office 1997, p.1) and emphasized its commitment to be tough on youth crime and its causes. It stated 'punishment is important as a means of expressing society's condemnation of unlawful behaviour and as a deterrent' (Home Office 1997, p.3). It proposed a wide-ranging reform of the youth justice system (Audit Commission 1996; Labour Party 1996) and subsequently set up a youth justice Task Force which undertook a review of all custodial provision ('the secure estate'), including local authority secure units (LASUs). The establishment of the national Youth Justice Board and multi-agency local Youth Offending Teams resulted from this review.

Although a wide-ranging piece of legislation, a key aim of the Crime and Disorder Act 1998 was to 'tackle' youth crime, providing national and local structures for intervention with offenders at a much earlier age, and it introduced some significant changes to the sentencing of young offenders. These include the abolition of the legal doctrine of *doli incapax*, which protected children from being treated by the criminal justice process as if they had the same mental capacity as adults; the introduction of child curfew orders and child safety orders against children under 10 years under the supervision of the Youth Offending Team, thereby treating very young children as offenders; court-ordered remands to local authority secure units for boys and girls aged 12 years and over; and the introduction of Detention and Training Orders to replace detention in a Young Offenders Institution for under-18s and the Secure Training Order for 12- to 14-year-old girls and boys which was provided by the Criminal Justice and Public Order Act 1994. An issue of particular concern relates to the power of the Secretary of State to reduce the minimum age for Detention and Training Orders from 12 (set by the Criminal Justice and Public Order Act 1994) to 10 years.

The criminal justice legislation introduced since the 1990s, particularly the Crime and Disorder Act 1998, has resulted in a substantial increase in the use of custodial facilities for children and young people under 18, which are provided by the Prison Service, Secure Training Centres and local authority secure units. Moreover, the continuing government investment in further capital development programmes throughout the secure estate will produce even more places for youth justice purposes (Children's Legal Centre 2000). Incarceration has been the main response to crime, justified on the basis of the claim made by the previous Home Secretary that 'prison works' in spite of evidence of the harmful effects on young people of placement in custody. This claim has been described as 'no more than a crude slogan. The evidence shows it is not true but evidence no longer seems to be required in policy making' (Kennedy 1995, p.4). These harmful effects are multi-faceted and result from removing children from their families and communities, which causes disruption to their health and development (Parker *et al.* 1991; Sinclair *et al.* 1995; Triseliotis *et al.* 1995) and from the experience of harsh custodial regimes which compound emotional disturbance and increase the risk of suicide and self-harm (Howard League 1995). The Government's guidance to the Crime and Disorder Act 1998 (Home Office 1999) claims that custodial penalties will be served by young people in 'a positive and constructive regime' but the continuing problems in the Secure Training Centres and other parts of the 'secure estate' must cast serious doubts on this claim. Young people whose criminal identity is confirmed by imprisonment face serious consequences following release with high rates of re-offending and social isolation. The policy of incarceration also ignores the evidence about the family circumstances of children in trouble, with high levels of family breakdown, poverty, abuse and loss (Boswell 1996; Bottoms 1995; Howard League 1995), which means that they are also undeniably children 'in need'. Some young people, mostly girls, are incarcerated as a direct result of behaviours which are survival strategies adopted to cope with such experiences, for example running away from abusive homes and institutional care situations. This weight of criminal justice legislation has been implemented against the background of the Children Act 1989 and the UN Convention on the Rights of the Child, which came into effect in 1991. The principles contained within the Act and the Convention emphasize both the welfare and the rights of the child, although many of the positive effects of these principles have been undermined in the context of other policy developments and legislation.

The Children Act 1989

The Children Act 1989 brought together public and private law proceedings relating to children and attempted to achieve a balance between the role and responsibilities of the state, the parents and family in the upbringing of children. It was the first English legislation to consider children's rights as distinct from notions of welfare and its provisions enhanced the legal relevance of the child's views. However, while some provisions seemed to take children's rights more seriously, this has proved to be highly qualified in practice as rights which the Act appeared to confer upon children have subsequently been overruled by the judicial system (Lyon and Parton 1995).

The 1989 Children Act enshrined in law rights for children looked after by local authorities. They include the right to an independent visitor, to complain, to have their views heard, their race, culture and religion respected, the right to contact with family and friends and the right not to be locked up unless the legal criteria to do so are satisfied. However, the Act does not deal with young offenders who are seen as offenders first and children second, and its provisions do not apply to penal institutions such as young offender institutions and Secure Training Centres. The children and young people who are incarcerated in these institutions and in adult prisons are subject to criminal justice rather than child-care legislation and are not afforded even the limited protection and rights due to them as children under the terms of Children Act 1989.

The UN Convention on the Rights of the Child

The UN Convention on the Rights of the Child is 'intended to promote and protect children's rights' (Franklin 1995, p.16), which have been broadly grouped into provision, protection and participation rights. The UK Government was equivocal about the Convention and failed to take seriously the implementation of its provisions following ratification in 1991 (CRDU 1994). Even at the time of ratification, the Government entered four reservations, expressing an unwillingness among other things to discontinue placing young people in adult offender institutions. In 1997 the High Court held that this practice in respect of female offenders was unlawful (R v Secretary of State for the Home Office *ex parte* Flood 1997), although it still continues, in breach of Article 37(c) of the Convention. Furthermore, in the UK Government's second report to the UN Committee on the Rights of the Child

(DH 1999a), this reservation was maintained although it was noted that work had begun on improving the custodial arrangements for young people. In October 1998, units for under-21s were set up in two women's prisons, although some facilities continue to be shared and plans have been announced for units for under-18s in four women's prisons (Howard League 1998b).

This is only one of the ways in which criminal justice policy runs contrary to Article 37 of the Convention[1] which states that 'no child shall be deprived of his or her liberty unlawfully or arbitrarily. The arrest, detention or imprisonment of a child shall ... be used only as a measure of last resort and for the shortest appropriate period of time' (UN 1989). Concern has been widely expressed about the policy of incarceration of young people in trouble in prison and other penal establishments (Howard League 1995) but there have also been increasing concerns about the detention of young people in local authority secure accommodation, many of whom have been assessed not to need secure placements (National Children's Bureau 1995).

The Children's Rights Development Unit (1994) monitored the implementation of the Convention and found a lack of commitment to children's civil rights. In 1995 the UN Committee recorded its concern at the Government's failure to take children's rights seriously and the lack of progress in the implementation of the Convention. Particular criticism was expressed about the UK's treatment of children in trouble and its recommendations for action included the abandonment of imprisonment in Secure Training Centres and an increase in the age of criminal responsibility (CRC 1995). The Committee concluded that not only had the position of children not been improved through a committed implementation of the provisions of the Convention, but the situation for many children, particularly those in trouble, had worsened as a result of repressive legislation.

Calls for the Convention to be incorporated into English law to prevent infringements of its articles have been ignored (Freeman 1993,1995), although the Human Rights Act 1998 which will be effective from October 2000 gives effect in UK law to the provisions of the European Convention on Human Rights. Many of its articles are similar to those in the UN Convention on the Rights of the Child and the Act has the potential to be of significant benefit to children.

Conclusion

This chapter has examined concepts of childhood and the legal and political context for children who are classified as 'troubled' and 'troublesome'. Although the discourse about children's rights and interests is controversial, it is clear that children who are classified as 'troubled' or 'troublesome' and conceptualized primarily as 'offenders' rather than children 'in need' will experience even greater inequality and discrimination than their peers (Adams 1986). Such young people, especially those regarded as 'extreme' (Stewart and Tutt 1987), who are placed through the care and criminal justice systems in custodial provision such as secure accommodation, are arguably the most disenfranchised group in contemporary society. The next chapter will examine the young people who are ascribed these labels, their behaviours and needs and the professional responses to them.

Notes

1 Article 37 is related to three other international agreements to which the government is formally committed: The United Nations Standard Minimum Rules for the Administration of Juvenile Justice 1985 (The Beijing Rules); The United Nations Guidelines for the Prevention of Juvenile Delinquency 1990 (The Riyadh Rules); The United Nations Rules for the Protection of Juveniles Deprived of their Liberty 1990.

TWO

Children in Trouble

The Professional Response

Introduction

This chapter will examine the concept of adolescence, described as the space between childhood and adulthood which is characterized by trouble and non-conformity, the classification of children in trouble and the responses and interventions of the different professional systems. It will review the institutional care provided for young people who are considered too troubled or troublesome to remain in the care of their families.

Adolescence

Adolescence is generally conceptualized as a process of transition from childhood to adulthood (Ollendorff 1972). Young people must redefine themselves in many areas of their lives, arising from physical, cognitive and social changes, and pressures can result from expectations placed on them by the family, school and peer group. The pattern of adolescent transition has changed and the period of time over which it takes place has lengthened (Rutter and Smith 1995) and it has been suggested that this may be related to the alleged increase in the incidence of emotional and social problems in adolescence (Hurrelman 1989).

Theories of Development

Theoretical models of adolescent development have offered various explanations of the transitional process. Traditional psychological and psychoanalytic theories suggest that adolescence is a period of particular psychological vulnerability with an increased likelihood of emotional or behavioural problems. They focus on the pathology of the individual or family. The developmental process of separation from the emotional ties with parents is seen as an essential prerequisite to the formation of mature emotional and sexual relationships outside the home. Rebellious teenage behaviour is viewed as an aid to this process of disengagement.

These models were constructed from the perspective of Western, white, middle-class males and they focus on male development, representing male experience as human experience (Erikson 1965; Freud 1905; Kohlberg 1981; Piaget 1932) and female behaviour as a deviation from the norm (Gilligan 1982; McClelland 1975). Erikson's (1965) model of eight life-cycle stages is defined by male experience. He regarded the formation of an individuated, integrated identity as an essential task in adolescence which requires a resolution of the tension between identity formation and identity confusion. Furthermore, he suggested that the resolution of the task ascribed to each stage of development was essential in order for the individual to progress to the next stage. The stage which follows identity is intimacy, suggesting that separation (identity), where successfully accomplished, leads to attachment (intimacy). The assumption from these traditional models is that adult identity is achieved through adolescent separation from parents and their values, in a so-called 'second individuation process' (Blos 1967).

The inadequacy of these traditional theories and the problems they create for understanding adolescent development become evident when applied to female identity development. These models interpret differences in girls' development in terms of developmental delay, failure to achieve a clear sense of self, failure to make moral judgements, or deviance. Apter (1990) challenges these assumptions, arguing that teenagers attempt to negotiate a new relationship with their parents which will reflect their maturity, and she stresses the importance of connectedness and individuation rather than separation and individuation. Alternative theories which propose that the relationship between self and other is different for young adult males and females have since offered different explanations of female identity development (Gilligan 1982/1993; Miller 1976). In Chodorow's (1978) analysis, femininity is defined through attachment whereas masculinity is defined through separation. Similarly, Gilligan contends that the developmental stages of identity and intimacy, expressed sequentially in Erikson's model, are fused for girls, so whilst the male experience of identity is of separation which serves to define and empower the self, the female experience is of 'the ongoing process of attachment that creates and sustains the human community' (Gilligan 1993, p.156). These analyses have in turn been challenged on the basis that they promote the notion of a generic female who is white and middle-class and fail to take account of black feminist ideas (Collins 1990).

Sociological and social-psychological theories also regard adolescence as an important transitional period with potential problems arising from external, rather than internal conflicts, associated with the process of socialization and role assumption and changes. During childhood, individuals have roles ascribed to them within the family, school and other social groups. In adolescence, individuals achieve roles in social groups of their own choice and the struggle to attain status and power is regarded as integral to the adolescent transition. As adolescence progresses, the individual achieves or is assigned more roles which impact on their sense of self and the development of an identity. The adolescent faces potential conflicts in values and in the expectations held of them in different situations such as the school, the family, peer groups, the media and political organizations. Potential stresses result from role conflict, where expectations of different roles are incompatible; role discontinuity, where there is a lack of transition from one role to another; and role incongruence, where the role ascribed to the individual is not the one they would have chosen for themselves.

While there are significant differences in the degree of psychological vulnerability ascribed by these theoretical models to this period of development, the majority of young people negotiate it without major trauma, and the concept of adolescence as a period of 'storm and stress' is not borne out (Coleman 1987; Coleman and Hendry 1980). However, a significant minority of the population of young people

(Rutter and Smith 1995) do experience emotional, behavioural or social problems, commonly referred to as 'psycho-social disorders'.

Psycho-social Adversity

Risk or stress factors have been identified which are said to provide indicators of the likely development of psycho-social problems, some of which relate to the individual child, others to their families and a third group to wider social and environmental issues (NHS 1995; Rutter 1993). These risk factors include the following: low self-esteem and communication difficulties for the child; parental conflict; family breakdown; physical, sexual and emotional abuse in the family; and socio-economic disadvantage and discrimination. There are more serious consequences where a combination of adversities or stresses exists (Caprara and Rutter 1995). A close association has been observed between poor relationships with parents, strong peer relationships and behaviour described as anti-social, which includes drug and alcohol abuse, running away, suicidal behaviour and criminal activity (Triseliotis *et al.* 1995).

However, not all young people who experience adverse circumstances in combination with these risk factors are equally susceptible to developing psycho-social problems. Protective factors which modify the influence of risk factors and enhance the resilience of young people and their resistance to adversity have also been identified. These protective processes include those that promote high self-esteem and autonomy, the absence of parental conflict and the availability of high-warmth, secure relationships and strong social support systems (NHS 1995). Attention needs to be given to processes which both enable people to overcome the harmful effects of past events and strengthen their ability to cope effectively with future stress. In this connection, attention to potential 'turning points' which increase resilience through exposure to beneficial experiences is important. Achievement in one area of life which enhances positive self-esteem is likely to increase the confidence and ability of the individual to address difficulties in other areas of their life (Rutter 1992,1993).

Self-Concept and Self-Esteem

Adolescence is regarded as a time of both change and consolidation in self-concept. Self-concept has been defined as a composite image of what we think we are, what we think we can achieve, what we think others think of us and what we would like to be (Burns 1979). This term includes within it the notions of self-image, that is the individual's description of the self, and self-esteem, which is the individual's self-evaluation. Self-concept develops through interactions between the individual and their environment. It is influenced by a combination of psychological and social factors and is subject to variables such as family background and cultural context. Global self-esteem is the overall positive or negative attitude toward the self (Rosenberg 1979). A positive self-image and high self-esteem are closely related to a stable self-concept. Well founded self-esteem in adolescence is regarded as essential for the individual to manage change successfully and make competent choices about important issues. There are different views about the development of self-esteem during adolescence. Some studies report positive development (for example O'Malley and Bachman 1983), others suggest that there are negative changes (Simmons *et al.* 1973) while yet others report very little mean change in self-esteem during adolescence (Bolognini *et al.* 1996; Wylie 1979). Gender differences have been reported, with lower self-esteem in girls, both globally and in specific domains (Block and Robbins 1993; Bolognini *et al.* 1996; Harter 1985, 1988; Rosenberg 1979). Various explanations have been proposed which include the importance attached to appearance by girls, overly high aspirations and the differences in the process of identity development of girls and boys (Chodorow 1978; Gilligan 1982; Miller 1976).

James (1968) and Cooley (1968) provided the first theories of the concept of self. James' cognitive-analytic model defines global self-esteem in terms of a person's accomplishments relative to their aspirations in specific areas of their lives. In contrast, Cooley suggests that the self is a social construction determined on the basis of one's perceptions of how one is seen by significant others and he introduced the notion of the 'looking-glass self'. Harter (1985, 1988) incorporated the principles of both James and Cooley in her self-perception profiles for children and adolescents. These instruments measure individuals' perception of their competence across a number of domains, the importance they attach to achievement in each domain, the relationship between competence and importance, and global self-worth. She contrasted the children with low self-esteem, who were unable to discount the importance of the domains in which their achievement was low, with the children with high self-esteem, who both discounted the importance of those domains and promoted the importance of others in which they were successful. Furthermore Harter (1987) reported that self-esteem was higher for those who felt they were valued by significant others, parents as well as peers, illustrating the continuing importance of parental influence in adolescence.

Social psychologists have argued that there are limitations in these traditional models which ignore the individual's capacity actively to construct their self concept through interaction. From the interactionist perspective self-concept is 'concerned with states of active becoming as opposed to passive being' (Gergen and Gergen 1983, p.255). It is constructed from the autobiographical stories that individuals tell to identify themselves to others and to themselves; social constructions which are altered through interaction and which are known as self narratives (Gergen and Gergen 1988; Jansz 1995). The process is described as reflexive and diachronic; that is individuals create themselves through self-reflection and the self that is created changes over time. Self narratives provide stability but at the same time are dynamic and open to change. The self narrative is a linguistic tool which serves the function of providing the individual with a sense of continuity, consistency and individual distinctiveness and thereby results in the construction of a stable self-concept.

The relationships between self-esteem, affect and motivation were examined by Harter (1987) and Rosenberg (1979). Harter (1987) found that self-esteem has a direct impact on the affect or mood of the individual, so that children who like themselves as people are happiest, while those who have a negative view of their worth are more likely to feel sad or depressed. In turn, the motivation of the happy child to engage in activities is greater than that of the child who is depressed or miserable. Relationships have been observed between low self-esteem and the behaviour of children regarded as troubled or troublesome. A strong association has been noted between low self-esteem and mental ill-health, particularly depression. In addition, many young people separated from their families have low self-esteem, which is also associated with deliberate self-harm and poor educational achievement (Hoghughi 1978). The behaviour of boys with a positive self-concept has been found to be less delinquent than that of those with a poor self-concept (van Welzenis 1997). Furthermore, low self-esteem has repeatedly been found to be a factor for young people in care, resulting both from the adverse experiences leading to admission and the stigma and risk factors associated with being in care (see for example Stein and Carey 1986).

Behaviours labelled as 'Troubled' and 'Troublesome'

Behaviours are labelled by professional systems in ways which identify the people exhibiting them as different from or 'outside' the normal. Labels serve to separate young people from their peers and re-establish them in new 'deviant' social groups. Becker (1963) suggests that deviance is a social construction which is illustrated by an examination of how what constitutes crime alters with changes in the law. The ages of criminal responsibility in the UK, which determine whether young people can be prosecuted for certain behaviours, have been subject to change during the last century and are now set at levels which are lower than those in most other European countries. Pearson (1993) contends that if young people were exempt from prosecution under the criminal law, even if they committed acts which in an adult would constitute a crime, it would be impossible for them to be labelled 'criminal'. Moreover, many young people are labelled criminal as a consequence of the commission of acts which in an adult would not constitute a crime, such as engaging in sexual activity and purchasing alcohol. The age limits are socially constructed, and are subject to change.

Traditionally, professional agencies were seen as passive respondents exercising control over behaviour which they labelled deviant, troublesome or disturbed. However, labelling theorists have shown that labelling behaviour as deviant or delinquent can reinforce the behaviour, create a deviant motivation and lead to further deviant behaviour; these theories suggest that social control leads to deviance (Becker 1967; Lemert 1967). In addition, the stigmatizing social labels attributed to young people can have a profound effect on their developing identities and self-esteem.

There are a number of behaviours defined as psycho-social disorders which have been found to increase in frequency during adolescence. These include suicide, suicidal behaviour including deliberate self-harm, depression, eating disorders and alcohol and drug abuse (Bailey 1997). Important links have been identified between some of the disorders, particularly alcohol abuse and crime, other psychoactive drugs and crime, conduct disorders leading to the use of drugs, depression and suicidal behaviour, and the use of alcohol and drugs and suicidal behaviour (Kerfoot 1996; Rutter and Smith 1995). These and other behaviours may result in intervention by the professional systems.

Professional Responses to Children in Trouble

Young people presenting behaviour which is regarded as unacceptable will usually be responded to on a random and unco-ordinated basis by one or more of four professional systems: education, health, criminal justice and social services. While each of these systems describes and responds differently to broadly the same type of behaviours, it has been argued that control is a key objective of the intervention (Malek 1991, 1993). Scraton (1997) contends that the discretion of classification is the most extensive power that professional adults exercise over children. Young people are rarely active participants in this process of definition of their problems, and their views on the labels ascribed to them are infrequently sought. Those in power define both the problem and prescribe its solution without the participation of the individual concerned (Becker 1967; Scraton 1997).

Much work with teenagers lacks coherence and it has been shown that inter-agency policies for adolescents are lacking despite evidence that their needs cross the boundaries of many professional agencies (NHS 1986) and the introduction of Children's Services Plans which emphasize joint planning and co-operation across departments (Berridge and Brodie 1998; DH 1996; Triseliotis *et al.* 1995). Whilst accepting that child protection has been a major preoccupation for health and social services it has been suggested that this cannot be the only explanation for the lack of attention to teenagers, particularly as this age group constitute a significant proportion of those on child protection registers. Parker (1996) proposed three possible explanations which relate to competing priorities, to an under-estimation of the needs of adolescents and the number of teenagers in the care system and finally to a sense of pessimism among professionals working with teenagers which results from a lack of clarity about the expectations of such work and conflicting interests between teenagers, their families, social workers and other professionals. Furthermore, their lack of political, economic and social rights leaves them in a weak position to argue for resources. Three studies which focused on teenagers in need of services (Biehal *et al.* 1995; Sinclair *et al.* 1995; Triseliotis *et al.* 1995) showed that life was grim for many of those who were disadvantaged in important areas of their lives, who had poor or non-existent relationships with family, discontinuities in education, unstable living conditions, poor social skills and low self-esteem.

Professional responses to young people are gendered and vary according to race. Within each system different assessments produce different plans and outcomes for girls and boys and for black and white young people. The stereotype of the 'juvenile delinquent' is male and, as already noted, little attention has been given to girls in the criminal justice system, who have been allocated an inadequate share of resources. Girls are more frequently responded to by mental health or social services on the basis that they are at risk of sexual or self-harm and are in need of care or treatment, and it has been repeatedly shown that protection can lead to punishment. As already noted, the social behaviour of girls is 'policed' in ways that the behaviour of boys is not and they are frequently labelled as deviant by professionals and the courts even when they are not delinquent (Cain 1989; Hudson 1989).

It has been suggested that some behaviours described as 'intolerable' may constitute no more than an extension of normal adolescent behaviour that is unacceptable to parents or others (NHS 1986).

Referral and assessment processes appear to be arbitrary and the involvement of a particular agency is frequently determined on the basis of factors other than the needs of individual young people, such as the perceptions of particular agencies held by parents and professionals, the professional discipline of the person who provided the first point of contact, the resources available and the willingness to fund services for young people. Different definitions are used to categorize the same behaviour in each of the four professional systems, thereby giving the behaviour a particular medical, legal, social or educational focus and setting the young person on a particular path of care, control, treatment or punishment in different institutional settings (Malek 1993). The catch-all nature of the classifications and labels allows for a very wide interpretation: 'young offender' includes behaviours ranging from petty theft to armed robbery; 'conduct disorder' in the psychiatric system includes behaviours ranging from lying to deliberate self-harm (Jaffa and Deszery 1989); 'emotionally and behaviourally difficult/disturbed' in the education system includes disruptive behaviour and neurological impairment; 'beyond parental control' used by social services includes non-school attendance, running away and family breakdown. The outcomes for young people are substantially different within each of these systems.

The unco-ordinated involvement of more than one agency has been described as 'system spillage' (Jaffa and Deszery 1989; Malek 1993; Steinberg *et al.* 1981; Townley 1992). Young people can be supported at home by one system only to be removed and placed in institutional care by another. Inadequate resources in one system can result in intervention by another system. As young people move between systems, their difficulties attract different definitions, they acquire additional labels and their legal status may change or become more complex. Rather than being viewed holistically as complete individuals, they are seen as having a series of discrete difficulties.

However their problem behaviour is defined, when young people are considered to be beyond the care or control of their families, institutional care is provided by all four professional systems in hospitals, schools, penal custody and residential care homes. Some children have experience of institutional care in more than one system and young people with similar problems have been found to drift around the different systems (Bullock *et al.* 1990). Widespread concerns have been expressed about the whole range of institutional responses to children, which fail to include adequate safeguards for their protection, leaving them at risk of abuse (DH 1997a). Furthermore, the greatest concern which emerged from Malek's study was that children do not benefit from the time they spend in institutions which may instead intensify their difficulties and deny them the experience of mainstream society to which they are expected to return (Malek 1993, p.91). The different approaches to children in trouble taken by the four professional systems will be briefly reviewed.

Education

UK legislation requires local authorities to provide education for all children up to the age of 18, but there has been increasing concern about the marginalization of those who present disruptive behaviour in school. The number of children excluded from mainstream education has risen steeply since 1993, particularly African Caribbean boys who, it is suggested, are up to six times more likely to be excluded than their white counterparts (Commission for Racial Equality 1996). Children have no formal right to participate in decision-making processes within the education system, including those which result in their exclusion (Lyon 1996), and the principle of the best interests of the child is not reflected in education legislation. Non-attendance or exclusion from school has serious implications for young people. Their educational opportunities, peer social relationships and longer term employment prospects are severely restricted, the risk of involvement in delinquent activity born out of boredom is significantly increased and their self-concept and level of self-esteem are likely to be negatively affected. Furthermore, they are deprived of social contacts at school which can improve the life chances of children from disadvantaged backgrounds (Quinton and Rutter 1988). Social services departments become involved with many such young people, whose experience in care or custody serves further to compound their educational and social disadvantage (Berridge and Brodie 1996; SSI/Office for Standards in Education 1995).

The Education Acts of 1981 and 1993 provide for the formal assessment and statementing of children with special educational needs and their placement in residential special education. It has been suggested that the increase in the labelling of such children has more to do with the extension of the professional definition than to an increase in the level of emotional disturbance (Barton and Tomlinson 1981). This has been attributed to the changes in legislation which devolved financial management to schools (LMS), emphasized performance over social integration and led to increasing competition between schools for the most rewarding and least problematic pupils (Cohen and Hughes 1994). The documented increase in the demand for statements and poor levels of co-operation between education and social services have led to problems with the assessment and statementing process (DH 1997a; Lunt and Evans 1994), particularly in respect of children identified as having behavioural difficulties, many of whom have been admitted to residential schools even before the preparation of a statement (Malek 1993). While there have been attempts to reduce the trend for segregated education, it has been noted that local authorities continue to refer children with emotional/behavioural difficulties to special schools and units (Lloyd-Smith and Davies 1995), and residential provision for those defined in this way has therefore continued to increase (Berridge 1990). In one study of four residential schools almost a third of the children were subject to a care order (Grimshaw with Berridge 1994) and a Government examination has been recommended of the extent to which residential special schools are being inappropriately used as a substitute for social services care and support (Waterhouse 2000).

Mental Health

It has been argued that political and professional interest in mental health services for young people intensified as a result of the moral panic about childhood following the death of James Bulger (Coppock 1997). One in five of the population is under 16, although the expenditure on child and adolescent mental health services is only five per cent of the total spent on mental health and it is estimated that two million children under sixteen have mental health problems (Kurtz *et al.* 1994). Furthermore, reviews (Kurtz *et al.* 1994; NHS 1995) found that child and adolescent mental health services were unplanned, inconsistent across the country and variable in quality. Although a strategic approach to the commissioning and provision of services was recommended, they continue to be patchy and unco-ordinated (DH 1997a).

There are conflicting views about the level of psychological disturbance at which the intervention of children's mental health services are required. Some professionals contend that there are now unprecedented levels of disturbed behaviour, including violence in young people (for example, Peter Wilson, in Sone 1994). In contrast, others suggest that many children are referred to the mental health services because of the lack of resources in other professional systems, particularly social services and education, which creates the impression of an increase in mental health problems (Jaffa and Deszery 1989; Malek 1991, 1993; Steinberg *et al.* 1981).

Ninety per cent of children and young people in psychiatric units are 'informal' patients admitted by their parents or responsible local authorities rather than 'formal' patients who are subject to the compulsory powers of the Mental Health Act 1983 (NHS 1986). Such 'informal' patients are in effect also 'in custody' because they cannot discharge themselves without the consent of their parents or the responsible local authority. It has been argued that the reluctance 'formally' to detain young people under the Mental Health Act leaves them without any form of protection against unnecessary placements or extreme measures of control (Bates 1994), although even that provided for compulsory patients by the Code of Practice and Mental Health Review Tribunal has been shown to be inadequate (Children's Legal Centre 1993).

A major issue of concern in the treatment of young people in the mental health system relates to the representation of practices designed to control children as therapeutic interventions which are administered in their own best interests. Young people exhibiting difficult behaviour in psychiatric care are particularly vulnerable to 'sanctioned abuse' (Stein 1993), as drug therapy, one of the most powerful methods of control, is legitimately used in addition to other forms of control (Hodgkin 1993). In recent years, the rights of young people to refuse medical treatment given by the Children Act 1989 have been overridden (see Re R, Re W and Re K, W and H) so that it is now virtually impossible for young people with a 'negative mental health label' to refuse treatment (Masson 1991). The use of the rhetoric of treatment to disguise practice which is designed to control has also been found in other forms of institutional care, including secure accommodation, and is an important issue in the care versus control debate which will be examined further (Children's Legal Centre 1991; Coppock 1997; Kelly 1992; Levy and Kahan 1991; Ogden 1991).

Notwithstanding these concerns about practices within the mental health system, young people in social services care and in custody have been found to have mental health needs which are greater than those in the general population of the same age (Berridge and Brodie 1998; DH 1997a; DH 1998; Farmer and Pollock 1998; Howard League 1995, 1997; Sinclair and Gibbs 1998). It seems that as well as children finding themselves in the psychiatric system because of the lack of resources in the other systems, some young people are in the care and criminal justice systems because of the failure of the adolescent mental health services to respond to their needs.

Criminal Justice

As already shown, there has been an increase in custodial provision for young people, particularly during the last five years as the number remanded and sentenced to custody has risen steeply (Howard League 1995). Legislation and policies have ignored the argument that only those young people convicted of serious, violent offences should be locked up, only then in a system of secure care rather than prison, and that resources should be re-directed into non-custodial alternatives (Howard League 1997). Young people can be detained in a range of custodial institutions: remand centres and young offender institutions which provide only for boys; Secure Training Centres; adult prisons and local authority secure units. The choice of placement is determined on the basis of a number of factors including age and gender, the nature of the offence and whether the offender is on remand or convicted, the length of sentence and the availability of places. Cost is also a significant factor, as placements in Secure Training Centres and local authority secure accommodation are substantially higher than those in prison. However, in practice the allocation of places is an arbitrary process.

As already noted, girls are neglected and marginalized in custodial and community provision in the criminal justice system (Howard League 1997). There have been no young offender institutions for girls, so those sentenced to detention have been held in adult prisons partly designated as young offender institutions where they live alongside convicted adult offenders (Howard League 1997). While some steps have been taken to remedy this situation with young offender units for under-21s set up in two prisons and juvenile units for under-18s in four women's prisons, these have been described as 'prisons within prisons' (Howard League 1998b) and concerns have been expressed that as facilities continue to be shared, the inappropriate prison culture will extend into the units. The inadequacy of community alternatives to custody for girls has been shown to be a contributory factor in the increasing use of custodial remands and sentences as an early rather than a last resort.

The use of penal custody for young people has been widely criticized and the operational regimes condemned as cruel, dangerous, dehumanizing and totally counterproductive in terms of reducing offending (see for example, DH 1997a; Goldson 1997c; Howard League 1995,1997). The welfare principle of the 'best interests of the child' is subjugated to factors such as punishment, retribution, protection of the public, risk and confidence in the system (Howard League 1998a).

Social Services

Social services departments have powers and duties under the Children Act 1989 to provide services to children in need or at risk of significant harm and their families, and to take steps to encourage children not to commit offences. Furthermore, policy initiatives such as '*Quality Protects*' (DH 1998a), which is designed to transform the public care system, and the Government's Objectives for Children Social Services have established clear goals for improvements in social work with children and their families.

The predominant problems resulting in intervention by social workers relate to school issues, family relationships and offending (Triseliotis *et al.* 1995), persistent non-school attendance, the 'moral' welfare of girls and health issues, particularly with regard to the use of drugs and alcohol (Farmer and Parker 1991; Sinclair *et al.* 1995). The precipitating factors for children admitted to substitute care have been found to be unacceptable behaviour, home-related and school problems (Packman and Hall 1995; Triseliotis *et al.* 1995) and a breakdown in family relationships (Sinclair and Gibbs 1998). More recently three main factors were identified for children being looked after: behaviour control problems, abuse of the child and more general concerns which included inadequate care and relationship problems (Berridge and Brodie 1998).

Children admitted to social services care have generally experienced deprivation (Bebbington and Miles 1989; Triseliotis *et al.* 1995) and frequently have histories of abuse and neglect (Kahan 1994; Madge 1994). As already noted, it is also increasingly evident that many have mental health needs and educational problems (Berridge and Brodie 1996; DH 1998; Farmer and Pollock 1998; Sinclair and Gibbs 1998). Teenagers, particularly those aged 14 and 15, are particularly vulnerable to admission to social services accommodation (Bebbington and Miles 1989; Rowe *et al.* 1989; Sinclair and Gibbs 1996) and girls are more likely than boys to request their own admission as an escape route from emotional pressures at home (Hudson 1989). Whether young people remain at home seems to depend on factors other than the degree of difficulty of their behaviour, such as the attitude of their parents and the availability of community services. Many admissions occur in circumstances of crisis, often due to inadequate support or the failure of intervention by other professional systems (Malek 1993). The admission process has implications for the success of a placement (Berridge and Cleaver 1987; Packman *et al.* 1986) and unplanned placements which fail can lead to a damaging pattern of multiple placements and the inherent instability which characterizes the care careers of many young people (see for example Stein 1993). The breakdown of foster placements may result in admission to residential care and, while difficult behaviour may not have been the reason for the initial admission, it can become an issue in residential care as children learn difficult behaviour from other young people.

There have been significant changes in the residential sector during the last two decades, with a substantial reduction in the numbers and sizes of homes, the numbers of children accommodated and in the more complex nature of their problems. Social policy during this time has emphasized the importance of family placements for children and given priority to foster care and adoption. This has resulted in less specialization in residential homes, meaning that children and young people with different needs are frequently accommodated together. A negative image of residential care has been compounded during the last decade as the plight of children has been exposed by a trail of independent inquiries into personal and institutional abuse in residential child care (for example DH 1997a; Kirkwood 1993; Levy and Kahan 1991; Waterhouse 2000).

This negative image of residential care has influenced its use as a 'last resort' by social workers and managers, rather than the placement of choice (DH 1991a; Sinclair and Gibbs 1998). As the number of residential homes has reduced, the relatively high costs (in comparison with non-specialist foster care placements) and limited resources have contributed to the difficulties in meeting the needs of young people. The lack of expertise and professional qualifications of staff have been identified as an important factor in the low status of residential work (Berridge and Brodie 1998; DH 1991a) and in the persistence of abusive regimes (Waterhouse 2000). The paradox of the most difficult and complex young people being looked after by the least experienced, trained and qualified staff is not new, but it has been sharply refocused by the inquiries into the abuse of children in residential care. The importance of training, supervision and staff development has been emphasized and initiatives developed (DH 1991a; DH 1992a; DH 1997a; DH 1998) but it seems that improvements in training have so far had only a limited impact on practice in residential care (Waterhouse 2000). It has been found that professional qualifications are frequently regarded by staff as a passport out of residential work and those returning from training often experience marginalization and leave (Berridge and Brodie 1998), giving among their reasons for so doing poor career prospects and low status (Hills *et al.* 1998).

Despite the requirements of Children Act 1989 and the Utting Reports (DH 1991a; DH 1997a), many residential homes continue to lack a clear theoretical orientation or method of work and have no clear statement as to their purpose and function (Berridge and Brodie 1998). Residential care has functioned within a 'theoretical void' (Stein 1993) which has allowed abusive regimes, legitimated as therapy, to become established (Levy and Kahan 1991). Regimes in residential homes are frequently organized on the basis of the needs of the institution rather than the young people and confusion about their purpose can contribute to institutionalized, potentially abusive practice. Issues of control have been found to dominate, with emphasis on discipline rather than care and therapeutic help, and powerful cultures of institutionalization (Parkin and Green 1997). The style of leadership and the prevailing cultures of staff and children powerfully influence the quality of the residential experience. The incidence of bullying by staff and children and running away have both been found to correspond closely to the culture and regime operating in the home (Millham *et al.* 1978).

Stein (1993) critically examined the concept of abuse in residential care and identified four distinct forms: sanctioned, institutional, systematic and individual. These different forms of abuse can only be fully understood through recognition of the inequalities of power across the range of dimensions which have already been mentioned. Powerlessness is experienced by children in their relationships with (particularly male) adults, and through the wider policies and practices in residential care. The powerlessness of children may be mirrored by staff who, being powerless themselves, are unable to provide protection for children (Morrison 1990). Particular difficulties have been identified for women workers (Aymer 1992; Parkin and Green 1997) whose powerlessness is institutionalized through the maintenance of traditional gender roles and their compliance with expectations to 'police' the sexuality of girls. This reinforces the stereotype of the 'predatory' young woman, denies 'their shared sexual vulnerability from adult males' (Aymer 1992, p.192) and means that women workers fail to provide empowering role models for girls.

Notwithstanding its negative image, residential care is regarded as an essential part of the range of services for children (DH 1991a; Frost and Stein 1989) and is the principal form of substitute care for teenagers, some of whom will have had previous placements in foster care (Aymer 1992; Berridge and Brodie 1998; Bullock *et al.* 1993; DH 1998; Madge 1994; Rowe *et al.* 1989). The opportunity to match the needs of such young people with the most suitable homes is limited by the absence in many homes of a clear theoretical orientation and statement of purpose (Berridge and Brodie 1998; Sinclair and Gibbs 1998). As well as an apparent reluctance by some managers, many others are not given the discretion to define objectives and implement more selective admissions procedures. In addition to the confusion in regimes, this can result in an inappropriate and even dangerous combination of young people, exposing those who are vulnerable to additional risks. There are particular concerns about the combination in residential care of girls and boys, of different categories of offenders and non-offenders and of abusing children with victims of abuse. They will be reviewed briefly here but examined in more detail later, as the effects of combining these groups of young people in secure residential institutions are matters of especial interest.

Girls have traditionally been in the minority in residential care and their different needs have not been recognized or given priority. However, even where they have been found to be in the majority, inadequate recognition has been given to their needs for positive gender role models and protection from sexual exploitation, particularly in establishments with predominantly masculine cultures (Berridge and Brodie 1998; Farmer and Pollock 1998). In residential care the sexual behaviour of girls attracts greater attention and surveillance than that of boys. Boys' sexuality is invisible and they are not seen as either potentially abusive or at risk of abuse while girls' sexuality is 'perceived as something to be punished, controlled, forbidden, made invisible and seen as taboo' (Parkin and Green 1997, p.80). Furthermore, Farmer and Pollock found that 'the sexualised behaviour of girls was a particularly neglected area, and their behaviour excited rejection by male workers and only a passive stance by many caregivers ... They were viewed as troublesome rather than troubled' (1998, p.131). It has been shown that staff lack a theoretical framework or practice ideas for working with sexualized girls (Hudson 1989). Furthermore, there is a lack of commitment by social services departments to the provision of services to girls (Jesson 1993) and a separatist strategy has been advocated as a way of reducing the marginality of girls in trouble and challenging 'the invisibility and misrecognition of girls' needs' (Hudson 1989, p.219).

The primary concerns expressed about mixing offenders with children admitted for other reasons relate to the difficulties of working with offenders within small residential units, the lack of specialist intervention to address offending behaviour and the dangers of 'criminal contamination' of the non-offenders (Berridge and Brodie 1996, 1998). This may be one of the factors which leads to young people in residential care receiving a criminal record. Other factors include the policy of many local authorities to report to the police young people who cause 'criminal damage' in their residential unit. In a recent study 40 per cent of young people admitted to residential care without any previous caution or conviction received one whilst they were in the home (Sinclair and Gibbs 1998).

Although it has been recommended that children who abuse should be separated from victims of abuse (DH 1991a), residential homes commonly accommodate them together (Sinclair and Gibbs 1998). Westcott and Clement (1992) found that abuse in residential care was being perpetrated by another child rather than an adult. It has been argued that children who abuse should only be placed in residential homes where their behaviour will be addressed (NCH 1992). However, the degree to which residential homes are equipped to work with such problems has been questioned (Barter 1997; NCH 1992) and children who do not know if a child has abused others may be at risk because they are both unaware of the need to protect themselves and inadequately protected by staff.

For many young people residential care not only fails to provide the required solutions but instead becomes part of the problem. The education difficulties of young people in residential care have aroused increasing concern in recent years (Berridge and Brodie 1998; DH 1997a; Sinclair and Gibbs 1998; SSI/Ofsted 1995). The health needs of looked-after children have been neglected, despite recognition of the increased vulnerability of this group (Biehal *et al.* 1992; DH 1997a). Low priority has been given to routine medical care, to health education, including sexual health, and to preventive work related to sexuality and personal relationships, drug and alcohol use. The mental health needs of young people in residential care have been the focus of increasing concern (Berridge and Brodie 1998; Farmer and Pollock 1998; Sinclair and Gibbs 1996). Many young people, particularly girls, are admitted to residential care because of concerns about their sexual behaviour and some because of sexual abuse. It is now emerging that residential care itself presents a risk of initiation into prostitution (Farmer and Pollock 1998; O'Neill *et al.* 1995; Shaw and Butler 1998). Adolescent prostitution is a survival strategy for many young people and those in residential care who lack close support are particularly vulnerable. There has been a lack of clear policies and few workers have an understanding of the behaviour of adolescent prostitutes or experience of developing appropriate interventions, and professional responses range from punitive to indifferent (Jesson 1993; Parkin and Green 1997).

Child prostitution is belatedly the focus of national and international attention as the extent and nature of the problem has been revealed (see for example Lee and O'Brien 1995; The Children's Society 1997), and there were calls from among others the Association of Chief Police Officers and the Association of Directors of Social Services for child prostitutes to be treated as victims of abuse in need of protection rather than criminals, and the adults who abuse them to be prosecuted. Government guidance on safeguarding children involved in prostitution which recommends these changes, and also specifically addresses the vulnerability of children living in and leaving care has now been issued (DH 2000a). This issue will be discussed later.

When residential care fails to control or change the behaviour of such young people, admission to local authority secure accommodation may be considered. It is frequently the inadequacy of the institutions rather than the needs of difficult children which results in the demand for a secure place, reflected in the differences between institutions and local authorities in the requirement for and use of secure accommodation (DH 1997a; DH 1997b; Harris and Timms 1993; Kelly 1992; Millham *et al.* 1978). It is argued that locking up such young people serves the primary function of punishment rather than protection, and that young people are punished as much for their disadvantage as their wrongdoing (Goldson 1997d). Local authority secure accommodation is substantially better resourced than other forms of residential care provided by local authorities, and secure units present themselves as specialist facilities, even in some cases as 'centres of excellence' which have the expertise to meet the needs of exceptionally difficult young people. But this image may be seriously misleading, as it seems that many of the problems associated with residential care can also be seen to characterize local authority secure accommodation.

Conclusion

This chapter has examined the concept of adolescence and the professional systems which respond to the social, emotional and behavioural difficulties young people manifest. Those in the care system who are considered to have 'extreme' needs (Stewart and Tutt 1987) which cannot be met in any other form of provision and those in the criminal justice system who are 'vulnerable' or whose circumstances are regarded as 'exceptional' (Howard League 1998a) are placed in local authority secure accommodation, that is locked institutional care. The next chapter will examine the role and function of this type of provision for children in trouble.

THREE

Local Authority Secure Accommodation

Introduction

Secure accommodation is a generic term which is used to describe locked accommodation for adults and children within the health, education, prison and child-care systems. This chapter will examine the secure accommodation which is provided in the child-care system by local authority social services departments in England and Wales and defined by the Children Act 1989 as 'accommodation provided for the purpose of restricting liberty'. Secure accommodation has an ambiguous, interdependent role in the child-care and criminal justice systems and is the interface where the conflicting philosophies of welfare and justice converge.

The issue of locking up children is emotive, and secure accommodation encapsulates many of the confusions in society's attitudes to young people in trouble. The reasons for depriving children and young people of their liberty within the welfare and criminal justice systems fall under five general headings: for retribution, for deterrence, for containment, to prevent them re-offending, because they are a danger to others and because they are a danger to themselves. However, the primary purpose of secure accommodation 'is continuous and effective control' (DHSS 1977).

The Historical Context

The current system of secure units has developed from 'special units' which were opened between 1964 and 1966 at three approved schools, Kingswood, Redhill and Red Bank, to provide a total of 60 places for boys who were 'exceptionally disturbed', 'exceptionally unruly and unco-operative' or persistent absconders. Other categories of young people were added later, for example those who had committed serious crimes (under section 53 of the Children and Young Persons Act 1933) were added in 1968.

The Children and Young Persons Act 1933 established the national system of approved schools, which were open institutions under the control of the Home Office to provide for those who were persistently delinquent. During the 1950s there was an increasingly punitive approach to young offenders and the lobby for secure, in addition to custodial, provision gathered momentum. The Criminal Justice Act 1948 provided for the establishment of junior (14–17 years) and senior (17–21 years) detention centres, institutions which were intended to be an alternative to short terms of imprisonment and to corporal punishment, operating under a punitive regime which subsequently became known as the 'short, sharp shock'. However, the objectives of detention centres were inconsistent and contradictory, reflecting both the view that punishment would act as a deterrent and that education and training would reform the offender. The more emphasis there was on 'treatment', the greater the contradictions. The early development was slow and controversial and the first four centres, set up between 1952 and 1957, were regarded as an experimental form of custodial treatment. Views varied about the type of offender who would benefit from a detention centre placement: the first offender or offenders for whom other forms of treatment had been unsuccessful. Although they were not judged a 'success', a rapid expansion of detention centre provision was approved and by 1961 it became the standard, short-term custodial sentence available to the courts, rather than a custodial sentence suitable only for a minority of offenders. In 1962 a centre for girls was opened, although it closed approximately 18 months later. It has been suggested that the detention centre was an experiment which could not be allowed to fail (Hall *et al.* 1975) because the demands on the penal system resulting from rising crime rates among the young meant that ten weeks in a detention centre was regarded by policy-makers and the courts as a preferable alternative to corporal punishment, a short prison sentence or longer borstal placement.

Punishments in approved schools were reviewed in 1951 by the Franklin Committee which reported that it had received strong representations for the establishment of locked provision for persistent absconders. The problem of absconding also led the Home Office Children's Department Inspectorate to set up a working party which recommended the establishment of closed blocks for boys attached to approved schools in the North West, Midlands and London areas. Even though the absconding rate from girls' institutions was greater than that from boys', closed establishments were not considered appropriate for girls. As most of them were not offenders, the need to protect the public was not an issue and detention facilities were available in the girls' schools. These recommendations were referred to the Approved Schools Central Advisory Committee which set up a further working party to examine in greater detail the possibility of closed schools. While the working party was sitting, disturbances at Carlton Approved School resulted in a Government inquiry which reported to Parliament in December 1959 (Home Office 1959). Although the report attributed the disturbances to poor personal relationships, and most of the boys' complaints of ill-treatment were upheld, it concentrated on the 'unruly and subversive boys' and recommended the introduction of secure establishments and detention rooms in schools for senior boys.

The Carlton report influenced the working party set up in 1960 by the Approved Schools Central Advisory Committee chaired by the Children's Department Inspectorate with representatives of the Home Office, which started with the assumption that secure facilities were necessary (Home Office 1960a). It identified four groups of boys who would be candidates for closed establishments: persistent absconders, exceptionally unruly and unco-operative boys, exceptionally disturbed boys requiring psychiatric care and medical misfits (sic) such as epileptics and diabetics. The working party endorsed much of the Carlton report in recommending closed units at three schools, detention rooms in senior and intermediate schools and provision to transfer unruly boys to borstal. Attention was paid by the working party to public opinion which it was felt would be opposed to the introduction of secure units and the detention of young children. It therefore recommended less conspicuous closed blocks within schools and a lower age limit of 13 years. The language to describe the facilities was also the focus of debate and some of the euphemisms introduced, which Cohen (1985) described as 'controltalk', are still in use. Euphemisms based on medical terminology such as 'treatment' and 'intensive care' were used both because custodial measures were thought to be inconsistent with child-care philosophy and because such language was thought to be reassuring (Cawson and Martell 1979). Simultaneously, a Home Office working party (Home Office 1960b) was undertaking a review of the approved school system to report to the Ingleby Committee on Children and Young Persons (Home Office 1960c). It referred to the report on closed facilities and endorsed its recommendations.

In all these reports the 'rotten apples' theory was accepted as the cause of all the problems of the approved schools (Cawson and Martell 1979, p.14). The language used compounded the stigmatization of the children it described. In addition, the pressure for closed units came from the belief that increasing numbers of children admitted to the approved schools were presenting violent or aggressive behaviour, although some commentators dismissed this as a 'myth' (Taylor *et al.* 1980). In the clamour for closed units, a few dissenting voices were heard. A representative of the Headmasters Association argued that problems could be solved by improvements to the approved school service and staff training, the first suggestion from within the system that the schools themselves might be responsible for the boys' absconding or disruptive behaviour. This recognition that demands for security reflect the needs of inadequate institutions rather than the needs of difficult children has been a recurrent theme (Harris and Timms 1993; Millham *et al.* 1978; National Children's Bureau 1995).

The three 'special units' accommodated boys from the age of 13 within an explicitly punitive regime, described in the reports as 'brisk'. Even before they opened, conflicts between the treatment philosophy of the approved school and the containment and control intentions of the Home Office were evident. In 1967, the Home Office reviewed the functioning of the special units (Home Office 1967) and this was followed by the general reappraisal of the child-care system which led to the introduction of the 1969 Children and Young Persons Act. A further review was then requested to update the situation of the special units and to provide guidelines for local authorities which were to take over responsibility for them from the Home Office (Home Office 1970). A number of worrying themes emerged from their report. The failure rate of the units was high, in that most of the boys were reconvicted, and the report complained of the 'dumping ground' function of the units, the lack of effective selection criteria and the inability of the units to manage severely disturbed boys who had a detrimental effect on others. However, the report confirmed the need for the special units and that they were appropriate placements for young people who had committed serious offences, while openly acknowledging the inability of staff to offer therapeutic intervention for disturbed and dangerous young people.

The issue of very disturbed boys remained at the forefront and was responded to by increased control in the form of padded cells in the units, increasing numbers of transfers to other parts of the system and calls for an institution which could cope with disturbed boys and girls where psychiatric treatment would be available. The focus on severely disturbed children became even more intense at this time with two children, including one girl, convicted of murder, which served to legitimate the various working party recommendations. The Working Party on Severely Disturbed Children and Young Persons in Approved Schools reported in 1968 (Home Office 1968) and although the report was not made public at the time it recommended the establishment of a new unit for severely disturbed boys and girls aged 12 to 19 and later formed the basis of guidance for youth treatment centres. The first Youth Treatment Centre, St Charles, was opened in Brentwood in 1971 providing a psychotherapeutic regime under the control of the Department of Health and Social Security rather than the Home Office. It closed in 1995. The second unit, Glenthorne, which provided a behavioural regime, was opened in Birmingham in 1978, also under the control of the Department of Health. An earlier decision that separate units for boys and girls should be provided was reversed on the basis that it would create an environment 'too artificial and removed from normal social opportunities for the promotion of growth towards maturity' (Cawson and Martell 1979, p.33).

Following the partial implementation of the 1969 Children and Young Persons Act, the demands for secure provision increased. This legislation 'institutionalised the confusion between justice, punishment and welfare' (Timms 1995, p.208) by blurring the boundaries between the welfare perspectives of social work and the control and punishment perspectives of the justice system. Deep, long-standing conflicts were revealed in philosophy and practice which were irreconcilable because of the differences in expectation and role performance of the different welfare and justice positions (Morris 1976). The establishment of a national system of Community Homes with Education in place of approved schools emphasized the diminution in the distinction between deprivation and delinquency. The replacement of approved school orders with care orders transferred the responsibility for young people from the probation service to social services departments. Reservations were expressed about expansion in the numbers of secure places and it was recommended that any future development should be restricted to larger secure units (DHSS 1972). However, there was a rapid expansion during the 1970s and early 1980s which was funded by Government and supported by professionals, including social services departments who reacted with what was described as 'the paranoia that characterizes "dustbins" under stress' (Millham *et al.* 1978, p.30). This highlighted a fundamental and continuing paradox: the social work profession supports the development of local authority secure accommodation while simultaneously opposing other forms of custody for children.

By the late 1970s objections were being raised more widely about the use of secure accommodation which had expanded virtually unplanned, unmonitored and without evaluation of its effectiveness or the alternatives available. From the 60 places available in the special units in 1966, by June 1981 there were at least 537 officially approved places for girls as well as boys in community homes with education, in observation and assessment centres, in single detention cells and in the two youth treatment centres (Children's Legal Centre 1982)[1]. One of the questions raised related to the appropriateness of secure accommodation as a response to young people who run away. A Committee Report concluded 'we do not consider that absconding in itself should result in a child being locked up' (House of Commons 1975, Para 78) and suggested, although failed to recommend, that such young people should simply be located and brought back, as was the practice in some other countries, notably Sweden. A second concern related to the type of young people who were being placed in the units. Less problematic children were being held in the units to fill empty places (the principle of demand following supply) and it was noted that some community homes were more likely to seek placement in secure accommodation than others which appropriately managed children's disruptive behaviour. The third area of concern related to the wide variation in the use of secure accommodation made by local authorities, and illustrated the very broad nature of criteria for admission and the lack of clear guidelines. Furthermore, locking up young people on executive decision rather than through a legal route by court order was seen to be contrary to the rules of 'natural justice' and in breach of the European Convention on Human Rights. These concerns were fuelled by the economic crisis of the late 1970s which highlighted the unacceptable cost of the increased use of institutional care and by the enhanced awareness of children's rights following the United Nations Year of the Child, the founding of the Children's Legal Centre and other campaigning groups which focused attention on the issue of children's liberty.

A working group set up to provide guidelines for the inspection of secure units (DHSS 1979) and the publication of the Department's own research (Cawson and Martell 1979) were followed by a third study which addressed the use to be made of secure accommodation by local authorities (DHSS 1981a). It recommended that admission should be by court authorization to provide some judicial safeguards for children deprived of their freedom. In November 1981 an adjudication by the European Court of Justice ruled that the arrangements for placement of young people in secure accommodation by executive decision were unlawful. Amendments to the Criminal Justice Bill 1982 and the Child

Care Act 1980 requiring local authorities to obtain a court order to hold children in secure accommodation for more than 72 hours in any 28-day period, and providing for the legal representation of children, came into force with the introduction of the Secure Accommodation Regulations 1983. This legislation was replaced in 1991 by the Children Act 1989.

The guidance and regulations accompanying the Children Act 1989 were informed by a review of secure accommodation undertaken in 1988 and published in a consultation document (DH 1989). The findings confirmed that secure accommodation was necessary but, consistent with the policies of decarceration and decriminalization, recommended that there was no need for increased provision and that it should be the duty of local authorities to provide alternative accommodation. It found an inefficient use of secure accommodation, variation in use between local authorities, a poor system of gate-keeping and inadequate court scrutiny of applications (Stephens and Hopper 1992). The apparent injustice in the position of children admitted for welfare reasons also caused increasing concern. There was a focus by the courts and professionals on what was deemed to be in the best interests of the child, thereby reducing the child to an object of concern whose rights to liberty were subordinated to their perceived need for 'treatment'. This fuelled the controversy about whether treatment, prescribed by the court and social services, could be anything but punishment (Morris *et al.* 1980), still an important issue in the debate about secure accommodation. An over-compliance by the courts with the recommendations of local authorities was reported, with no independent assessment of the child's rights and interests and a 'rubber stamping' of applications (Harris and Timms 1993a). To remedy this, applications under section 25 of the Children Act 1989 were included in the list of specified proceedings in which guardians *ad litem* are appointed.

The Criminal Justice Act 1991 abolished penal custody for 14-year-olds and ended remands of 15- and 16-year-olds to prison, introducing provisions for their placement instead in secure accommodation. In response to this and the provisions in the Criminal Justice and Public Order Act 1994, and despite the findings of the earlier review, a Government-funded capital development programme of secure accommodation was initiated to provide 170 additional places for three groups of young people in the criminal justice system: 15- and 16-year-old boys who would otherwise be remanded to penal custody; 12- to 14-year-olds remanded and convicted under the Criminal Justice and Public Order Act 1994; and 10- to 13-year-old children convicted under section 53[2] of the Children and Young Persons Act 1933. This represented a massive investment in secure accommodation to cater for the needs of young people in the criminal justice system. However, even before completion, it was described as 'woefully inadequate' (Jarvis 1996) in the context of the changing criminal justice climate from 1993 onwards which saw a radical return to the incarceration of young offenders. The substantial expansion in secure accommodation was not met with any corresponding decrease in the use of other forms of custody. On the contrary, a significant change in policy introduced by the Criminal Justice and Public Order Act 1994 enabled private and voluntary organizations to provide secure accommodation and increased custodial provision in the criminal justice system with the establishment of a military training centre (which has since closed) and the opening in 1998/1999 of the first three privately run Secure Training Centres.

Local authority secure accommodation is part of the provision for children in need under Part III of the Children Act 1989, yet this expansion programme occurred simultaneously with a significant decline in other forms of residential care. Cautions against increases in secure provision have been expressed repeatedly (Harris and Timms 1993; Millham *et al.* 1978; National Children's Bureau 1995). More places mean that more children are locked up, particularly where the lack of investment in non-secure provision means that the number, choice and quality of non-secure alternatives has declined, and community alternatives to custody are regarded by politicians and the courts as less acceptable than custodial penalties for young people in the criminal justice system. Local authority secure accommodation is now part of the 'secure estate', with the majority of places purchased for young offenders by the Youth Justice Board, and as such is primarily a facility for offenders. In the discourse about youth justice and the preoccupation with young offenders, the position of non-offenders in local authority secure accommodation, the majority of whom are girls, has received little attention.

The Legal Framework

The statutory framework which provides for the placement of young people in local authority secure accommodation is complex and has been described as a 'legal labyrinth' (Dawson and Stephens 1991). Young people may be placed in secure accommodation through welfare and criminal justice routes. Theoretically, there is a third route through mental health legislation, but it is rarely used. Young people admitted through the welfare route are considered to be at risk of significant harm while those admitted through the criminal route will either have been remanded or detained to await trial or sentence, or convicted and sentenced under the Crime and Disorder Act 1998 or the Children and Young Persons Act 1933. The admission route through which young people are placed in secure accommodation is a gendered issue, reflecting the different attitudes to girls and boys in the care and criminal justice systems. More than three quarters of the girls in secure units are admitted through the welfare route while almost the same proportion of boys are admitted through the criminal justice routes (DH 2000).

Welfare Route

The criteria that determine admissions to secure accommodation through the welfare route are set out in section 25 of the Children Act 1989. Prior to the Children Act 1989 an order could be made on two main grounds: the child had a history of absconding, was likely to abscond again and if he (sic) did so was likely to put his physical, mental or moral welfare at risk; or that the child was likely to harm himself or others. The Children Act 1989 replaced the phrase 'physical, mental or moral welfare' with the concept of significant harm and introduced a guardian *ad litem* into the proceedings. The criteria apply to children who are the subject of a care order, accommodated or remanded by a court to local authority accommodation. It is notable that local authorities have the power to make decisions concerning the restriction of the liberty of some children for whom they do not exercise parental responsibility.

There are several groups of children to whom section 25 of the Act does not apply: those who are detained under any provision of the Mental Health Act 1983; those in respect of whom an order has been made under section 53 of the Children and Young Persons Act 1933; those who are accommodated under section 20[5] of the Act (accommodation of persons over 16 but under 21); and those in respect of whom an order has been made under section 43 of the Act (child assessment order).

Section 25 states that a child who is being looked after by a local authority (or who is remanded to local authority accommodation but does not meet the Regulation 6 criteria, described below) may not be placed, and if placed may not be kept, in accommodation provided for the purpose of restricting liberty (secure accommodation) unless it appears:

1. that -
   (a) he has a history of absconding and is likely to abscond from any other description of accommodation; and
   (b) if he absconds he is likely to suffer significant harm; or
2. that if he is kept in any other description of accommodation he is likely to injure himself or other persons.

While the prior approval of the Secretary of State is required for the placement of children under 13, the local authority has the primary responsibility for deciding whether the criteria are met. It has the power to place a child in secure accommodation for up to 72 hours in any 28-day period without a court order. Concern has been expressed about the use of this power, which can result in young people being deprived of their liberty without prior knowledge and placed at a considerable geographical distance from family and community. Although the regulations provide that children accommodated by health or education authorities may also be placed in a secure facility the majority of applications are made by local authority social services departments.

There are some significant problems with these criteria and with the court process. The criteria are 'opaque' and arbitrary decisions continue to be made of the sort which characterized proceedings before the criteria were introduced (Littlewood 1996). Section 25 is the only section of the Act which severely limits the discretion of the court. As already noted, if the criteria are met an order is mandatory and the only discretion which lies with the court is the maximum period for which the child can be kept in secure accommodation. The court has no power to consider some fundamental issues set out in section 1 of the Act, such as the likely effect on the child of a placement in secure accommodation, the ascertainable wishes and feelings of the child involved and whether making the order will positively contribute to the welfare of the child. This section of the Act gives local authorities the power to place in secure accommodation, in company with convicted and unconvicted offenders, children who have been abused or whose behaviour such as prostitution may indicate prior abuse, regardless of the general regulations (DH 1991c) and the recommendations of Sir William Utting (DH 1991a, 1997a).

The court has the power to make an interim or full order for up to a maximum of three months on a first application and up to six months on subsequent applications. Once the order is made, the applicant has the power to detain the child for the whole or part of the period of time ordered, without any review by the court. If the criteria cease to be met the child's liberty should be restored, but there are no means by which this can be ensured. The difficulties for children attempting to demonstrate that criteria are no longer met when they are locked up will be self-evident and the local authority is not required to seek the opinions of others in reaching a decision. Regulations 15 and 16 of the Children (Secure Accommodation) Regulations 1991 require that the review panel, which should meet within 28 days of placement and subsequently at 3-month intervals, include an independent person, but there is no obligation for the local authority or the secure unit to follow the recommendations made by the panel. The system of renewal of orders at six-month intervals has been described as 'the worst of all possible worlds' (Harris and Timms 1993, p.167). There is no provision for children to apply to the court for their detention to be reviewed, and once a full order has been made the Act prevents the continuing involvement of the guardian *ad litem.* It has been argued that in such circumstances the making of an order is in breach of both the Convention for the Protection of Human Rights and Fundamental Freedoms (Article 5) and Article 37 of the UN Convention on the Rights of the Child (Butler and Hardy 1997) and it seems likely that this will be legally challenged following the implementation in October 2000 of the Human Rights Act 1998.

Absconding is the behaviour most likely to result in a secure accommodation order in welfare proceedings and the abandonment of this ground has been recommended (National Children's Bureau 1995). There is no legal definition of absconding, a term which is used only in this part of the Act. The Collins English Dictionary defines it as 'to run away secretly, especially to avoid prosecution or punishment'. In the context of secure accommodation proceedings the term is used to describe diverse behaviours and carries assumptions about young people who abscond with little assessment of their behaviour or the reasons for it. Running away is itself deemed to put children at risk of significant harm by the definition contained in the Children Act 1989. The criterion of absconding is very easily met and although no significant gender differences have been found in the pattern of running away (see for example Stein *et al.* 1994; Wade *et al.* 1998), girls are more vulnerable to the use of this criterion than boys. In these legal proceedings the reasons why young people run away become irrelevant, even though there is increasing recognition that many young people run away from home and care because of abuse (Waterhouse 2000).

The criteria that refer to self-harm relate closely to mental health legislation. There is an overlap between secure accommodation and psychiatric services, but little co-ordination or coherence in the decision-making process which determines where young people are placed. The limitations on the discretion of the courts to consider the effects on young people of making an order mean that no attention is given to the potential increase in the risk of significant harm which can result from placement in secure accommodation. Why young people who self-mutilate, abuse drugs, overdose or suffer sexual exploitation are locked up rather than in health care is an important question that remains to be answered (National Children's Bureau 1995).

In civil proceedings children have no right to be present and can be excluded by the court. This is a matter of particular concern where the children's views and those of their guardian *ad litem* differ and the children are directly instructing their lawyer. In a recent case a boy's guardian and solicitor were denied access to him because it was considered not in his best interests even to be told that an application had been made to place him in secure accommodation (Baum and Walker 1996). In a criminal court by contrast, a custodial sentence cannot be imposed unless the defendant is present even where the defendant is a child, and they have the right to instruct a lawyer. This seems to produce a double standard with apparently less justice for those involved in civil, welfare proceedings which, under the guise of 'protection', may be more punitive.

Criminal Justice Route

There are three groups of young people admitted through the criminal justice route: those who are remanded or detained; those who have been convicted of an offence punishable by imprisonment in the case of someone aged 21 or over; and those who have been convicted of grave offences.

REMANDED OR DETAINED

Regulation 6 of the Children (Secure Accommodation) Regulations 1991 modifies the criteria under section 25 and applies to children under 17 years looked after by a local authority who have been:

1. Detained under section 38(6) of the Police and Criminal Evidence Act 1984; or
2. Remanded to local authority accommodation under section 23 Children and Young Persons Act 1969 (as amended by the Criminal Justice Act 1991); but only where either
   (a) the child has been charged with or convicted of a sexual or violent offence or an offence punishable in an adult with a custodial sentence of 14 years or more; or

(b) has a recent history of absconding while remanded to local authority accommodation and has been charged with or convicted of an imprisonable offence while on remand.

Both detained and remanded children can only be placed in secure accommodation if it appears that any other accommodation is inappropriate because: (a) the child is likely to abscond from other non-secure accommodation or; (b) the child is likely to injure himself or other people if kept in any other non-secure accommodation. There is no requirement to satisfy the criteria to show that young people have a history of absconding or that if they do abscond they will be at risk of significant harm. The maximum period a court can authorise placement in secure accommodation is the period of the remand itself.

SS 97, 98 of the Crime and Disorder Act 1998 amend s.23 of the Children and Young Persons Act 1969 to allow for the implementation of court ordered secure remands to local authority secure accommodation of children aged 12 years and over (effective from 1 June 1999).

CONVICTED

SS 73–79 of the Crime and Disorder Act 1998 provide for Detention and Training Orders (DTO) for children aged 12 years and over (replacing s.1 Criminal Justice and Public Order Act 1994). A DTO is made for a minimum of 4 months and a maximum of 24 months with half the period being served in detention and half in the community under supervision (effective from 1 April 2000).

Children can be placed in secure accommodation when they have been convicted of 'grave offences'. Section 53 [1] of the Children and Young Persons Act 1933 provides that a person under the age of 18 years convicted of murder be detained during her Majesty's pleasure. The indeterminate sentence is the only sentence a court can dispense when children are convicted of murder and it has not been significantly varied by subsequent legislation. The Secretary of State determines where young people are detained.

Section 53[2] provides for longer terms of detention with no statutory minimum and up to a maximum of 'life' for a range of grave offences defined as those which in the case of an adult would carry a custodial sentence of 14 years or more. They include manslaughter, rape, arson, robbery, aggravated burglary and aggravated driving offences. The Criminal Justice and Public Order Act 1994 extended the provisions of this section to apply to children from the age of ten years. Unlike section 53[1] which has remained unchanged by subsequent legislation, the provisions of this section have been increased reflecting changes in the political climate towards young offenders.

The procedure was introduced in 1984 by which those sentenced to 'life' receive a 'tariff date' from the trial judge setting the earliest date by which they could be released. This is subject to executive as well as judicial review and it is suggested that while judicial discretion is more powerful in relation to section 53[2] detainees 'it is the discretion of the executive which prevails in relation to section 53[1] detainees and, especially in a punitive climate, bears far-reaching consequences for young people convicted of murder' (Boswell 1996, p.7). This concern was justified by Government attitudes to the sentences of some high-profile children convicted of murder, and the power of the Home Secretary to set tariffs has been challenged in the European Court of Human Rights (T and V v UK 1999). The Court's judgement requires the Government to bring forward legislation to provide for the tariff to be set in such cases by the trial judge in open court (included in the Criminal Justice and Court Services Bill).

Different attitudes to placement in local authority secure accommodation are evident in the welfare and criminal justice systems. Secure accommodation should be used only as a 'last resort' for those admitted through the welfare route, never because no other placement was available and never for punishment (DH 1991c, p.118). Although this has been shown in practice to be more rhetoric than reality, it is not usually the placement of first choice for those admitted through the welfare route. In contrast, local authority secure accommodation has been recommended as the only form of custody which should be used for young people under 18 whose offences are serious enough to justify the loss of their liberty (Howard League 1995).

The Secure Units

There are 31 secure units run by local authorities in England and Wales providing almost 500 places. Secure units are licensed and monitored by the Department of Health but there is no centralized co-ordination or management of secure accommodation as a service or coherent strategy for its use and each unit functions autonomously, resulting in a lack of consistency between units. Increasingly, secure units are run on an income-generating basis with the pressure to keep occupancy rates high, and the costs of providing services, including therapeutic services, low. The roles and relationships between local authorities and central government, particularly the Department of Health, the Social Services Inspectorate and the Home Office, are complex. The national Youth Justice Board has recently taken responsibility for commissioning and purchasing places for offenders from local authority secure units, as well as the Secure Training Centres and the Prison Service, and for monitoring performance to ensure that regimes are of an appropriate standard. Whether the Youth Justice Board will develop the national strategy for the use of secure accommodation which has been widely called for remains to be seen (for example, National Children's Bureau 1995; Howard League 1995).

There is a lack of co-ordination in the allocation of places which severely restricts any opportunity for matching children's needs with the most suitable unit or achieving any consistency in the implementation of selection criteria. The strongest correlation with admission has been found to be the persistence of professionals rather than the needs of children (Cawson and Martell 1979). The availability of beds also appears to be a determining factor (Littlewood 1987; National Children's Bureau 1995). There are differences between local authorities in the number of applications which are made and in the use of secure accommodation. It has been shown that the most powerful predictor of high admission rates is a local authority's ownership of a unit and children are most likely to be placed in a secure unit if they live in an authority which runs one (Harris and Timms 1993; National Children's Bureau 1995).

As already noted, secure accommodation is substantially better resourced than other residential provision in the care system. The cost of a placement is comparatively high, ranging from £2500 to £4000 per week, and what is purchased for that fee, apart from locks and keys, is an important question. A major issue of concern is the inadequate level of training and lack of professional expertise of staff. This has been identified as a crucial issue in residential care and several reports have called for an increase in the number of qualified residential staff (for example Department of Health 1991a; Waterhouse 2000). In secure residential care the concerns about the quality and expertise of staff are intensified (Harris and Timms 1993) and the majority of staff have been found to be untrained, unqualified and lacking professional expertise (Harris and Timms 1993; Howard League 1995; Kelly 1992; Millham *et al.* 1978; Stewart and Tutt 1987). An important related issue which will be examined further concerns how far therapeutic interventions are provided for young people and the availability of specialist consultation for staff.

The Regimes

The units operate regimes which have variously been described as educational, social educational, custodial and psychotherapeutic (Jarvis 1996). In practice they are all based on behaviour modification models, with sanctions and rewards used to exercise control. The primary objective of all the regimes is security and the buildings reflect the philosophy of control (Stewart and Tutt 1987). Within units high levels of surveillance and control over all aspects of behaviour and day-to-day living are exercised. Within any one unit all the young people are subject to the same regime and methods of control, irrespective of the reason for their admission or their individual needs. The conflicting philosophies of care and control in an overtly custodial setting results in inconsistency in the practice between staff in the units and differences in emphasis between units.

Some units do not have statements of purpose, setting clear objectives and methods of working and even where they exist, there are questions about the extent to which they are implemented and shared by staff. It has been argued that the needs of the institutions are frequently given higher priority than the needs of children (Kelly 1992). All the units provide educational facilities, although there are differences in the range and quality of provision. Concerns include children's isolation from mainstream education provision, resulting in discontinuities in education, the limited curriculum and the wide age range of young people which limits the opportunity for education to be provided to meet their individual needs and abilities.

Resident Group

Government policy has been to promote the development of mixed-gender units, to provide accommodation for young people through all the admission routes and across the whole age range, from 10 to 17. Government and managing local authorities have argued that maximum flexibility in the use of scarce resources is achieved in this way and is most likely to achieve their desired target of 100 per cent occupancy. This policy has resulted in a significant and continuing reduction in the number of places in single-gender units (DH 2000). The marginalization which girls experience in the care and criminal justice systems is perpetuated in secure accommodation itself, particularly where they are alone or in a small minority in a unit with boys. Although the design of the newer buildings allows for some separation of different groups, it appears that this happens infrequently because of the ideological commitment to mixed groups. Those who advocate mixed-gender units argue that they provide a more normal and beneficial living experience for young people. However, where the needs of girls have been considered, concerns have been expressed that although boys frequently benefit from mixed-gender placements, girls are disadvantaged (Gabbidon 1994; National Children's Bureau 1995). The position of girls in secure accommodation is therefore of particular interest and will be explored further.

The combination of non-offenders and different categories of offender within units is a complex and controversial issue. It is the policy promoted by Government and local authorities and is consistent with the blurring of boundaries between welfare and punishment introduced by the Children and Young Persons Act 1969, and with the conceptualization of all children in trouble, offenders and non-offenders, as children 'in need'. However, rather than producing a 'welfare' approach to all children in trouble, it seems that the changes in the criminal justice system during the 1990s which have led to the increasing criminalization of young offenders have in fact resulted in the criminalization of all children in secure accommodation, whatever the reason for their admission. Those convicted of offences or on remand awaiting trial or sentence, many of them for violent or sexual offences, comprise approximately two thirds of all admissions and the majority of them are male (DH 2000). Policy and practice is based on an ideology that focuses on the similarities between young people, particularly their background experiences of abuse and loss (Boswell 1996), rather than the more complex analysis that is needed of the differences between them in welfare or justice admission route and 'career route' (Bullock *et al.* 1998). The dangers of a global approach to young people in trouble which minimizes the importance of differences in individual background experiences, problems, risk factors and likely outcomes, have been repeatedly expressed (Brogi and Bagley 1998; Bullock *et al.* 1998; Hodgkin 1993; Howard League 1995; National Children's Bureau 1995; Timms 1995). How far, if at all, it is possible to reconcile the different welfare and criminal justice functions within one institution is an important question. It would seem to be extremely difficult for staff to create a regime that can meet the conflicting needs of 'intensive care' and custody (Millham *et al.* 1978) and incorporate irreconcilable philosophies of care, justice, containment and treatment within one system (Timms 1995). In practice it seems that all children in trouble in secure accommodation are being criminalized rather than treated as children in need of care. This important issue will be explored in greater depth later.

Conclusion

This review of local authority secure accommodation and its role and function in the care and criminal justice systems has revealed many concerns about the legislative framework, policies and practice, some of which have a history as long as secure accommodation itself. It might be argued that some problems which have been repeatedly articulated have almost been accepted as an inevitable part of a system which is characterized by conflicting ideologies and inconsistent policies and practices. The young people concerned seem to have been regarded as objects of concern in need of 'treatment', control, punishment or a combination of all of these, and stigmatized by the labels which attach to all young people in the care and criminal justice systems who are deprived of their liberty.

Implicit in the capital investment and development of local authority secure accommodation is government and professional endorsement of this type of provision for children in the care and criminal justice systems. However, since the implementation of the Children Act 1989 and the changes in criminal justice legislation, there has been relatively little investigation (for example Goldson 1995; Bullock, Little and Millham 1998) to find out how far the longstanding and more recent concerns about secure accommodation have been addressed, and whether young people admitted through the different legal routes are benefiting from their placements. The research study that follows investigates the current situation in local authority secure accommodation from the perspectives of those most directly affected and associated with it, that is the young people inside, their social workers and the managers and staff working in the secure units.

Notes

1 These figures were obtained following a survey by the Children's Legal Centre in the absence of published Government statistics on the use of secure accommodation.

Part II

The Context of the Research Study

FOUR

The Children in the Study

Characteristics and Background Circumstances

Introduction

The young people in the study were aged 13 to 17 years and placed in 6 secure units in England. Of the 35 young people who expressed their wish to participate: 3 did not proceed beyond an initial, individual meeting – 1 ran away prior to the first planned interview, 1 was moved from the unit at short notice, 1 boy on remand was advised not to participate by a parent – and a further 3 withdrew after the first interview. This left 29 young people – 11 boys and 18 girls – who completed the work in two or three interviews. Although this sample is small and not claimed to be necessarily representative of the wider scene, the characteristics of the young people and differences in terms of gender and legal status are typical of children in secure accommodation nationally.

Legal Admission Route

An analysis of the legal admission routes into secure accommodation of the 29 young people, illustrated in Table 4.1, shows that 41 per cent were admitted through the criminal justice routes, 59 per cent through the welfare route and none under mental health or other legislation. This contrasts with the national figures for admissions to secure accommodation during the same period, with 58 per cent admitted through the criminal justice routes, 40 per cent admitted through the welfare routes and 2 per cent admitted under other (non-specified) legislation (DH 1997b).

Table 4.1 Legal admission routes

Legal category	**No.**	%
Criminal routes:		
s.53[2] CYP Act 1933	8	27
s.23 CYP Act 1969–Regulation 6	4	14
Welfare routes:		
s.25 CA 1989 (s.31, s.38)	9	31
s.25 CA 1989 (s.20)	8	28
Total	29	100

None of the young people had been convicted under section 53[1] of the Children and Young Persons Act 1933 and all those convicted under section 53[2] of that Act had received determinate rather than life or indeterminate sentences.

Of the young people in secure accommodation in England and Wales on 31 March 1997, 71 per cent of the girls had been admitted through the welfare route while 79 per cent of the boys had been admitted through the criminal routes (DH 1997b). These national gender differences in admission routes into secure accommodation are reflected in this sample, with 15 of the 18 girls (83 per cent) admitted through the welfare route and 9 of the 11 boys (81 per cent) admitted through the criminal routes. This is shown in Table 4.2.

Table 4.2 Legal admission route and gender

Legal category	**Female**		**Male**	
	No.	%	No.	%
Criminal routes:				
s.53[2] CYP Act 1933	2	7	6	21
s.23 CYP Act 1969	1	4	3	10
Welfare routes:				
s.25 CA 1989, s.31, s.38	8	27	1	3
s.25 CA 1989, s.20	7	24	1	4
Total	18	62	11	38

Young people may be subject to more than one legal order made separately in care and criminal proceedings. In this study, one girl convicted under section 53 of the Children and Young Persons Act 1933 was also the subject of a care order, under section 31 of the Children Act 1989; the girl on remand under section 23 of the Children and Young Persons Act 1969 and Regulation 6 of the Secure Accommodation Regulations 1991, was also the subject of an interim care order under section 38 of the Children Act 1989; one of the girls who was the subject of an order under section 25 of the Children Act 1989 had originally been admitted to secure accommodation on remand criteria. Two boys and one girl had been convicted of offences listed in Schedule I of the Children and Young Persons Act 1933 and were thereby deemed to be 'Schedule I Offenders'.

The age of young people on admission is related to their admission route. The national statistics show that the peak age for admissions is 14 through the welfare route and 15 through the criminal justice routes. The proportion aged 14 and under has increased since 1995 (DH 2000) and this trend is likely to continue as changes to the criminal justice legislation, discussed earlier, will result in an increase in the number of younger boys and girls being admitted to secure accommodation through the criminal justice routes. In this study, the mean age of the boys was 15 years 5 months and of the girls, 14 years 6 months.

Table 4.3 illustrates the age and gender of the young people in the sample.

Table 4.3 Age and gender

Age	Female		Male		Total	
	No.	%	No.	%	No.	%
13–14 years	7	39	2	18	9	31
15 years	9	50	3	27	12	42
16–17 years	2	11	6	55	8	27
Total	18	100	11	100	29	100

Government statistics do not include information about the ethnic origin of young people in secure accommodation. Almost a quarter of the young people in this study were black, that is African Caribbean, or Asian or of dual heritage. Table 4.4 illustrates the ethnic origin of the sample by gender.

Table 4.4 Ethnic origin and gender

Ethnic Origin	Female		Male		Total	
	No.	%	No.	%	No.	%
White/British/Irish/ European *	13	71	9	82	22	76
Asian	1	6	1	9	2	7
African Caribbean	1	6	1	9	2	7
Dual heritage	3	17	0	0	3	10
Total	18	100	11	100	29	100

*This group included two young people who were Welsh, two whose parents were Irish, one whose grandparents were Polish and one from a travelling family.

Placements in the public care and criminal justice systems

There are notable differences in the histories and patterns of placement of the boys and the girls in this sample, and in the use of care orders. Only one boy was the subject of a care order (9%) in contrast with ten girls who were the subjects of interim or care orders (55%). Four boys had experience of placement in public care: two had been accommodated at age 11 and 13 years because they were beyond the control of their parents, and two had previously been remanded to local authority accommodation and placed with foster carers. Six boys had been in young offender institutions or remand centres prior to placement in secure accommodation. Only one boy had no previous placements in public care or custody.

In sharp contrast, all but one of the girls in the study had been in residential and foster care prior to placement in secure accommodation. Furthermore, the girls' histories in public care were significantly longer and more complex than those of the boys. In addition, two girls had received in-patient psychiatric care. None of the girls had been in prison custody although some of them had experience of being held in police custody, overnight or longer, in police cells. Table 4.5 illustrates the age of admission to public care of the girls, and shows that those admitted to secure accommodation through the criminal justice routes, as well as the welfare route, had histories in public care.

Table 4.5 Age at first admission to public care of girls (n = 18)

Girls' age at first admission	**Welfare route**		**Criminal justice routes**		**Total**	
	No.	%	No.	%	No.	%
Age under 5 years	3	17	0	0	3	17
Age 5–13 years	7	38	3	17	10	55
Age 14–16 years	5	28	0	0	5	28

Although this sample is small, it is nonetheless interesting to contrast these figures with the findings of Bebbington and Miles (1989) that those under 1 year old and those aged 14 and 15 are particularly vulnerable to entry to care. They found the lowest rate of entry to occur between age 5 and 12 but as they did not differentiate on the basis of gender, no direct comparison is possible.

Placements in Secure Accommodation

Secure units operate as single- or mixed-gender facilities, although as already noted Government policy has promoted mixed-gender units and there now remains very little single-gender provision. In this sample of young people, 38 per cent were accommodated in single-gender units and 62 per cent were in mixed units. Table 4.6 sets out the type of placement by gender and admission route into secure accommodation.

Table 4.6 Type of secure unit placement by gender

Secure Unit	**Female**		**Male**		**Total**	
	Welfare	Justice	Welfare	Justice	No.	%
Single gender	7	1	0	3	11	38
Mixed gender	8	2	2	6	18	62

As previously noted, one of the factors which influence the choice of unit for young people is bed availability and consequently young people can be placed at considerable geographical distances from their families and home communities. Four boys, that is only a third of the total, were placed in secure units in their home area or in the nearest unit to their home area. In this respect the girls fared better with 13, that is almost three quarters of the total, placed in units in their home area or in the unit nearest to their home area. However, even they were often at a distance from family members and professional workers visiting them.

There are gender differences in the role that secure accommodation played in the care careers of the young people, which partly reflect the gender differences in legal admission routes and previous care experiences. The number and frequency of previous placements in secure accommodation was greater for the girls than the boys, with 11 of the girls (61%) having had previous admissions to secure accommodation in contrast with only two (18%) of the boys. However, some of the boys without previous placements in secure accommodation had been held in custody in young offender institutions or remand centres. Table 4.7 shows that while many of those admitted through the welfare route had had previous admissions to secure accommodation, the majority of those admitted through the criminal justice routes had not.

Table 4.7 Previous admissions to secure accommodation by gender and legal status

Admissions	Female		Male		All	
	Welfare	Justice	Welfare	Justice	Welfare	Justice
No previous admissions	6	1	0	9	6	10
One previous admission	5	2	2	0	7	2
Two or more previous admissions	4	0	0	0	4	0
Total	15	3	2	9	17	12

Nine of the eleven boys (81%) were in secure accommodation for the first time. Each of the remaining two boys who had been admitted through the welfare route had one previous placement in secure accommodation and one of these had experience of placement in more than one secure unit. Seven boys (63%) had been in custody in young offender institutions or remand centres. One boy had no previous placements outside his family, having been admitted directly to secure accommodation following conviction under section 53.

In contrast, only 7 of the 18 girls had not been in secure accommodation before, although 6 of them had been in local authority non-secure residential or foster care. Just one girl had no previous experience of care outside her family.

Of the 11 girls with previous admissions, 7 (38%) were in secure accommodation for the second time. Four of them were placed in the same secure unit on the second admission as on the first, two were initially placed in a different unit and then transferred to the same unit as on the first admission and one had had a previous placement in the Youth Treatment Centre.

Of the remaining four girls, all admitted through the welfare route, one had three previous admissions to three different secure units, another had two previous admissions to the same unit and one to a different unit, a third girl had five admissions to the same unit and the fourth girl had more than six previous placements in the same unit. The reasons for these re-admissions were not clear. They may provide an indication that the previous secure placements had been ineffective in addressing the needs of the young people. Additionally or alternatively, inadequate exit plans might have resulted in young people returning to unsuitable placements to face the same problems and to find themselves in a 'revolving door' back into secure accommodation.

The length as well as the number of placements is important and must be considered in the context of findings by Bullock and Little (1991) that children can suffer serious psychological and social damage from their placement. If the placement is for less than a month, the harmful effects may be minimal but there are serious risks of institutionalization for those whose stays are longer term. As already noted, the length of placement is determined by the child's legal status, although all the orders are characterized by uncertainty. Young people convicted under section 53[2] of the Children and Young Persons Act 1933 and given a determinate sentence may have a planned timescale and date of release, and they might also know whether they will serve their whole sentence in the secure unit. The position for young people on remand is uncertain as the order is subject to renewal by the court at least every 28 days and may result in young people returning to secure accommodation, being transferred to a young offender institution or to prison or being remanded to non-secure provision. As already shown, young people who are subject to orders under section 25 also face uncertainty. Full or interim orders can be made for up to three months on a first application and for up to six months on subsequent applications. There is no total maximum period specified for placement in secure accommodation, and some young people face repeat applications and long periods in secure accommodation.

The mean length of stay in secure accommodation of the 11 boys was 10.5 months and of the 18 girls was 6 months. These figures relate to the length of the orders current at the time of the study and do not include the time spent in secure accommodation on previous admissions. The length of placements are set out in Table 4.8. In the context of the research findings referred to above (Bullock and Little 1991) it is of note that only one young person in the sample was due to be discharged after a stay of one month.

Table 4.8 Length of stay in secure accommodation by legal status

Length of stay	**Welfare s.25**		**Remand s.23**		**Convicted s.53**		**Total**	
	No.	%	No.	%	No.	%	No.	%
< 1 month	1	3	0	0	0	0	1	3
1–3 months	2	7	2	7	0	0	4	14
3–6 months	11	38	1	3	0	0	12	41
6–12 months	3	11	1	3	1	3	5	18
>12 months	0	0	0	0	7	24	7	24
Total	17	59	4	14	8	27	29	100

It appears from the figures in Table 4.8 that the young people convicted of offences under section 53 of the Children and Young Persons Act 1933, the majority of whom were boys, had the longest stays in secure accommodation. However, it is important to note that many of those admitted through the welfare route were expecting further court applications to be made to extend the length of their secure accommodation orders. For example, applications for further 6-month orders had been made in respect of 2 girls who had already been in secure accommodation for 11 months and 9 months; an application for a further 3-month order had been made in respect of a girl who had been in secure accommodation for 6 months; and applications for 6-month orders had been made in respect of a boy and a girl who were completing 3-month orders. It is also significant that those admitted through the welfare route had the greatest number of re-admissions so that the combined length of their stay in secure accommodation would have been for as long a period as for some of those in secure accommodation following conviction of serious offences.

The differences in length of stay in secure accommodation by admission route are reflected in gender differences, because 83 per cent of the young women were admitted through the welfare route and 81 per cent of the young men were admitted through the criminal routes. The gender differences in length of placement are shown in Table 4.9.

Table 4.9 Length of stay in secure accommodation by gender

Length of stay	**Female**		**Male**		**Total**	
	No.	%	No.	%	No.	%
< 1 month	1	3	0	0	1	3
1–3 months	2	7	2	7	4	14
3–6 months	10	34	2	7	12	41
6–12 months	3	11	2	7	5	18
> 12 months	2	7	5	17	7	24
Total	18	62	11	38	29	100

These figures can be compared with the national figures for discharges from secure accommodation during the same period which show the length of stay (DH 1997b). Thirty-one per cent of the boys and thirty per cent of the girls had had stays in secure accommodation of less than one month. Of the young women discharged, 27 per cent had been in secure accommodation for longer than 3 months and 7 per cent for longer than 6 months. Similarly 34 per cent of the young men discharged had been in secure accommodation for longer than 3 months and 15 per cent for longer than 6 months.

Reason for Admission

The reason for admission to secure accommodation is important to provide a context for examining the young people's perspectives about their experiences and placements. Eight young people (two female and six male) were admitted to secure accommodation following conviction under section 53 of the Children and Young Persons Act 1933. Table 4.10 shows the offences for which they were convicted.

Table 4.10 Section 53 convictions by gender

Offences	Male	Female	Total
Rape/Indecent assault	2	0	2
Arson	1	0	1
Armed robbery/Street robbery	2	1	3
Causing death by driving	1	0	1
Wounding	0	1	1
Total	6	2	8

Four young people, three male and one female, were placed in secure accommodation on remand. Table 4.11 sets out the offences with which they had been charged and remanded to secure accommodation.

Table 4.11 Offences leading to remand by gender

Offences	Male	Female	Total
Attempted murder	1	0	1
Robbery	1	0	1
Robbery and arson	1	0	1
Child abduction	0	1	1
Total	3	1	4

Eight girls and one boy, who were the subjects of care or interim care orders, were admitted through the welfare route. All of them had been living in residential care, with the exception of one girl who had been living with foster carers. The young man was admitted because he was considered to be at risk of offending, particularly taking cars, and because of a suicide attempt. The girls were all admitted because they were running away and were considered to be at risk of harm and, with one exception, specifically because they were considered to be at risk of sexual harm. This is consistent with findings from previous studies that intervention with girls is more likely to be because of concerns about their sexual behaviour than because they have committed criminal offences (for example, Carlen 1987).

The behaviours which resulted in admission for these nine young people are set out in Table 4.12. More than one reason for admission was given for all the young people and it is noteworthy that running away was a consistent factor for them all.

Table 4.12 Behaviours resulting in welfare admission for young people on interim or care orders (n = 9)

Behaviour	Total
Running away	9
Sexual harm/abuse	7
Prostitution	3
Alcohol/Drug use	5
At risk from violence	3
Suicide/Deliberate self harm	3
Violent to others	1
Taking cars	1

Seven girls and one boy who had been accommodated by the local authority under section 20 of the Children Act 1989 were admitted through the welfare route. The patterns of behaviour leading to admission were the same as those of the young people who were the subjects of care orders and all but one of them had been living in residential care. Table 4.13 sets out the behaviours which led to admission.

Table 4.13 Behaviours resulting in welfare admission for young people accommodated by local authority (n = 8)

Behaviour	**Total**
Running away	8
Alcohol/Drug use	6
Sexual harm/abuse	6
Prostitution	5
Suicide/Deliberate self–harm	4
Violent to others	2
Taking cars	1

It is interesting to note that prostitution, suspected prostitution and the risk of sexual harm figured in the reasons for admission through the welfare route of most of the girls. How far, if at all, placement in secure accommodation is an appropriate response to this behaviour will be considered in subsequent chapters. It is also of interest that there were no equivalent concerns expressed in relation to any of the boys, illustrating that girls' sexuality is placed under closer scrutiny than that of boys (Aymer 1992; Farmer and Pollock 1998; Hudson 1989). A final issue of interest in the reasons for admission is that the young people admitted through the welfare route on more than one occasion were admitted each time for the same reasons.

Circumstances Prior to Admission to Secure Accommodation

The different care career patterns of the boys and the girls provide some indication of the differences which existed in their family circumstances. The birth or adoptive parents of the majority of young people (93%) were separated or divorced with those of only three young people still living together. Two of the girls were living with a birth parent and step-parent prior to their admission to secure accommodation, with the remaining 16 living with foster carers or in residential care. In contrast, seven of the boys were living with a birth parent (three also with a step-parent) and one was living with both birth parents prior to their placement in custody with only three living with foster carers or in residential care.

Relationships and Contact with Parents/Primary Carers

Continuity in relationships between the young people and their parents or substitute carers and positive family support were thought by the social workers to be important factors influencing young people's prospects following release from secure accommodation and their longer-term life chances. Of the ten boys whose parents were separated or divorced, four maintained contact with both parents, whilst six of them had no contact with their fathers, one of whom had died. All of them had continuing relationships with their mothers. A more complex and fragmented picture emerged in respect of the girls. Six girls maintained contact with their birth parents, although the parents of five of them were separated or divorced; four girls had no contact with either parent; a further six had no contact with their fathers; and one girl had lost contact with her mother. Two girls had been adopted following removal from their birth families because of abuse or neglect and they maintained contact with their adoptive parents. One of them had also re-established contact with her birth mother although her birth father had died. Only one girl had a child of her own, who was placed in local authority accommodation. These gender differences in contact and family support were reflected in the social workers' evaluations of the future prospects of the young people, which will be examined later.

Education

Ten of the eleven boys and seventeen of the eighteen girls had experienced disruption in their schooling, some of them dating back to primary school. More than two in five had been permanently excluded from mainstream school and one in five of the young people were the subjects of Statements under the Education Act 1996. At least three boys had basic literacy problems on admission to secure accommodation. There are notable similarities between the experiences of these young people and those in non-secure residential care. For example,

Berridge and Brodie (1998) found that of 25 young people in adolescent homes, 7 (28%) were permanently excluded and 1 was subject to a fixed-term exclusion while Sinclair and Gibbs (1998) found that nearly a third of school age young people were not in school.

Table 4.14 sets out the education provision for the young people in the study prior to their placement in secure accommodation or custody.

Table 4.14 Education provision prior to placement in secure accommodation or custody

Education provision	**Female**	**Male**	**Total**	
	No.	No.	No.	%
On roll – day comprehensive	6	5	11	38
Excluded – no provision	5	4	9	31
Excluded – PRU/ home tuition	2	1	3	10
Residential school	3	0	3	10
CHE	2	1*	3	10
Total	18	11	29	100

* This boy was placed in a community home with education on site, following permanent exclusion from a five day boarding special school for pupils with emotional/behavioural difficulties.

Physical Health

The physical health of young people is affected by their risk behaviour, with major issues of concern relating to cigarette smoking and the use of alcohol and drugs.

ILLEGAL DRUG/ALCOHOL/CIGARETTE USE

All the young people discussed their attitudes to and use of cigarettes, illegal drugs and alcohol. A number of them had been injecting drug users prior to admission to secure accommodation and several felt that their use of alcohol and illegal drugs had contributed to the reason for their placement in secure accommodation. Table 4.15 sets out the extent of their substance use.

Table 4.15 Extent of smoking, illegal drug and alcohol use by gender

Substance	Frequent use - No.		Occasional use - No.		Total use %		No use No.	
	F	M	F	M	F	M	F	M
Cigarettes	18	9	0	1	100	91	0	1
Alcohol	9	5	7	2	88	64	2	4
Illegal drugs	14	7	1	0	83	64	3	4
Solvents	1	1	1	1	11	18	16	9

Nearly all the young people said that they were aware of the danger to their health of their use of drugs and alcohol, and also of their misuse of prescribed drugs, but few appeared to be aware of or take seriously the risk involved in smoking cigarettes. Restrictions on cigarette smoking in the secure units was a contentious issue for them. One exception was a boy who said he did not smoke cigarettes (or use drugs or alcohol) because he regarded himself as a serious sportsman with a commitment to health and fitness. A wide range of factors is involved in the take-up by children of cigarette smoking. It has been suggested that those with low academic achievement and those with low self-esteem or who feel alienated from school are more likely to take up smoking and poor knowledge of the health risks has also been identified as a factor (Royal College Physicians 1992). There has been more attention paid to the risk factors than to the protective factors which deter children from taking up smoking and which influence cessation.

There were also concerns about the health of some of them who had spent extended periods of time running away when they had received inadequate physical care and nutrition, and some girls had health needs arising from the effects of injuries sustained in violent relationships. In addition, four young women had asthma for which they received medication. The self-care of some of the young people in this study appeared to have been erratic, which might be explained by a number of factors including their low self-esteem which will be discussed later.

Sexual Health

Thirteen girls (72%) but none of the boys had been admitted to secure accommodation because they were considered to be at risk of sexual harm. Although the girls were not directly asked about pregnancy, one young woman who had given birth to a child at the age of 13 years said that she had also had one termination of pregnancy and another young woman said that she had suffered two miscarriages, one following a rape. Some of the young people were tested for HIV and other sexually transmitted diseases following admission to secure accommodation, although in this regard also there appeared to be greater emphasis on the girls who seemed to be considered to be at higher risk than the boys.

The young people's level of knowledge about matters of sexual health appeared to be sketchy and those who discussed the issues minimized the risks to their health. This might partly be explained by the likelihood that many of them will have failed to receive basic sex education at school because of their inconsistent school attendance at secondary school level. In addition, although the Education Act 1993 made the biological aspects of sex education compulsory at secondary school level, other aspects such as contraception, relationships and sexually transmitted diseases remain at the discretion of individual schools. Parents are another important source of information and support but prior to admission to secure accommodation 94 per cent of the girls and 18 per cent of the boys had been living away from their parents or primary carers in residential or foster care, where issues of sexuality are frequently ignored or neglected (Aymer 1992; Farmer and Pollock 1998).

Mental Health

The inadequate provision of mental health services for children and the difficulties in the relationship between mental health services and other agencies have already been considered (Kurtz *et al.* 1994; NHS 1995). The particular mental health needs of children and young people in care have received little research attention. However, some recent studies have highlighted the problems and the limited response from mental health and other therapeutic services. For example, Sinclair and Gibbs (1998) found that four in ten of their sample had considered killing themselves in the previous month, Berridge and Brodie (1998) expressed astonishment at the lack of therapeutic services for young people whose emotional and behavioural difficulties were significant, while Farmer and Pollock (1998) found that over half the sexually abused and abusing children in their study had never had the opportunity to talk about their experiences in a therapeutic setting.

Suicidal and deliberate self-harming behaviours are obvious indicators of mental distress and may result in placement in secure accommodation if community mental health services, appropriate in-patient care or other therapeutic services are unavailable (Katz 1995).

Psycho-social Stress and Adversity

The work on post-traumatic stress disorder (Pynoos and Nader 1993; Wilson and Raphael 1993) has shown that children suffer the after-effects of traumatic stress in a similar way to adults and that unresolved grief or fear can manifest itself, particularly in males, in later aggressive or violent behaviour and in females in psychiatric disorder, depression and deliberate self-harm. There are implications for the development, self-concept and self-esteem of young people when even their basic needs for love and security, new experiences, praise and recognition and responsibility (Kellmer Pringle 1980) have not been met and normal childhood experiences have been distorted. Maslow (1970) proposed a hierarchy of needs in which fundamental needs must be met before higher needs can be addressed and stressed the importance for children of love, friendships and control over their lives through knowledge and understanding. A high proportion of the young people in this study had experienced childhood adversity in the form of violence, abuse and loss, and some of them had also suffered trauma from the circumstances of the offences which they had committed. Some of their parents had also suffered adverse life experiences which might have affected the levels of protection that they were able to provide to their children. As the young people were not asked specific questions about stress in childhood, it is likely that some of those who had suffered adverse experiences did not feel able to include them in their stories. However some common themes emerged such as family violence, physical and sexual abuse, bereavement, suicide and deliberate self-harm and the use of drugs and alcohol.

Family Violence

Violence against women is reported to be the most common form of family violence (Levinson 1989). Feminist analyses of male domination have linked power, sexuality and violence and argued that the relations of male power and female subordination are achieved and maintained through sexual violence (Kelly 1996; Radford and Stanko 1996). Research has shown that family violence also has an impact on the health and well-being of children (Hester, Pearson and Harwin 2000). Jaffe, Wolfe and Wilson (1990) contend that the effects on children of witnessing violence towards their mothers are profound, with the impact compared with the effects of other overwhelming life experiences. Children can be affected by violence as witnesses, as triggers or justification for the violence, as accessories and by intervening in the violence, trying to offer protection to their mothers (Mullender and Morley 1994; Radford 1995). While there are reports of emotional distress and disturbance among children living with violence, no fixed pattern of response has emerged and it is important to understand the perceptions, needs and responses of the individual child (Mullender 1995; Harold 1997).

In this study, 5 boys and 10 girls (51%) described witnessing repeated serious violence between their parents and life-threatening assaults by their fathers on their mothers. Some of them reported that as well as witnessing violence, they had also become involved indirectly or directly by intervening to try to stop the violence. For example, Stacey described an assault on her which was triggered by her step-father observing her witnessing his assault on her mother:

> They started arguing and then he hit her in the face with his hand and she fell on the floor crying ... the kitchen door was open and I was hiding behind it and he turned round and saw me and grabbed me by the hair and he ripped his belt off and he was hitting me with the belt ... Mum was crying and she told me to get upstairs and phone the police but he came after me and pulled me down the stairs again ... He broke my arm.

REPEATING PATTERNS

Several young people described a repeating pattern of violence in which they intervened and summoned help, which resulted in the arrest of their fathers, only for them to return to the family to continue the violence. For example, Mandy said:

> I can remember all the violence at home between my mum and my dad and us lot ... the first time I phoned the police, I was so scared that my dad would kill me if he caught me but he was proper out of order doing what he was doing to my mum and I couldn't handle it no more ... Two policemen came and the next thing I know my dad's walking out with handcuffs on and my mum was hugging me and thanking me for phoning the police. She said my dad had a pair of tights round her neck strangling her and if the police hadn't got there when they did she would have been dead ... after that, phoning the police was a regular thing, my dad always got arrested and then let out the next day. I suppose it did do good because it meant that my mum was still alive the next day ... she's nearly been dead six times ... she's been beaten up really, really bad ... Sometimes I didn't have the guts to phone the police, I was too scared because if my dad had caught me phoning the police I would have got as bad a beating as my mum.

DISRUPTION AND REFUGES

Disruption of home and school life is one of the consequences of family violence, and was reported by several young people. For example, Stephen said:

> My mum and dad used to fight all the time ... I started going into refuges from the age of two ... when I was about six we came back

> to the house and it was all smashed up so we went to another refuge, we spent about five months there but after about the first three months my dad found out where we was and he was coming down and trying to get into the refuge so after that they shipped us off to another refuge ... the last refuge I was in I was fourteen, we were there for about nine months ... I started getting used to being in and out of refuges because it had been like that since the age of two.

RENEWED VIOLENCE

Some of the young people witnessed serious violence between their parents which resulted in their separation, only to witness renewed violence between their mothers and new partners. For example, to escape his father's violence Kevin moved with his mother and siblings to live in a refuge, but further violence then occurred between his mother and a new partner:

> My mum was getting beaten up by my dad ... he had tied her to the bed and he had a knife in his hand ... he told us to 'Say goodnight to your mother, kids' and after that I picked up his pool cue and hit his wrists to stop him killing her ... he was on the floor and my sisters untied my mother ... I jumped through the window to get the police ... after that we moved to a refuge. After about two months my mum met another man but then he was the same, he kept beating her and also he was beating me too.

The connections between domestic violence and child abuse have been well established. Whilst it is generally accepted that living with violence is a form of emotional abuse of children, in some families abuse of women and children occurs at the same time. Bowker and colleagues (1988) found that in 70 per cent of cases where children were present, men who were violent to their wives also physically abused their children, while Farmer and Owen (1995) found that 59 per cent of children taken to case conferences because of physical abuse, neglect or emotional abuse came from families where there was violence, usually by male partners to mothers. Further important evidence of the link between domestic violence and child abuse can be found in the report of the death of Sukina Hammond (Bridge Child Care Consultancy 1991) and a number of other child death inquiry reports (O'Hara 1994). Stark and Flitcraft (1985, 1988) argue that domestic violence provides the typical context in which child abuse develops and that abuse of women and children have a common source in terms of power and male control.

Attacks on children during domestic violence incidents provide one example of the ways in which abuse of women and children may be interconnected (Hester *et al.* 2000; Morley and Mullender 1994). It is impossible to define some abusive behaviour as either domestic violence or child abuse; for example, where there is a 'double level of intentionality' – when an action is directed at one person but designed to affect others as well, such as hitting or threatening a child in front of the mother in order to threaten or maintain power or control over the woman (Kelly 1994).

Physical Abuse

Five boys and fourteen girls, that is almost two thirds of young people in the study, described physical abuse or ill-treatment of them by their parent or another member of their family. All the young people who described living with violent parents also reported physical abuse. A recurrent theme which emerged was abuse inflicted by male family members, particularly fathers, step-fathers and brothers and the powerlessness of mothers to prevent the abuse or protect the children. All the young people described their own sense of powerlessness at their inability to protect themselves and their siblings. One example of this was given by Stephen, who attributed his father's violence to his use of drugs, and the failure of his mother to prevent the abuse or protect the children:

> My dad was taking LSD … when I was about five he got me and my brother and he put our hands on the cooker and he burnt them … he done it to my brother first and I could see my brother screaming and crying and I knew I was going to be next and my mum and my sister was screaming at my dad to stop.

An additional dimension which emerged concerned the complex relationship between the young people and their mothers. Many of the young people felt a strong sense of responsibility to protect their mothers from violence whilst at the same time feeling betrayed when their mothers were unable or unwilling to protect them. Several young people described situations where their mothers colluded with their father's violence. For example Mandy suggested that her mother colluded by pretending not to see her father's violence toward the children, as a means of protecting herself:

> He used to beat us up as well … he'd line us all up – oldest to youngest – I suppose that was good in a way that the oldest went first because by the time it got to the little ones he didn't have any anger left inside him. He still hit them,though not as bad as us.

An example of more active collusion by her mother was described by Jane who was abused by her brother:

> My brother was in boarding school but every time my brother came home it was horrible. There was arguments, fights, my mum crying, me walking out. It was really bad and I felt like killing myself… she just cries when he hits me, she fell apart when he started hitting me. I'd go to school with bruises, he nearly broke my jaw, he's broke my toe and my finger and he's stabbed me with scissors … my mum don't do nothing … when I tell the police my mum says that I'm telling lies but she's there while he's hitting me.

Furthermore, several young people described situations where their mothers joined in the abuse perpetrated by their fathers. For example Marie said:

> I used to get beaten up by my step-dad which started when I was about nine … sometimes I couldn't go to school because the bruises were really bad … and then when my mum and dad found out they both used to hit me even more.

A second recurring theme relates to the connection between physical abuse inflicted on the young people by family members and their subsequent placement in care. For example, Jackie was physically abused by her step-father and step-brother and her mother was unable to protect her and so supported her step-father's demands for her placement in care:

> He sent me to my room … I started crying and he shouted at me to 'shut up you spoilt bitch' … I started arguing with him and he

> smacked me round the face with a leather belt. After that whenever I got in trouble he used to beat me up … my dad and brother used to beat me up all the time but my mum couldn't do anything about it because she was scared of my dad so in the end I just got moved away into care.

A third theme concerns the longer-term impact on the young people of the violence and abuse they suffered in childhood. Some of them said that they had become violent and others saw themselves repeating the disadvantage and problems of their parents. For example, Jackie said:

> When you get beaten up as a child and someone has a go at you, you end up turning to violence because you grow up thinking violence is the right thing.

Karen was aware of her mother's history of being abused and then herself becoming violent, a pattern which she saw herself repeating:

> I went into care when I was ten years old because of the way I was treated at home … My mum worked on the streets and she injected drugs and she used to hit me and pull my hair and do all those things to me … My mum was a violent person, I was brought up with violence … if I had never seen my mum beating up or using drugs or working on the streets then I wouldn't have done it … I have done exactly what my mum did.

Sexual Abuse

The relationship of physical and sexual abuse is complex in that sexual abuse is also physical abuse with additional power dimensions (Hearn 1990). Secrecy surrounds sexual abuse, children are ambivalent about telling anyone and boys are less likely than girls to talk to anyone about abuse (Hooper 1992). Fewer boys than girls are recognized in adolescence as sexually abused. A more common form of discovery of sexual abuse of boys is in the process of identification of them as an abuser (Finkelhor 1984; Glaser 1993). The reluctance of boys to talk about sexual abuse has been attributed to a number of factors: the notion of male victims is less acceptable than female ones; boys are less frequently 'supervised' and more often befriended by men who are strangers, sometimes operating in sex rings (Christopherson 1989); disclosure by boys is less easily heard and more shameful and furthermore, since the majority of abusers are male, disclosure of abuse may amount to a declaration by the boy of involvement in a homosexual relationship (Nasjleti 1980). Furthermore, as already noted, there is significantly less attention given to the sexuality of boys than to that of girls.

Glaser (1993) identified symptoms of post-traumatic stress in many young people who had suffered sexual abuse. Depression is not uncommon, particularly in girls, as a result of the abuse and society's response to it, even when this response is intended to be protective and supportive. Although depression does occur in boys it is less common than externalized responses, such as angry and aggressive behaviour. The cumulative effect of many of the feelings is one of significantly lowered self-esteem in both boys and girls (Tong *et al.* 1987). Finkelhor and Browne (1985) developed the Traumagenic Dynamics Model of Child Sexual Abuse to provide a better understanding of the problems that are characteristic in those who have been sexually abused. They proposed four traumagenic dynamics: traumatic sexualization; betrayal; stigmatization; and powerlessness, and described the distortions which affect a child's self-concept, sense of worth and ability to cope with their own lives. Powerlessness can be 'exacerbated when children resist by fighting back, running away or trying to outsmart the abuser' (Finkelhor 1988, p.72) only to be met with control and 'unwanted events' such as court proceedings and placement in secure accommodation.

In this study, 9 young women (50%) revealed sexual abuse within their families and outside. Several were sexually abused by their mother's partner. While none of the boys revealed that they had been sexually abused, it would be unsafe to conclude that none of them had experienced such abuse, particularly as there was a history of sexual abuse within some of their families. Most of the girls did not report the abuse or seek help. For example, Nicola said:

> My mother had this boyfriend ... and I used to be in my bedroom playing, he used to drink from morning till night and he used to come in the bedroom and sexually abuse me ... He used to tell me

> he'd go mad if I did say something and that he'd do horrible things to me.

The effects on them of sexual and physical abuse were described by the young people, many of whom had been suicidal, had self-harmed and run away. For example, Charlotte said:

> When I was about five I got abused by both of my parents and my step-brother and this carried on until I was fifteen … I started taking overdoses and starving myself so I could go to hospital … Whenever I complained at home or whenever my dad felt like it I got beaten up … I kept on running away, taking overdoses, cutting my wrists … I got admitted to hospital and then went to a children's home and then came here … I tried to strangle myself … then I told people about what had happened and my parents got arrested … now I've found out that my older brother was sexually abused by my dad and he's been in and out of psychiatric placements for ten years … Finding out that I wasn't the only one in my family that had been abused, I got really upset and cried for days.

Several studies have found a high incidence of sexual abuse as a precursor to running away and observed the vulnerability of such young people to further sexual abuse and exploitation (see Janus *et al.* 1987; Stein *et al.* 1994; Weisberg 1985). An example of this is provided by Jane who was sexually abused within her family and ran away, and was abused again by a trusted adult who was aware of her vulnerability:

> All the bad stuff started when I was about seven … I was sleeping over at my auntie's house and my uncle came into my room and said 'you're uncle's special niece' and then he started touching my breasts and everything … that carried on every weekend until I was eleven when I did a runner with my best mate and her uncle gave me some drugs and alcohol and I got drunk and I must have fallen asleep and when I woke up my best mate told me that I'd been raped by her uncle.

The complex relationship between a child being victimized within their family as a result of violence, physical and sexual abuse and that child running away only to be revictimized within the care system or on the streets emerged as an important theme in this study. It will be explored further in subsequent chapters.

Bereavement/Loss

Children who experience the permanent or semi-permanent loss of significant relationships can suffer trauma which may result in serious emotional disturbance (Bowlby 1951; Rutter 1972). This emerged as a significant issue for the young people in this study and the extent of their loss of important relationships is summarized in Table 4.16.

Table 4.16 Experience of loss

Type of loss	Mother	Father	G'parents/ Siblings	Other	Total
Death	1	2	4	3	10
Contact	4	12	4	2	22

Suicide and Deliberate Self-Harm

Suicidal behaviour presents a problem for health and welfare services (see Coleman, Lyon and Piper 1995; Harrington and Dyer 1993; Kerfoot 1996; Pritchard 1995). There are differences in the characteristics of those attempting to commit suicide and parasuicide (deliberate self-harm), not least that there are more boys in the first group and more girls in the second. There are dangers associated not only with the act of deliberate self-harm itself, which increases the risk of another attempt, as well as the risk of later completed suicide (Hawton 1993), but also because such acts are often indicators of other severe and persistent social or psychiatric problems (Kerfoot 1996). Some studies have recognized deliberate self-harm as an attempted solution to relationship problems and as a means of control over or escape from an intolerable situation (Reder, Lucey and Fredman 1991; Riggs, Alario and Mchorney 1990). A number of factors associated with deliberate self-harm in childhood have been identified, notably parental problems such as criminality and poverty and a disrupted upbringing resulting from separations from parents and long periods in local authority care.

Factors intrinsic to the child such as depression and behavioural problems have also been noted (Kerfoot 1988, 1996).

As already mentioned, 12 young people in the study, that is 2 in 5, had attempted suicide, deliberately self-harmed or endangered their lives by their reckless behaviour. Some of them engaged in self-harming behaviour with suicidal ideation, that is thinking about or planning either suicide or parasuicide, while the self-harming behaviour of others appeared to be without suicidal intent, although was sometimes life-threatening and indicated a high level of mental distress. These findings compare with those of Sinclair and Gibbs (1998) that four in ten of the children and young people in non-secure residential care in their sample had considered killing themselves in the previous month. Treatment and aftercare for such young people varies considerably and there is a lack of consensus about what is needed. The response of some medical and professional staff to young people who repeatedly self-harm can be unsympathetic and rejecting and experienced as punitive.

One boy had attempted suicide on three occasions, once prior to admission to secure accommodation and twice by attempted strangulation in the secure unit. Three other boys had also endangered their lives, although they did not suggest that there was suicidal intent. Eight girls had attempted suicide or engaged in serious deliberate self-harming behaviour such as taking overdoses of legal and illegal drugs, cutting themselves and starvation. Five of them continued to deliberately self-harm when in secure accommodation. All the girls described themselves as very miserable, for example:

> I just wanted to kill myself … I started taking overdoses and I tried to starve myself, I kept on trying to strangle myself and I cut my wrists … I cut myself and leave scars … taking overdoses. The temptation doesn't go away. I've done it loads of times before and I'll do it again … it makes it easier to do because I've done it loads of times.

> I felt like I wanted to die, that I didn't deserve to be alive … I would climb on high roofs and try to jump off them.

Another girl who described herself as 'just too miserable to live' took two serious overdoses of heroin and only then faced the implications of her behaviour:

> Ending up in hospital made me realize I was killing myself and it didn't dawn on me until a couple of days later that I did nearly die ... and I thought 'What am I doing, if I don't stop I am going to be dead within a month?'

Alcohol/Illegal Drug Use

The use of drugs and alcohol compounded the adverse childhood experiences of a significant proportion of the young people in the study. As already shown, 14 said they regularly used alcohol, 9 said they used it infrequently with just 6 (4 male and 2 female) who said they did not use alcohol at all. Seven boys and fourteen girls, that is almost three quarters of the young people, said they had regularly used illegal drugs ranging from cannabis and 'E' tablets to heroin and crack cocaine, with one girl reporting only infrequent use. Four young people said they had used solvents in conjunction with other illegal drugs. Seven young people, four boys and three girls, said they had not used illegal drugs.

A number of themes emerged from the young people's descriptions of their use of alcohol and drugs. The first of these themes concerns the use made of drugs and alcohol by most of the young people when things went wrong in their lives, as a means of escape from their unhappiness. However, they all described how their dependence on alcohol and drugs had compounded their misery and many talked about 'a vicious circle' in which they felt trapped. For example, Anna said she started using drugs because she felt suicidal:

> I was permanently depressed and suicidal ... so to make myself feel better I started taking heroin ... gradually I started trying cocaine, rock and temazepan, the green jelly ones which are injectable ... and gradually I found myself in a deeper hole which I thought I couldn't get out of ... I got so down I started not to be bothered about the consequences of taking drugs even if it would kill me. I would just shrug my shoulders because I felt let down and it was the only thing that made me feel better. It gave me an escape from my

> problems for a couple of hours and made me feel good about myself again but when I look back I can see that it was just a vicious circle.'

The second theme concerned the link that was explicitly made by a number of young people between their use of drugs and alcohol and their offending behaviour. For example, Julie attributed her offending behaviour to drinking alcohol:

> I started drinking and that's when I started offending ... I was waking up in the morning and going down the shop and nicking a bottle of vodka. I was just like drinking all the time ... I was just doing street robberies. I only done it when I was drunk. I was quite bad but it's only through the drink.

Some young people described how their offending and their use of drugs escalated in proportion to each other. For example, Jason said:

> I started offending and I was sniffing gas and aerosol stuff and smoking draw ... My dad caught me sniffing gas and I had an argument with him and then I went into care ... then I was getting worse in care, I was taking heavy drugs and robbing cars ... when I was under the influence of drugs I was robbing all the time ... then I went to this children's home and started on brown heroin ... I was doing burglaries and spending all my money on drugs.

A third theme emerged from the accounts of the young women who had been working as prostitutes who said they used drugs/alcohol to help them cope with the difficulties which they faced, and to feel better about themselves. They also described a vicious circle in which taking drugs helped them to cope but meant that they had to continue working as prostitutes to obtain the money to buy the drugs. For example, Vicki said:

> I started taking cocaine and I injected it to block everything out of my mind ... I wasn't happy when I was working, I used to sniff gas to block it out ... I took ecstasy every time I went out.

Family Adversities and Inter-Generational Links

Associations have been made between adverse childhood experiences and later psycho-social disorders. While it has been shown that adverse experiences, particularly disrupted parenting, are likely to increase the risk of problems in adult life, it has also been shown that many opportunities exist to limit the inter-generational transmission of family problems so that children do not repeat the disadvantages of their parents (Quinton and Rutter 1988). The transgenerational effects of post-traumatic stress have also been recognized (Wilson and Raphael 1993) and an analogy drawn with the effects of alcoholism.

Many of the young people reported that their parents had experienced adversity in their own lives. Their parents' difficulties were described by the young people in telling their own stories, and are therefore likely to be incomplete, although some common themes emerged and some confirmatory and additional information was obtained from the social workers.

Physical and Sexual Abuse

The mothers of four young people were reported to have been sexually abused as children. The fathers of two young people had been convicted of offences under the Children and Young Persons Act 1933 and were 'Schedule 1 Offenders', one for sexual abuse of the sister of one of the boys and the other for physical abuse of the brother of one of the girls in the study.

In Care

The mothers of three young people spent part or all of their childhood in care and one of these was adopted.

Alcohol/Illegal Drug Use

Ten, that is more than a third of the young people in the study had lived in families where adults experienced problems with alcohol and/or drugs. In summary, two young people had lived with parents who were drug dependent, eight with parents who were alcohol dependent, and of these, four lived with parents who were dependent on or had problems with *both* drugs and alcohol.

Suicide, Deliberate Self-Harm and Mental Health Problems

Seven girls and two boys, that is almost a third, had parents, step-parents or siblings who had been identified as having mental health difficulties, including suicidal behaviour.

Criminal Offences

Twelve young people, that is two in five, came from families where there was a history or culture of criminal behaviour. Five boys and seven girls had parents or siblings who had been convicted of criminal offences and eight of them, that is more than a quarter, had close relatives who had served custodial prison sentences.

Conclusion

This exploration of the circumstances and childhood adversities of the young people in the study provides the context for the research which will examine professional views on the role of secure accommodation and the young people's perspectives on their lives and problems and the circumstances which resulted in their placement in secure accommodation. It contributes to an understanding of the vulnerability and the extent of the physical, emotional and educational needs of young people placed in secure accommodation. Local authority secure accommodation was judged to be the only provision suitable to meet the needs and provide for the best interests of the children in the study, or in some cases, the best interests of others. A key question must be how far a non-therapeutic, custodial environment such as secure accommodation can meet the needs of young people who have experienced such severe psycho-social adversity.

Part III
The Professional Context

FIVE

The Roles of Secure Accommodation
The Views of Managers and Staff

Introduction

Investigating the views of staff as well as residents in closed institutions is important to avoid 'uncomplimentary stereotypes' (Millham *et al.* 1978, p.125). In this and the next chapter, the perspectives of managers and staff on policy and practice in secure accommodation will be examined to provide the professional context for the research with the young people. Next to the children, the staff most directly experience the system and 'the unresolved abstractions which constitute its ideology'(Kelly 1992, p.6). The value of their perspectives lies in the insights they provide into the regimes, practice and quality of care in the units. Problems for staff in secure accommodation result from the lack of clarity or consensus about their function and from paradoxes in the ideology, objectives and practice of secure units (see Harris and Timms 1993; Kelly 1992; Millham *et al.* 1978; Stewart and Tutt 1987).

The process of engaging the managers and staff has been described. In summary, a total of 65 managers, members of the management teams and staff participated in discussion groups or interviews about secure accommodation. In two units representatives of the teaching staff also participated. Staffing structures in all the units operated on traditional, hierarchical lines with a principal, unit manager or officer in charge, one or more deputies, senior staff and a complex structure of grades and levels of seniority. Their backgrounds, levels of experience, training and qualifications varied, replicating the situation in the wider residential care world. All the principals, managers or officers in charge were male and five of them had a Certificate in Social Services, Certificate of Qualification in Social Work or Diploma in Social Work qualification. In addition, the majority of those in senior positions had social work or other relevant qualifications. There were female deputies or assistant principals in three units and women were represented in senior positions in all the units. The ratios of staff to young people differed between units. For example, one unit nearing completion had its full complement of staff but not of young people, so the ratio was more than 1: 1, while in another unit the ratio was 1: 3 because of staffing difficulties.

The Purpose of Secure Accommodation

The place secure accommodation occupies in the wider child welfare system was discussed by staff and some of them expressed concerns about the way it is perceived and the functions it fulfils within the wide range of service provision for young people. Their first concern related to professionals' use of it as a threat which reinforced its negative image, a concern which highlighted the tension between secure unit staff and field social workers:

> Well it was always used as a weapon towards the kids, like a threat, 'If you don't toe the line this is where you'll end up and it's a pretty horrific experience'. I mean a lot of social workers threaten kids with secure accommodation with no real knowledge of what it is.

The second concern related to the containment of young people who were admitted because of inadequate community services, which many staff felt was a misuse of secure accommodation:

> It can be used as a place to contain a young person when they can't find anything else ... sometimes you wonder why their liberty is being restricted. It's easier to understand a section 53 because they've been sentenced but with some of the young people here on welfare orders, it seems that it's just that there's nowhere else for them to go ... if there was more effort in the community they wouldn't need to come to us in the first place.

The lack of community resources was contrasted with the recent investment in secure accommodation:

> Residential care is expensive and we've seen so many places close down ... Secure units are maybe the last growth industry in the country ... It's ironic that they're throwing millions of pounds into secure units at the same time that they seem to be cutting non-secure provision hand over fist.

The third, related issue raised by staff concerned the principle of 'demand following supply' as newly opened beds were immediately filled by children who would previously have been accommodated elsewhere:

> I think secure is an easy option ... Sometimes the authorities use it to get rid of a problem instead of dealing with it and that's the way I see it being used at the moment ... Since we opened, the minute the beds were available it was like heads on beds and you have to ask what did they do with them before they had the beds because there was a stage where it was all local children in there, so where did they put them before and how did they deal with them?

Secure accommodation is isolated from the wider child care world and mainstream services, and this issue aroused ambivalent views among staff in the discussion groups. Relationships between staff and field social workers appeared to be difficult, frequently based on mutual mistrust. Moreover, what also emerged was the extent of the isolation of individual secure units from other secure units. The problems which resulted from this lack of communication and cohesion between units ranged from the repetition of design faults in buildings to 'justice and care by geography', with young people receiving very different care in different units. Only a small minority of staff had experience of working in different secure units, although a few more had visited other units. There appeared to be a climate of competition between units rather than a sense of shared purpose and mutual support, and those advocating increased co-operation were in the minority:

> Let's face it, there aren't that many secure units in the country and there's virtually nil co-operation or cohesion between them and I think that's appalling ... there needs to be a secure service with units building up areas of specialization.

> I'd like more links with other secure units, with other people who are doing the same kind of work, because the problem with these places, any institution, is that they are very insular ... I think in this kind of work you need the network, you need support.

A lack of consensus also emerged about whether it would be desirable for secure accommodation to be more integrated into the wider child welfare system. Some units identified the isolation as a positive factor in that it enabled them to 'take over' and control the young people without interference from outsiders:

> It's still a detached part of the overall child care provision, it's out on a limb, it doesn't fit comfortably, it doesn't fit into the legislation, it doesn't fit into what people's understanding of child care is and I think that actually serves our purpose ... There is a tendency once you get the youngster in for the other people to back off and it is the opportunity for the staff in the secure unit to actually say right, let's throw everything we've got out and start again.

Residential care has been described as an essential service most appropriately used for adolescents who 'present challenging behaviour' (Aymer 1992; DH 1991a; Madge 1994). While there has been confusion about whether the purpose of residential care was to provide care or control, secure accommodation which was designed with security as its main objective has been seen unequivocally as providing control. The increasing emphasis on control has been evident in the escalating demand for placements in secure accommodation and is reflected in staff views about its function.

The primary purpose of secure accommodation was described by staff in the discussion groups as to deprive young people of their liberty. Some staff who saw this as its main or only function felt that the emphasis was increasingly placed on containment and that secure units were seen as 'holding' centres, 'like child prisons', particularly for young people on remand. Nonetheless, the deprivation of liberty, containment and control were regarded by many staff as pre-requisites to achieve change with young people, particularly in their behaviour. Some staff argued that some young people living in the community are not receptive to help while, in contrast, in secure accommodation young people are available for staff to work with them. There was some acknowledgement that this involved a high degree of coercion with young people, which was justified on the basis that it was judged to be in their best interests.

This theme of having children 'available' and 'protected' from key people and influences in their lives was seen as fundamental to the other functions of secure accommodation. Some staff talked about changing young people's experiences of relationships which had often been harmful, by promoting quality relationships between young people and between adults and young people. However, this raises questions about the nature and quality of relationships which are possible for young people in secure accommodation, an environment where there is no privacy, little choice in friendships and unequal power relationships between young people and adults. In this context, relationships are likely to have an artificial quality (Millham *et al.* 1978).

Managers in one unit described the type of young people they considered secure accommodation was designed for:

> We are set up to deal with young people who are the victims of their own life experiences and if we are ever offered a child who is not the victim of his or her own life experiences that is the child we should not have.

Although young people admitted through the different legal routes are accommodated together, staff drew some distinctions between these general functions of secure accommodation and those which relate to the different requirements of welfare and criminal justice legislation.

Criminal Justice Admissions

In relation to offenders, staff focused on the provision of safety, emphasizing the importance of public protection:

> It makes them safe, first and foremost, safe from themselves, safe from others and ... There should be some respite for the community ... some young people have been terrorizing the local populations in the various parts of the country they come from.

The role secure accommodation plays in the criminal justice system as an alternative to other forms of custody was regarded by many staff as its overarching function, almost its *raison d'être.* Mixed views were expressed about the extent to which this was an appropriate function and about its effectiveness in preventing young people re-offending. Concern emerged about the changes in legislation and government policy which have led to increases in the admission of young people on remand and altered the nature of the units. Staff who saw this as a valid function expressed the view that 'this environment is far better than the harsher environment of a young offenders institution' and they also felt that young people would be less likely to re-offend than if they were exposed to criminal influences in young offender institutions:

> I think it is far better for them to be here mixing with people of their own age rather than going to young offender institutions or prisons which just make them harder and more criminally minded.

However, other staff expressed doubts about its effectiveness both as a deterrent and in preventing re-offending. They argued that the harsher environment of a young offender institution would be more effective for some young people:

> There are some young people and I fear that until they have had something unpleasant happen to them, an unpleasant experience, they will carry on doing what they were doing.

Welfare Admissions

Some confusion was evident in staff views about how young people admitted for welfare reasons fit into what are seen essentially as offender institutions, although many said it provided an escape or 'sanctuary' from the risks in the community. The guidance and regulations accompanying the Children Act 1989 stress the use of secure accommodation only as a last resort. Current practice does not always comply with this guidance which is partly explained by the reduction in residential care options which has left little in between children's homes and secure accommodation. Furthermore, many managers and staff members appeared to be uncomfortable with its function as a facility of last resort and some argued that more effective work could be undertaken if children were admitted to secure accommodation at an earlier age:

> I have always had a problem with secure accommodation being used as a placement of last resort. I would love to be locking up 8- and 9-year-olds for three months when the learning process can be much more intense ... by the time we get 14-, 15-, 16-year-olds we are just having to keep them contained in an environment which is secure ... which often proves to be an expensive sojourn before they go on to the prison system.

The Regimes

As has been noted, secure units manifest many of the features of total institutions (Goffman 1961). In all the units, symbols of control and surveillance such as locked doors within the units, staff visibly carrying keys, high fences and closed circuit television were evident and the language used was the language of control. Young people were locked in their rooms at night and at other times determined by staff. The ambiguity of the message this gave to young people admitted for 'protection' frequently left them bewildered. The institutionalized nature of secure units creates opportunities for those in control to exercise considerable power, and the potential for institutional regimes to become abusive has been repeatedly demonstrated (for example, Levy and Kahan 1991; Kirkwood 1993; Waterhouse 2000).

The behavioural regimes and the nature and quality of education provision in all the units were different. The reasons for the widespread inconsistencies between units were attributed by managers and staff to the complexity of management which created 'a number of overlords' and to the lack of clarity in the relationship between local authorities and central government, particularly the Department of Health, the Social Services Inspectorate and the Home Office. An example which preoccupied staff in all the units, related to the inconsistent policies regarding young people smoking cigarettes. Practice varied from one unit which allowed no cigarette smoking to others where cigarette smoking was restricted. The emphasis on non-smoking was widely seen as inappropriate in the context of the young people's other problems:

> We get kids who are addicted to cigarettes, who have smoked 30, 40, 50 cigarettes a day and probably dropped all the Es they want … we do not allow anybody under 16 to smoke but stuff gets passed over by visitors … If they were allowed to smoke at 15 there would be so many less searches done … I can remember one occasion when we had a boy destroy his cell purely so he would get taken down to the police station so he could smoke.

Regimes in institutions for children have been described on a continuum from 'child centred' to 'institutionally oriented' (King *et al.* 1971) and treatment-oriented institutions are those which adopt a highly individualized approach within a permissive atmosphere where staff are observers not surveillants (Street *et al.* 1966). By this definition none of the units in this study could be described as treatment-oriented or providing a therapeutic environment. Although all the units implemented behavioural regimes, staff were not all able to identify or describe a theoretical framework which informed the regime and their practice within the unit. The manager in one unit explained their system:

> It's a simple behaviour modification system based on normal rules of social interaction … we don't feel it's punitive … and it's a graphic way for the young people to assess how they've done that particular week … secure accommodation is crisis interventionist by nature … we are the final safety net for kids who are going off the rails.

The success of behavioural approaches can only be judged on whether the changes in behaviour achieved in the institution can be sustained following release. However, there did not appear to be any formal mechanism by which staff evaluated the effectiveness of their behavioural approaches. Whatever the theoretical framework, control was the primary objective of all the regimes and took precedence over care. They all exercised a high level of surveillance over the young people and relied as a means of changing behaviour on the use of sanctions, with privileges earned for 'good', compliant behaviour. The view of one manager that 'the emphasis is on security' was reflected in all the units:

> Elements of control are implicit in the structure of the building and the staff procedures and routines ... sometimes we have to make some uncomfortable decisions in the interests of security. Earlier on today an example of good practice for a young person from a social work point of view was declined because it compromised the security of the building.

One of the questions which emerged from the discussion about the regimes related to the purpose of the control. Some staff regarded control as beneficial in itself, in that it ensured a clear structure, provided stability and re-established norms of behaviour for young people whose lives were regarded as chaotic. Others argued that it provided consistency, but this was not borne out by the variable practice of individual staff members and teams. One member of staff described the inconsistency:

> It was primary control, care was a secondary issue ... it was a very, very oppressive environment ... it's probably more balanced than it was with care and control now almost fifty fifty ... but depending on who you're working with will depend on how the shift is run ... you've still got staff who are totally controlling.

The majority of staff argued in favour of the high levels of control. For example:

> There has to be control. The environment itself is a very controlling environment but I would see it as protection, it's not a punishment place ... you can see we've got locked doors and the daily routine is strict.

Notwithstanding this emphasis on control, some staff expressed the need for change from 'institutionally oriented' to more 'child centred' regimes and felt that the balance was shifting:

> It has been a regime of containment, more a regime of control and the emphasis has been on the restriction of liberty more than child-centred work ... I think it's been more of a kind of jailer approach but I think it is moving more toward a child-centred approach.

However, scepticism emerged about whether the stated commitment to more child-centred regimes represented any more than rhetoric, and doubts were voiced across the units about whether practice had really changed:

> I am disillusioned by the pretence that we care when all we want to do is keep young people under control and make sure that they cause as little problem as possible.

> It's very much a control atmosphere, macho ... We have a very confrontational approach with the young people. There is nothing wrong with confrontation but it's got to be a planned tool and one part of the tool kit, not the entire works. Here it's 'You will or ...'. The second a kid steps out of line there is a sanction slapped on.

An important question is whether the high level of control was serving the interests of the institution, the staff or the young people. Institutional benefits were evident in one unit, where young people were routinely locked in their rooms for an hour over lunch time at weekends and for half an hour on weekdays. In another unit it was seen primarily as beneficial for the staff:

> You've got control here ... the kids are in their rooms at 9.00 pm and you're off duty at 10.00 pm whereas in a children's home they could be coming back at all hours and then you've got to be out to see to them ... it's much better here, you've got much more control.

The high level of control was commonly argued to be an essential pre-requisite to engage in work with young people who have chaotic lifestyles and are unresponsive to help in the community. However, this environment of control contrasts with the characteristics of a treatment-oriented institution. The extent to which therapeutic interventions or specialist services are provided to meet young people's needs and the basis on which such work is judged to be effective emerged as important questions for investigation.

Punishment

Widespread differences emerged from the discussion about whether secure accommodation was, or should be, used as a punishment and whether the regimes in the units were punitive. Many staff acknowledged that young people would be likely to experience the deprivation of their liberty as a punishment:

> I think if you deprive anyone of their liberty it's a punishment ... to deprive children of their family and friends we have to acknowledge that can be extremely difficult so I suppose the word punishment fits it quite well.

Uncertainty was evident among staff in some units about what was the required approach to the young people, and the balance between 'punishment' and 'help', and differences also emerged between the 'official' version of practice and what actually happens:

> There is tension between the view that they should be punished, make it tough and unpleasant, and we're here to help them ... it has always been very much in favour of them being punished ... An awful lot of staff will justify harsh treatment by saying 'They are here to be punished, you mustn't forget they are here to be punished ... they ought to be in bloody prison anyway'.

Staff also acknowledged the high likelihood of confusion for young people when told by staff that they were not in secure accommodation for punishment, whilst the attitudes of people outside the unit reinforced the opposite view that they were:

> When young people first come in they do see it as punishment but that begins to diminish whilst they are in this environment, but out there it is still very much seen that they are here to be punished ... they have some difficulty making the link between the two.

Staff who felt that some young people should be punished more severely regarded placement in secure accommodation as an easy option. However, while insisting that secure accommodation was not used as a means of punishment some members of staff paradoxically conceded that they differentiated in their own practice between those young people who they felt were there for punishment and those who were not. At the same time, there was acknowledgement of the impossibility of distinguishing between young people on a day-to-day basis when they lived in a group and were all subject to the same regime. This is illustrated in one workers' description which is 'Kafkaesque' in its lack of recognition of the reality of young people's experiences:

> When we're operating as a group we don't separate out those who are here for punishment and those who are here for protection and if those who are here for welfare reasons are feeling punished by what happens in the unit then the time to address that is in key worker time in looking at why they're here and trying to present it to them to show that it isn't really punishment even if it feels like it.

Sanctions

Sanctions, also referred to as 'consequences', were imposed on young people whose behaviour did not comply with the required standards. The ultimate sanction was to lock young people in their rooms, with all their possessions removed and, in some units, the electricity supply off. The range of other sanctions included early bed times, loss of electricity, loss of cigarettes, loss of pocket money, restriction on mobility within the unit, loss of mobility out of the unit, loss of access to facilities such as the gym in the unit, restriction on access to the telephone, restriction on visits. The authority to impose sanctions lay within the power of individual members of staff. Inconsistency in practice was evident even within units with regard to the nature and degree of the sanctions imposed, resulting in confusion for young people and staff alike.

Staff and Child Cultures in the Units

The differences in culture between the units were influenced by many factors including the size and gender make-up of the groups of staff and young people. Staff said that the make-up of the resident group influenced the atmosphere in the unit and the attitudes and practice of staff. For example, they said that the levels of control, surveillance and restraint (also euphemistically known as 'physical management') would be likely to increase where young people were unco-operative:

> If the kids themselves are not co-operative then the staff group 'up the ante' and the regime changes … they're not allowed out and things that are part of normal life get taken away from them.

The staff cultures in the units also influenced staff morale and sickness rates which were described by staff in three units as high and in one as 'unbelievable'. During the time of this study, tension was particularly evident in three units and alarms frequently summoned staff, creating an atmosphere of crisis. How far all the incidents required this level of crisis response was unclear, and some staff appeared uncertain about whether the degree of physical restraint exercised with young people was necessary.

This 'climate of crisis' appeared to be one of the features of a 'macho' culture. Staff in one unit said that it permeated from the 'top' through the whole institution and resulted in a very controlling, intimidating approach from management to staff and from staff to young people:

> Some staff have this power thing and rely very heavily on 'Do what I tell you now' … I think this comes from the way we're treated. We'll be told 'I'm the fucking boss and you'll do what I fucking tell you' and that's the manager of a social services establishment. I mean in the army you'd expect it … but not when you're doing residential work in social services … It's an extremely macho atmosphere to work in … Most places I go I would be a big bloke but I am nowhere near a big bloke here … they want big men who will be able to subdue quickly any insurrection and put, 'Bang', people in their rooms … and the percentage of male to female staff is odd … we'll be down to three out of twelve … in open units my experience has been that it is more fifty-fifty or more female than male … it suggests more control and the way the place is run it becomes a self-fulfilling prophesy … staff it with big people who

> can afford to push it because if it all goes off they can control it and you're going to get a unit that runs that way.

A female member of the management team in the same unit described sexism among staff, intimidation of women workers and stereotyping of the girls. These important gender issues will be examined in the next chapter. The presence of a 'macho' culture is one of the common themes which emerged from inquiries into abuse in residential homes (Berridge and Brodie 1996). Intimidation was reported in four units by managers or staff who described its effect on staff and young people:

> You do get staff who have the attitude, 'When I walk in the room everybody is going to behave' and the message the kids get is very much, 'You'd better behave because if you don't there'll be a consequence' and it's by sheer intimidation.

One manager described how intimidation by managers could result in disempowerment and staff copying inappropriate methods of working:

> If you have a manager who operates in that way it hugely disempowers the staff team who either feel they cannot operate in an appropriate way or who hide behind that mode of operation so that they are ... unable to operate for themselves. Some really quiet and ineffectual people are hugely effective as members of staff. Those people are the ones who are easily intimidated.

Intimidation on the basis of race was also reported:

> Well I've heard a member of staff calling one of the boys a nigger and that's totally unacceptable ... I would like that to be stamped out or to be dealt with by management, but it wasn't, so I think the person may still be saying things ... obviously if he can say that once he can say it again.

However, male members of the management team in the same unit took a different view. As one said:

> I would be surprised if you could sustain an argument that either the individual or institutional practice here was sexist or racist.

Cultures which allowed people to do 'their own thing' aroused particular concern because of the fragmentation in practice and inconsistency which resulted for young people. Staff in one unit described the problem:

> People here think they're not being monitored and that they can't be disciplined and that sets up an ethos of what I call a cowboy mentality … There really is a big cowboy mentality here which is 'I'll do it my way and if they don't like it screw them' … Kids do need consistency and without consistency of approach you're going to confuse them.

This brings into sharp focus the issues of staff supervision and training. In one unit, staff described a culture where those who requested supervision were regarded as 'weak'. The practice in the other units was varied and not always clear, although there did not appear to be an established culture of regular supervision, appraisal and staff development. Some staff expressed anxiety about their lack of supervision and the potential 'dangerousness' of practice where supervision was only regarded as necessary in response to a problem. In one unit, staff talked very positively about the opportunities to participate in external training and some in-unit training was also arranged, but in the other five units staff described training opportunities as inadequate or non-existent. Staff reported that their units could not afford to send them, or release them from work to attend training courses provided by the local authority. Opportunities for participating in training with workers in the wider child-care field were therefore very limited and none of the staff had had the opportunity to participate in any training with staff from other secure units. However, training which included some work on gender issues had been provided for the staff group in two newly developed units and an external training agency had been commissioned to undertake some training with staff in a third unit. None of the units had provided formal induction training for new staff, although an open learning manual providing a structural induction process has since been published (Gabbidon and Goldson 1997) which might improve the opportunities for new staff. It is perhaps significant that a primary concern for staff in five units was their lack of training in restraint techniques, despite guidance from government on control of children (DH 1997c).

Notwithstanding these training opportunities, in four units staff reported a negative attitude to training on the part of their managers and peers. Those who had undertaken training or who were appointed with qualifications were described as threatening to the existing staff group, and they experienced criticism and intimidation. In one unit a pattern was described of trained staff being recruited who then became disillusioned and de-skilled by the negative responses they received from managers and staff to their attempts at improving practice:

> It's the fourth time in a year that somebody has said 'We've got to do something about the medical room' and somebody with nursing experience has said, 'I used to be a nurse, I'll do that' and they spend time and effort getting a system together and nothing happens. There's no commitment from management to make sure it happens ... We're talking about kids who have epilepsy who aren't getting their medication, kids with infections that go on twice as long as they should because their antibiotics aren't given on time ... It's not just down to laziness ... things happen here, so you're rushing off to do a restraint or something serious has gone wrong somewhere but there is no commitment to see the job followed through and that particularly comes from the senior level staff who all seem to wear a 'Been there done that' tee shirt ... When anyone comes up with any suggestion people sort of tut tut and roll their eyes to the ceiling and 'Oh we tried that 15 years ago and it didn't work then, so ...'.

Staff in three units reported that those who had completed professional training frequently became disillusioned as their expertise was not acknowledged and many left to work elsewhere, while workers in two units said those who were just completing social work training were expecting to seek alternative employment. One worker described his experience:

> If you have some skills that can be utilized and you try to do something, you get slagged off by the rest of the staff team ... 'Oh yeah he's making his own little empire' ... It's not seen as a positive thing by the rest of the staff team and you get a hard time.

Some staff said their access to professional training was deliberately restricted because it was regarded as an 'escape' route out of residential care. They felt that this presented something of a 'double-bind' for staff and militated against achieving a higher proportion of qualified staff in residential care:

> A lot of people want to get onto a DipSW because they want to get out of residential, but they're not going to give us the opportunity. The major reports about residential care say 'Get these people qualified and raise the standards of training' but they're not going to do it because as soon as you get qualified you're going to bugger off out because you get so disillusioned.

The limited opportunities for training and the attitudes to training which emerged in some of these units are matters of concern particularly as inadequate staff training has been identified as a common theme in the inquiries into abuse in residential care (DH 1991a, 1997a; Waterhouse 2000).

Bullying and Intimidation

The culture of an institution is influential in the occurrence of bullying. Where young people feel valued there is less likelihood of bullying but where the institution fails to take the issue seriously and where staff use intimidation to control young people, bullying frequently occurs (Lane and Tattum 1989). Bullying is defined as any action such as threats or violence intended to cause fear or distress on more than one occasion (Lane 1989). Bullying and being bullied is often an interactive process and there are severe psychological consequences for the bullies and the victims of bullying (Browne and Falshaw 1996). Incidents of bullying are strongly associated with unhappiness and the extent of bullying and intimidation in residential care is much greater than generally appreciated (Sinclair and Gibbs 1998). It seems likely that the incidence of bullying in secure accommodation has also been underestimated.

While there was some degree of acknowledgement in all the units that bullying and intimidation occurred, a rather complacent attitude which minimized the problem emerged. This was surprising as the young people identified it as a substantial problem. Different attitudes were evident between staff in the units. In one unit one worker said 'it's very rare' while another said:

> Well, we say it doesn't happen but I do believe it does happen ... a young man came to see me and said he was being bullied and you'd never believe it was happening but it happens underground.

Similarly, in another unit a marked contrast emerged between the views expressed by the managers who dismissed the existence of bullying, staff who minimized the problem and the experiences of one girl:

Managers: 'We've never had bullying as an issue.'

Staff: 'We haven't had physical bullying ... I think we've had a level of intimidation which the staff have been aware of ... it's not totally resolved because there are still mechanisms these kids can use to intimidate, even where there are staff stood in front of them.'

Jenny: 'I got attacked last Thursday ... The manager said it's just an everyday occurrence, you have to put up with it ... that doesn't do anything for me. I'm going to feel afraid until I leave.'

Many staff appeared to condone bullying, suggesting that it was inherent in the system and that young people had to be prepared for it. For example:

> [Young people] have to change in here anyway as you do in any institution because of the pecking order. If you come in here as the mildest of people, you have to change that somehow because you're going to get picked on ... You'll always have your hierarchical system ... the person who's the loudest gets the most done for them because they're the loudest.

Furthermore, a victim-blaming approach emerged in the argument that some bullied young people were themselves responsible for the bullying:

> There's the ones that go looking for it, no matter how you try you can't help them, they go looking for aggression from the other people. They provoke it because they have a need to be bullied.

Some intimidation was attributed to sexist attitudes and behaviour. However, in one unit a rather muddled attitude to sexism emerged, which suggested that the boys were not responsible for their attitudes and behaviour because they had been brought up in and were therefore also the victims of a male-dominated society.

The potential for bullying was said to be increased by mixing young people with violent backgrounds with others unused to aggressive behaviour. One manager explained the dilemma for staff who tried to be observant and sensitive to the atmosphere, but found that in this context it was difficult to prevent bullying:

> Ostensibly we're a safe and secure environment and yet at any given time [we have] eight complete strangers with a myriad of problems, some of them involving aggression and violence and you're expected to carry on providing a safe and secure environment … You can't always square that particular circle can you?

This highlights one of the implications of combining in units young people admitted through different legal routes, which will be considered in the next chapter. The issue of safety for all young people, but particularly those specifically admitted for their own protection, is important and will be examined further.

The Effectiveness of Secure Accommodation

Previous research has highlighted the similarity between young people in secure accommodation and those in non-secure provision and shown that admission is frequently arbitrary and determined by factors other than their individual needs (for example, Harris and Timms 1993; Millham *et al.* 1978). A key question must therefore be whether young people's needs are met by their placement in secure accommodation. Moreover, it is important to consider whether secure accommodation is any more effective than other non-secure care in meeting the needs and safeguarding the rights of young people and how far these are forfeit to the requirement for security and control.

Staff in all the units felt the expectations placed on them by social workers were high and at times inappropriate, revealing social workers' lack of understanding of the nature of secure accommodation and of the problems peculiar to working in a secure setting – 'they expect us to wave a magic wand and be able to do something that they could not do'. Some staff felt that they were given a 'herculean' task and unrealistically expected to transform young people, while insufficient credit was given to their achievements:

> These kids have been chucked out of every school, out of their parental homes, out of relatives' homes, out of foster homes and nobody can cope with them because they are that dreadful, so they give them to us and pay us a pittance ... We feel undervalued and the message we get from everybody is that our work isn't important ... The way people feel about themselves needs to be changed ... it has always irked that as a residential social worker working with a young person for months and months, somebody who has visited twice will turn up with a report telling you what is the best thing.

Some managers said that the relatively high cost of a placement meant that high expectations were inevitable and probably justified, but they also said that many professionals were unrealistic in their view of what secure accommodation could achieve:

> It costs a lot of money ... an authority paying £10,000 a month for a child in secure wants something done and therefore it is our job to ensure that happens ... but there's an issue between residential and field services because social workers often apply a medical model to a child who has problems, sends the child to us and wants treatment and expects a cure and that's not what we're about.

The level and quality of information required by units about young people prior to or at the point of admission varied, and staff in several units identified as one of their biggest problems the lack of accurate information provided about young people. It was suggested that social workers sometimes withheld information, 'giving us the nice bits and saving the bad bits', which could result in inappropriate placements for individuals or a group mix which was potentially harmful and jeopardized the needs of young people already placed in the unit. The level of information available to staff regarding the childhood adversities of the young people or the social circumstances of their families was reported to be inadequate, replicating the situation in open residential care where staff were poorly informed about the background of children (Berridge and Brodie 1998; Farmer and Pollock 1998). This seems to reflect wider historical, social and political issues affecting the nature of relationships between social workers and residential staff.

None of the managers were autonomous in the decision-making about admissions and were subject to external social, economic and political pressures. They could be overruled in decisions relating to admission by senior managers in their own local authority and by the Home Office. Such situations could present difficulties in meeting the needs of the individual admitted and the group as a whole – 'If you haven't got the group dynamics right, that just hinders any work you can do. You end up just containing the situation and doing nothing else'. This highlights the potential conflict between the needs of individual young people and the needs of the group and the institution. Staff complained about difficulties in some situations where they had been 'required' to meet the cultural, religious or sexual orientation needs of individual young people which were different from those of the group and which led them to conclude that the placements were inappropriate. The lack of flexibility in practice described in all the units indicates that the needs of the group and the institution will almost always prevail over the needs of the individual, despite the rhetoric of 'individualized programmes' and care plans.

Individual Care Plans

The requirement for care plans for children is contained within the Children Act 1989 and the accompanying regulations and guidance. Individual care plans should be prepared for all young people in secure accommodation based on an assessment of their health, educational, psychological and other needs, including those arising from their religion, culture, race or language and a social history of the young person and their family. Workers in five units referred to their use of individual care plans and managers in one unit talked about care plans which provided a holistic view of young people and included their care and education needs 'hand in glove'. However, sharp differences emerged between this rhetoric and the practice described in relation to the use of care plans, the role of keyworkers and the balance of individual versus group needs. These differences were evident throughout the process, from admission to discharge, summed up by one member of staff who said, 'We just do the same thing with each one of them as they come in and go out'.

The practice in relation to care plans was raised as an issue of concern. Care plans should contain details of how young people's needs are to be met, set the timescale and identify any specialist services to be provided and in all the units they were the responsibility of the keyworkers. An important element of care planning, particularly with teenagers, is their right to participate in the process, but only a minority were involved in the preparation of their care plans and some young people were not shown care plans prepared by staff. Staff in one unit used identical care plans, regardless of the needs of the individual:

> We don't even talk to the young person or look at the file or whatever, you just include the same things ... it's just there, we don't change it ... It's not something you go through with the young person to see what they think ... I don't think I've ever done that, actually spoken on a one-to-one with a young person to say what would you like us to work with ... they just get told.

The absurdity of this was manifest in relation to young people who had more than one admission whose care plans were the same each time, regardless of what had happened to them since their previous admission. There was general agreement that care plans should set achievable goals and many staff felt that they were often unrealistic, particularly where young people would return to the same environment from which they had been admitted. Uncertainty about the length of placement often meant that no care plan was prepared, resulting in 'drift':

> If you knew from the start they were getting three months or six months you could plan something, whereas if it's a month then you think, oh it's not worth it, so you give up, but then that month and another and suddenly four months has gone by and you haven't done anything.

Many of the managers said that there had been changes in their practice from working with the whole group, 'what was relevant for one was relevant for the whole group' to working with the individual, with the commitment to individual care plans recited almost as a mantra. Some justified the mix in units of young people admitted for different reasons on the basis that they had individual care plans. But while managers in one unit insisted that individual care plans ensured individual needs were met:

> The main aim is working with the individual so no two care plans or programmes for those individuals are the same … They will all be working towards different aims and working on different levels.

Staff in the same unit described what was actually happening in practice:

> Well they all have individual care plans but you have to interact with them as a group and do things as a group, so therefore they're all treated the same even though they've got individual care plans, it makes no difference at all.

This contradiction was evident in all the units. The focus on the group was further illustrated by staff who said that they were only familiar with the care plans for the young people to whom they were allocated as keyworker, so although interacting with other young people on a group basis they would be unaware of their individual needs or the work being undertaken with them:

> The way care plans are done, we don't read other people's care plans, so we've got to complete them but we don't know what other people are doing with them … we don't actually know what we're trying to do with the young person.

The failure of staff to share information about individual young people extended beyond knowledge of their care plans. In five units the poor quality of information-sharing at staff meetings was also raised:

> We never really sit down and discuss the youngsters … we have our staff meetings but the only thing we discuss about them is when it

> comes to their ratings or if there has been a specific serious incident … we rarely talk about them.

Role of Key/Link Workers

Keyworkers were allocated by managers to young people in all the units. It was generally acknowledged that the quality of the work undertaken with young people was likely to depend on the expertise and commitment of the keyworker and that it was inevitable that some young people would fail to experience any effective work with their keyworker. Variation emerged in the role played by the keyworkers and in their understanding of what was expected in their individual sessions with young people. Some staff found there was less importance attached to the quality of the work undertaken with young people, than to demonstrating that sessions had taken place:

> Sometimes there'll be a drive on doing keywork sessions, you're told you must have one, you might not get on with your key work kid at all, there might be a big personality clash, but you're the key worker so you do the key working session. It won't produce anything worth while but you've had one, so it looks good.

Although it appears that only a minority of staff had training or qualifications which would equip them to undertake counselling work or provide them with a theoretical framework to understand many of the young people's behaviours, the primary responsibility for one-to-one work with young people lay with the keyworkers. At the same time, staff in one unit said that they were criticized very heavily for becoming too involved if they tried to engage in work of any depth with young people.

Access to Specialist Services

In this context, it might reasonably be expected that staff and young people would have access to specialist services. But this was not the case and a picture emerged of *ad hoc* arrangements and an absence of clear policies between secure units and local authorities regarding the use and funding of specialist services. Two units employed clinical psychologists on a part-time basis, who were available to engage in some assessment and direct work with young people and to provide a consultancy service to staff. One of these units also employed staff who had previously worked in the health service. None of the staff in the other units had ready access to specialist psychiatric or psychological advice or consultation in relation to the young people with whom they were working. Staff in one unit observed, 'We don't have any support externally. We support each other but there is nowhere to go other than our own staff group'.

Young people in secure accommodation have needs which require therapeutic interventions. However, staff in one unit reported that no specialist services were provided at all unless they were arranged and paid for by the placing local authority and it emerged that local authorities were usually unwilling to fund specialist interventions because 'extra services are regarded as extra to requirements'. A typical battle about funding was described:

> We were trying to get a psychiatric assessment of a young person here and there was a problem because the local authority wouldn't fund it and we wouldn't fund it and then they said, 'Oh well, by the time the referral's gone through she wouldn't still be here anyway.'

This highlights the particular difficulty for young people admitted through the welfare route where therapeutic interventions are not arranged because of uncertainty about the length of placement or because the waiting time from referral to intervention is longer than the young person's placement. However, staff in several units also described long delays in the provision of services for some convicted young people resulting from demarcation disputes in responsibility between the secure unit, field social workers and the Home Office. It emerged that the lack of specialist services meant that decisions were sometimes taken not to address particular issues which were beyond the abilities of the unit or could not be resolved in the time available, and they were left in abeyance to be addressed at a future unspecified time.

Evaluation of Practice

Most of the staff had difficulty evaluating the effectiveness of their work, particularly as there appeared to be a lack of clarity about their aims. It appeared that they largely relied on informal feedback from social workers and they spoke anecdotally and impressionistically about work with young people and whether it had been effective. It was not clear how education provision was evaluated. Distinctions were commonly drawn on the basis of the legal status of young people in what could be achieved. None of the units had any formal system of follow-up or evaluation of the outcomes for young people following their release from the unit.

The units did not expect to be able to meet all young people's needs and in some cases said they could do little to address the reason for admission, which lay in their social or family circumstances. Staff observed that the work undertaken with young people often bears no resemblance to the reason for admission, for example 'a child might come in for street robberies but it is attendance at school or bedtime behaviour which we focus our time on'. Some suggested that the objectives of the placement could frequently be as basic as demonstrating that 'you care for them, you do not judge them and you take them for what they are'. Staff generally felt that the primary requirement for containment and control for all young people was met, although it is of note that during the time of the study young people went missing from two of the units.

Staff in several units observed that some young people appeared to achieve change, only to revert to previous patterns of behaviour following their return to the community, which would seem to indicate the ineffectiveness of the behavioural approaches without follow through after discharge. Staff in all the units questioned how far they could be effective in achieving change with young people if they were to return to the same situations and negative influences:

> I think you will find the staff could give you countless examples of young people … they have really brought about change in a young person's life and they go out and after a few weeks, or a few days or even a few hours sometimes have committed further offences and slipped back to where they were four years before and … it's of no value at all.

Staff expressed greater clarity about the needs and the aims of placements in relation to those admitted through the criminal justice routes, where the focus was on the offending behaviour. However, it emerged in at least three units that very limited work was undertaken with offenders, particularly when they denied offences of which they had been convicted. There was also less confidence that emotional and psychological needs could be addressed and staff suggested that this would only become apparent when the external control provided by secure accommodation was removed. Even more doubts were expressed that the needs and reasons for admission of those admitted through the welfare route could be effectively met. Managers in one unit acknowledged the limitations on what they could achieve:

> If we do nothing else ... I always like to think that if they come to us in a bad state of health, the very least we would do would [be to] attempt to give them a sort of MOT ... we would at least like to send them on their way ... with a clean bill of health and if you can't do the bigger things then you should be able to do the smaller things.

Concerns were expressed about the inability of secure units to address the needs of many of those admitted for welfare reasons and the complex issues associated with behaviours such as deliberate self-harm:

> These young people who are here on care orders ... I think we've let them down, we've failed ... we've let them down drastically. They shouldn't be in this unit even if they say they're a danger to themselves and others. You could still do things in the community ... I do feel strongly that these people are inappropriately placed and I think it's an indictment to say that this is all we've got to offer them.

At the same time some staff argued for longer stays because the limited time available in many cases made it impossible to resolve their problems:

> If you only get 28 days you question what you can actually achieve in that time and quite often you can discharge a kid you really don't feel you ever got to grips with and you feel is going out and will quickly re-fulfil the criteria for a secure order and that sort of

> in-out-in-out isn't good and you would prefer a situation where they did come on a longer order.

Tangible evidence that the needs of young people have not been met is provided by requests for re-admission. However, where the responsibility for this lies is contentious and workers in the units largely attribute the failure to the social workers, rather than the behavioural regimes which are implemented. One manager expressed his concern that, 'We've had one girl who has been admitted to the unit five times, which speaks volumes for what was not available to her when she left us ...' and another manager described a similar experience:

> It's not uncommon to hear a social worker asking to place a kid back in the unit ... it's a really sad indictment of just how little there was for her in the wider community ... if she meets the criteria and there really is no alternative, we have taken girls back in, in the certain knowledge that at the end of their stay when we've managed to stabilize them again, they're going to go back to an unworkable situation ... and they're quickly going to find themselves repeating the exercise.

Conclusion

This chapter has examined the perspectives of the staff and managers in six secure units on the role and function of secure accommodation, the regimes operating within the units and the ability of secure units to meet the individual needs of the young people. Some striking inconsistencies emerged in attitudes and practice between staff within units and between units, reflecting the lack of clarity about the ideology, function and objectives of secure accommodation. In the ideological conflict between control and care, control emerged as the overriding priority, resulting in institution- rather than treatment-oriented regimes. Emergent concerns include the cultures in some of the units, negative attitudes to supervision and training and the limited training opportunities available to staff, many of whom acknowledged their lack of expertise to understand the needs and undertake work with the young people in their care.

The lack of flexibility in the regimes in all the units meant that in practice young people were treated as a group by staff, despite individual care plans and the rhetoric of individualized programmes. Although in all the units keyworkers were seen as responsible for the individual work with young people, inconsistency emerged in their understanding of the role and in their practice. Furthermore, while a function of secure accommodation is said to be to contain and control young people in order to treat them, there were very limited structures in place to provide the required treatment. The next chapter will examine these issues further in exploring staff views on the young people who make up the secure unit population.

SIX

Secure Unit Residents

The Views of Managers and Staff

Introduction

This chapter will examine staff perspectives on the young people resident in secure accommodation and the debate about the secure unit population. The first aspect of the debate is the placement of young people considered to be in need of protection together with unconvicted and convicted offenders. Although government policy promotes the mix of admission routes into secure units, the practice is contrary to the UN Convention on the Rights of the Child and other international conventions. The second aspect relates to gender, and the benefits and disadvantages of single- and mixed-gender units, particularly for the minority group, the girls.

These are both gendered issues which are linked because the majority of boys are admitted as offenders and the majority of girls are admitted for protection. While there are issues arising from the mix of offenders and non-offenders in single-gender units, there are additional factors in mixed-gender units. Staff views on children's age will also be considered, although this issue appears to have attracted less attention and children across the whole age range are currently admitted to all units.

The Combination of Offenders and Non-Offenders

The combination of offenders and non-offenders in secure units is a contentious issue which impinges on one of the key debates in secure accommodation, that is the relationship between care and custody. Offenders can be conceptualized as 'children in need' just as easily as non-offenders in that their backgrounds have been shown to be strikingly similar (Boswell 1996), but whether this is sufficient to justify placement together, thereby emphasizing the similarities rather than the important differences between them is a complex question. Previous research studies have reached different conclusions about the merits of this practice. Whilst Millham and his colleagues (1978) stress the importance of separation of young people placed for 'intensive care' from those placed for 'custody', Harris and Timms (1993) argue that in secure accommodation it ceases to matter whether children have committed an offence or are troublesome in some other way. In rejecting this view and arguing that it does matter to those who are in secure accommodation, Littlewood (1996) contends that it is indefensible to place children who have not committed serious offences in secure accommodation, even if one of its functions is care, while Brogi and Bagley (1998) argue that it is 'neither fair nor logical' to lock up young people who are the victims of prior sexual abuse with those who have a history of sexual assault.

All the units in this study accommodated a combination of offenders and non-offenders. One mixed-gender and two single-gender units accommodated up to eight young people together. In the other three larger mixed-gender units, the accommodation was divided into smaller sub-units. These arrangements provided limited opportunities for separation on the basis of legal status and/or gender. However, only one unit used a six-bed facility to accommodate girls and 'vulnerable' offending or non-offending boys. The paradox of this lay in the fact that the boys regarded as the most vulnerable were frequently those who had been convicted of sexual offences. Whatever their views about the ethics of this practice, all the managers and staff were confident that they 'managed' the mix of young people well, and some said that the issue presented more of a problem philosophically than in practice.

The Arguments in Favour of 'the mix'

Although there was widespread discussion about the 'gambling' involved in balancing the risks presented by mixing offenders and non-offenders, the units' ability to manage them was cited in support of the argument that it was appropriate practice. The most popular argument advocated by staff in favour of combining offenders and non-offenders was that young people's needs are likely to be similar because they emanate from similar backgrounds. The greatest differences between them were thought likely not to be their admission route; for example, a young man who has committed sexual offences may himself have been sexually abused and repeatedly run away. Furthermore, they argued, somewhat pessimistically, that they all show similar behaviour patterns and were all likely to end up in secure accommodation one way or the other, sooner or later.

By emphasizing the similarities, rather than the differences between young people, uniform treatment of them within the units is justified. One member of staff reflected, 'I think it's important for us as an institution to be able to believe that they have the same needs'. As already shown, this practice flies in the face of research which emphasizes the importance of disaggregating groups of young people who have different needs and potentially different outcomes (Bullock *et al.* 1998) and sexually abused and abusing young people and tailoring services to meet the needs of each group (Farmer and Pollock 1998).

Those who advocate this practice stress the importance of the individual care plan and the ability of the secure unit to address the needs of the individual. They argue that the use of care plans minimizes the harmful effects of living within a regime which, in adopting the lowest common denominator in terms of control, surveillance and punishment, treats everyone the same. However, as already shown, widespread concerns emerged about the value of care plans, described in one unit as a 'complete irrelevance', within regimes which do not have the flexibility to differentiate between the needs of individuals. This suggests that some managers are advocating an ideology which is in conflict with the reality of what is happening in practice, leaving both the young people and the staff in confusion, trying to 'square the circle'.

A number of arguments were advocated against more specialization. The first proposed that if units accommodate only offenders or only welfare cases, there would be a tendency to move to an establishment regime and a group mentality with the subsequent loss of individualized plans. But it has already emerged that even with a mix of offenders and non-offenders, units are operating establishment regimes and working with a group mentality. The second suggested that separation of young people would lead to competition and claims of élitism by staff working with 'the difficult, meaty stuff who need all the specialist skills' with the consequent marginalization of the others.

The third argument related to the situation of young people convicted of offences (mostly boys) who it was felt had most to lose by any changes. A primary concern was that, if they were in specialized units for convicted offenders, they would not be given the care and experiences they need as children, but rather those they would be deemed to need as *convicted* children. However, it has emerged that within the present system, whether offenders or not, they are all treated as 'criminal' children. This argument is also gendered in that it seems to matter to its proponents that the boys may lose out through any changes to the system, but not that the current practice disadvantages the girls.

The fourth argument against more specialization relates to the threat to the overall flexibility of secure provision and constitutes a management argument. It is argued that specialization in units on the basis of admission route or gender would reduce the flexibility of units and that if places were specifically designated, young people needing a place at a particular time might not match the place available. However, one manager said that this flexibility was itself disadvantageous in that it meant not enough thought was given to how young people were brought together and that the needs of very vulnerable and damaged young people were not uppermost in people's minds when places were sought. He said:

> It's not very nice to put some of our very vulnerable kids in with some out and out villains and I've never been happy with that aspect of secure accommodation but unfortunately you can't pick and choose.

A final argument made against specialization was that it could result in young people being placed at greater geographical distance from their homes. This did not carry significant weight, both because the problems resulting from it were felt to be superable, and because young people were frequently placed at geographical distance from their homes in the current system.

The Arguments in Favour of Specialization

Considerable disquiet emerged about the current practice in relation to the mix of admissions, with views ranging from outright opposition to confusion and uncertainty. Staff highlighted the fundamental conflict:

> The emphasis for section 53s is on punishment ... the restriction of their liberty is a punishment for what they've done so how can you mix that group with a welfare group who are in for a place of safety where the emphasis isn't on punishment ... you've got conflict straight away.

Staff in the two single-gender units described the difficulties of combining offenders and non-offenders and expressed misgiving at the additional implications of doing so in mixed-gender provision. Even those who supported this policy expressed their concerns about it:

> It is incongruous to have children for such widely differing reasons entering the same establishment for similar periods of time which are disproportionate to the offences or life experiences they have had, so you will get murderers in with very vulnerable young girls, you get rapists in with victims of rape – so the issue of mix is a real issue, although it tends not to cause problems in the secure unit itself because it can cope with the mixes, but I wouldn't like to be a young girl who had been the subject of sexual abuse who finds myself living in a secure unit with a rapist. It would cause me a lot of grief.

Staff identified differences between young people admitted through the different legal routes, particularly that those convicted of offences had a different philosophy on life and attitude to their placement, which was that they were there to 'do their time' and then leave. Staff observed that ironically they frequently felt less punished than those admitted through the welfare route. Although the impact of this practice on young people admitted through the welfare route caused most unease, some concerns were expressed about the implications for convicted offenders, which will be considered first.

OFFENDERS

In the five units which accommodated convicted offenders, they were regarded as significantly easier to manage and presented fewer behavioural problems than those admitted through the other legal routes. The suggestion of one member of staff received widespread support:

> Give us a whole unit of section 53s because they cause the least trouble because most of their problems, which are of a criminal nature, have been dealt with whereas the problems of the other kids are emotional and psychological and much harder to deal with.

Concern was expressed about the ability of convicted offenders to make and maintain relationships in units where the majority of young people were admitted through other legal routes and the turnover of residents was high. The placements of convicted offenders were usually long-term, in contrast to the short(er)-term placements of those admitted through the other legal routes. Other concerns related to their morale and self-esteem, which was thought likely to be negatively affected as they saw other people gaining mobility at an earlier stage and leaving the unit after shorter stays, and as a result of the limited facilities available in units for them over the long term. Furthermore, as many faced transfer to prison system accommodation at or around age 16, their needs and the focus for work were very different from those admitted through the welfare route.

However, the primary concern for this group related to their treatment by their peers and by staff. For example, some young people who had committed grave offences were treated harshly by staff who considered that they 'deserved' more severe punishment and they were also ostracized by their peers. Staff described the treatment of one girl convicted of an offence against a younger child: 'She really did get a very hard time, the others were actually cruel with her, so much so that she couldn't cope in the classroom and we saw her deteriorating before our eyes.'

Notwithstanding these concerns, most unease was expressed about the position of young people admitted through the welfare route and the difficulties in ensuring that they received the protection for which they had been admitted.

WELFARE ADMISSIONS

Some staff felt that secure accommodation was not an appropriate placement for young people in need of protection. There were concerns about young people who presented a risk to themselves, particularly those who were deliberately self-harming. Many staff felt that such young people had been failed by the professional systems and that secure accommodation provided an easy alternative to the development of suitable community resources. The majority of staff regarded secure accommodation as a facility for offenders, and some described it as 'a criminalized environment' which was an inappropriate place for those who had not committed any offences at all, or whose offences were minor and frequently a consequence of their placements in residential care. One of the implications of this was that non-offenders were 'treated as a criminal' because regimes and behavioural systems were applied across the board, without any differentiation between those who had committed violent and other serious offences and those admitted for their own protection. Staff described the absurdity of seeing young people deprived of their liberty to protect them from perpetrators of abuse, sitting across the table from other young people convicted of abuse or violent offences.

There was recognition that this practice influenced young people's perception of themselves, reinforcing the sense of guilt that many victimized young people already felt: 'It's very unfair for the welfare kids … they complain that being in here they feel as if they're criminals.' One member of staff articulated more widely voiced concerns about the harmful effect of placement on self-perception and self-esteem and highlighted the muddled nature of the message given to young people:

> I don't think the welfare cases should be in secure accommodation. I think they should be dealt with out in the community, there should be alternatives ... it can't do them any good, it can't do their self-esteem any good being locked up with alleged and convicted offenders ... what messages are we giving them, is it a school to learn crime ...?

The issue of risk referred to above is important. Staff talked about the daily 'gambling' in which they engaged, balancing the risks to young people presented by their peers and situations in which staff felt they 'diced with danger'. The danger of 'criminal contamination' is one of the risks faced by young people who have no previous history of offending or whose offences have been minor in nature. There were mixed views about the extent to which this happened as most staff said they discouraged young people from discussing the offences they had committed and intervened where necessary. However, there was also acknowledgement that young people were generally aware of the offences committed by their peers and that the effect could be either to 'glorify' or 'terrify'.

The risk of violence was identified as a significant issue and some concerns were expressed about the harmful effect on young people who had been victims of violence placed in the same units as those convicted of violent offences. Interestingly, staff in all the units, many of whom had *minimized* the extent and effect of bullying, nonetheless shared their disquiet about the distress caused to very vulnerable and frightened young people by those who were violent or abusive.

The risks of sexual and emotional harm associated with combining young people who have been abused with those who have been convicted of abuse were identified as the most serious and challenging for staff. It was an issue of concern for staff in the boys' unit, as well as in the mixed-gender units, who said, 'it causes a lot of anger, with mixed feelings in the staff group as well as in the kids ... it makes the whole situation difficult to cope with'. However, most anxiety related to the combination of girls who had suffered abuse with boys convicted of sexual offences. One member of staff personalized the issue:

> If I were a father and my daughter was here because of running away and being at risk and I knew she was living with convicted rapists, I wouldn't be happy, I would feel as though the system had let me, and her, down.

It was clear that some staff who struggled with this dilemma justified the practice on the basis that the offender had to face up to what he had done and learn that it was inappropriate, but this inevitably meant that the offender's needs were given priority:

> You're gambling, but you can argue that the situation has got to be faced at some time in that person's life ... they've got to be able to mix at some point ... it's not fair on the innocent party but the person who's in for a serious rape has got to face that situation.

While staff in all the units felt that they managed these risks well, there were divergent views about whether it was desirable practice. For example, one manager supported the policy on the basis that it had not presented any concerns which could not be managed by good staff practice. However, another questioned whether it should have to be managed: 'It's a situation that neither the young people, the victims, the perpetrators or the staff groups should have to deal with.'

Single- and Mixed-Gender Units

Government policy during recent years has been to promote the development of mixed- gender units. One manager talked about the lack of consultation by government in the change in policy from single- to mixed-gender units: 'I can't comment on what sort of forethought or planning went into it ... but somebody obviously thinks that single-sex units are not the way to go.'

In this study, two units were single-gender (one male and one female), one new mixed unit had replaced two single-gender units, and one unit had been developed from a single-gender to a larger mixed-gender unit. The remaining two units were mixed-gender, one with some separate living accommodation which was used primarily for girls. There were male and female staff working in all the units. In the two single-gender units the gender balance of the staff groups reflected that of the young people. Three mixed-gender units had a higher proportion of male staff (two of them were significantly higher), and the remaining unit had approximately equal numbers of male and female staff. Staff in the two single-gender units had no experience in mixed-gender units, while staff in the mixed-gender units had varying degrees of experience in single-gender units.

An interesting but disturbing emergent issue concerned the attitudes to girls. Girls were widely regarded as more difficult and demanding to work with and the majority of the staff in the mixed-gender units, as well as perhaps more predictably the staff in the boys' unit, said they would prefer to work with boys. Staff appeared to attribute many of the difficulties they encountered in mixed-gender units to the presence and requirements of the girls and it was worrying to find that many male staff felt threatened by girls they regarded as 'dangerous'. These difficulties seem to have been compounded by staffing issues, particularly a shortage of female staff. The perspectives of staff on gender issues relating to the young people will be examined first, followed by those relating to the staff.

Notwithstanding the concerns about mixing offending boys with non-offending girls, the predominant ideology was that mixed-gender units provided the opportunity for greater 'normality' for young people, who would in any other circumstances be living and interacting socially together. It was suggested that this practice reflected the movement in residential care away from gender segregation. Care and education staff argued that the placement of boys and girls together added another dimension to work that could be undertaken with young people on their own relationships and the impact they have on other people. Staff expressed particular concern in relation to young men serving long sentences who were considered to need contact with girls during their placement as part of their preparation for release. And yet, there was broad agreement that it was more difficult for staff to supervise and work with a mixed group, and that staff faced some significant problems in mixed-gender units.

The majority of staff also said that all-female units were essential for some girls who would be disadvantaged by placement in mixed-gender units. They suggested that effective pre-placement assessment would identify these young women. However, the dearth of places in all-female units and the practice reality that placement is frequently determined by bed availability with very little 'matching' or choice possible must lead to the conclusion that many young women whose needs would be more appropriately met in girls' units are placed in mixed-gender units.

This ideology of normality was challenged by some staff on the basis that secure accommodation does not provide a normal living environment, that there is gender segregation in the alternative forms of custody and the risk in prioritizing the need for mixed-gender social interaction is that other equally or even more important needs will be overlooked. Furthermore, it was argued that in mixed units with a male culture, the different and frequently conflicting needs of girls and boys can result in more rather than less difficulty for everyone. Indeed, it was striking that the benefits of mixed gender units identified by staff, confirmed that they were predominantly benefits for the *boys*, with the girls most likely to experience the disadvantages.

As already shown, girls are in the minority in mixed gender units and the proportion of male to female residents fluctuates. A common view was that unless a reasonable balance could be maintained, girls should be placed in single-gender provision. It was suggested that the vulnerability of a young woman at risk can only be increased if she is placed, without adequate female support, in a unit of offending young men. However, the pressure for flexibility in the allocation of places means that in practice situations will recur such as that evident during the time of this study, where in one group of eight young people there was only one girl.

The prevailing cultures in the mixed gender units were described by managers and/or staff as 'male dominated', 'blokish' and 'macho', with a preponderance of male staff in all three units. It was evident that services and activities were male-oriented or majority (that is male) driven and that the girls had to fit in with what was on offer. There was some awareness of this marginalization of young women, although there was variation in the extent to which it was seen as a problem and its effects appeared to be minimized. This evidence of marginalization is particularly worrying in that it compounds the exclusion already experienced by these girls as a consequence of the behaviour which resulted in their placement in secure accommodation. This issue relates to the gender issues for staff, such as the proportion and role of female staff in units, which will be examined later.

In all the mixed units, concerns were expressed about the boys' negative sexist attitudes, abusive language and intimidation of the girls and the female staff. Staff observed that stereotypical views of women were held by the majority of the boys, many of whom had experienced very poor relationships with women, and also by some of the male staff. There were opposing views on this. One school of thought suggested that mixed-gender units were advantageous because sexist behaviour could be challenged directly as it occurred with the girls present, which was beneficial for the boys and also helped the girls to develop skills to deal with this type of male behaviour. Furthermore, the issue could be followed up in education more successfully with mixed-gender groups than with boys alone. The contrary view was that girls who have been victimized, frequently sexually, and whose self-esteem is very poor should not be exposed to further abuse by young men in the very environment to which they have been admitted for protection from abuse. Furthermore, it is not the responsibility of vulnerable young women to provide teaching material for the young men. It must be noted that the majority of girls in this study would have had more sympathy with the second view than the first.

As the numbers of young women in mixed-gender units are small, there is very limited opportunity for them to develop peer relationships. This was regarded as a disadvantage for the girls and also for the female staff:

> The boys seem able to form stronger relationships with their peers than the girls ... because there are many more of the boys if the relationship with one boy breaks down they just move on to another, whereas with the girls, they form a relationship and it breaks down, then they generally go to staff because there isn't another girl to go to.

The relationships between boys and girls frequently appeared artificial. Whilst staff said they encouraged contact in an attempt to 'normalize' their experience in the unit, they exercised high level surveillance to control the sexuality of residents and prevent the development of sexual relationships. The sexual double-standard was evident in the closer scrutiny of the girls' sexuality than the boys. Staff suggested that this was necessary because the majority of girls admitted to secure accommodation had been sexually active and could be provocative and flirtatious. Extra surveillance of the girls was exercised in relation to other matters, such as the type of clothing they were required to wear to avoid any possible sexual provocation to the young men. In this way staff reinforced the stereotype of the 'predatory' young woman (Aymer 1992). This illustrates how differently girls' sexuality is viewed from that of boys. There was no equivalent recognition or even reference to the previous sexual activity of the young men, even though it appears they had been no less sexually active and some of them had been convicted of sexual offences. A situation was described in which staff had become 'paranoid' about the activities of the young people:

> We got really paranoid about the relationship between the boys and the girls. If anyone was talking for too long we got worried, we had to make sure there was a space between them if they were sat on the chairs watching television and if the girls were outside at the same time as the boys we had to go out to make sure there was no physical contact.

Another related issue which worried staff concerned the competition between young people for attention, for relationships with each other and claims about 'who was going with who' which frequently led to frustration and confrontations. Whilst this was acknowledged as normal adolescent behaviour, the environment and circumstances of the young people were not normal and they were unable to utilize their usual coping mechanisms to deal with frustrations and disappointments. Many staff suggested that as they could pick up on difficulties when they occurred and help young people learn how to deal with them, they were of positive benefit. However, others felt that rivalry between boys and girls was unhelpful to them in the context of secure accommodation and that it distracted them from focusing on their own problems and needs. Some staff also conceded that as they were not always aware of everything that was happening, they could not intervene or effectively protect. Protection from sexual competition was seen as one of the benefits afforded by single-gender units. One manager explained this viewpoint:

> There's no competitiveness about it, you don't have to play the mating game, you don't have to show off to each other. If you're a boy you don't have to pretend that you're a big macho man and try and get off with the girls in the unit and as a girl who don't have worry about responding ... Many of the girls are victims, with low self-esteem and a poor self-image and they are very vulnerable as regards members of the opposite sex, so to come to an all-female unit is a bit of a respite from that.

The protection of young people in secure accommodation is a primary objective, particularly for those admitted because they were considered to be at risk in the community. Some staff questioned how far it was possible for young women to feel safe living alongside young men and as suggested above, they felt they were 'gambling' on a day-to-day basis, increasing or relaxing the levels of control and surveillance in an attempt to manage the risks.

Gender Issues for Staff

The proportion of female to male staff was an issue of concern, particularly in the three mixed-gender units, where female staff were in the minority. This is in contrast with the almost even gender balance in non-secure residential homes for adolescents (Berridge and Brodie 1998) and the situation in residential care generally where female staff are in the majority (DH 1998). These three units were described as having a masculine culture, which presented different problems for male and female staff and difficulties for them as colleagues working together. In one unit there was a strong culture of overtime working where some male staff doubled their salaries in overtime, adding to their power status. Some female staff who were unable to undertake overtime because of other commitments were subjected to intimidation and pressure by their male colleagues, who suggested that they were not pulling their weight in the unit and could not stand the pace. In two units there was general agreement that more female staff were needed. However, there was no money available to fund additional posts and no willingness to use existing posts to employ more female staff because of the need to maintain the level of male staff to control difficult young people.

It emerged that gender stereotypical roles continue to be played by male and female workers:

> Male staff are seen as the ones to provide the heavy bit ... we have a situation going down, so where's the male staff, where's the big six foot four inch male, if you're a male you provide this aspect, if you're a female you provide something else.

Female staff were expected to take primary responsibility for providing the role model and meeting the girls' needs, protecting the girls from predatory males and protecting the male staff from the girls. The reason for this was succinctly described by one manager as 'the fear factor', that is the fear of male staff that allegations of sexual or other misconduct might be made against them by the girls. Aymer (1992) suggests that many heterosexual male staff, anxious that their own sexual feelings may be aroused by the girls, project their feelings onto them and she suggests that little attention has been given to the role of women workers in protecting their male colleagues from 'dangerous' girls. However, it was an explicit expectation in the secure units in this study. The fears of male staff and the resulting defensive practice were based on the myths that allegations were made only by girls and only against male members of staff. These stereotypical views were challenged by the female and some male staff, and there was some theoretical acceptance that there was no greater risk of allegations being made by girls than by boys, and that they could be made equally against female and male staff. However, this was not reflected in the practice in the units where the emphasis by male staff was firmly on self-protection against 'dangerous' girls.

Whilst there was general acceptance that girls had some needs which would be most appropriately responded to by female staff and that some would experience difficulties relating to male workers, it appears that male staff abdicated responsibility for young women. The female staff were expected to deal with everything for the girls as well as sharing responsibility for meeting the needs of the boys. One manager expressed concerns that whilst a degree of self-protection was necessary, at the same time staff had to be effective as workers, and that important issues and clues about behaviour could be missed by staff holding young people, particularly girls, literally and metaphorically, at arm's length. As already discussed, girls were considered more difficult to work with, not least because of the limited opportunities for them to develop peer relationships and the consequent need for them to turn to staff for individual attention. The pressure experienced by female staff was described by one worker:

> You're usually the only female on shift and the girls tend to use the female member of staff for absolutely everything ... and they are a lot more demanding than the lads, so it's not shared out very equally.

It also emerged that many male workers avoided engaging with girls because they felt unable to address and respond to their needs and were fearful of their behaviour, such as deliberate self-harm, which they were unable to understand. One member of staff described his apprehension in responding to girls, and his anxiety about exercising restraint. His concerns were shared by male colleagues, many of whom failed to understand why many young women were in secure accommodation at all:

> The boys will fight if they're upset, they'll thump someone in the face and that's a lot easier to deal with. You restrain them, sit on them until they calm down, let them cool off, but with the girls, you can't do that ... I'm very nervous that somebody's going to cut themselves, someone's going to try to hang themself. It's happened on my shift ... I find working with the girls much more stressful.

Differences emerged in the expectations of male and female staff. Managers in one unit suggested that they would always ask a male member of staff if he were willing to work with a young woman, and provide him with support. However, managers did not appear to adopt the same approach or offer the same degree of choice to female members of staff working with young men. Female workers experiencing sexual harassment from the boys, as well as from male colleagues, were expected to tolerate it as an unavoidable part of the work. Concerns were also expressed about the vulnerability of female staff, who could be left on their own with a group of young people, without adequate support.

The pressure on female staff to meet all the needs of the young women and share the responsibility for the young men highlights the unequal nature of the relationship between male and female staff operating in a male-dominated environment. An example of this emerged in the description of arrangements for mobility, which also illustrated the inconsistent attitudes of male staff to girls:

> There's a rule that there has to be a female there all the time, so what happens if there's any mobility ... the senior can't leave, the female can't leave so that leaves the bloke to go out with the girls, so the girls rarely if ever go out on mobility with a female ... But the bloke can take them for a walk in the woods and if he's going to do something he's more likely to do it in the woods in the middle of nowhere than in a unit where he's got to identify himself with his key tag to get into the room ... They haven't stopped to think this through at all.

On the issue of mobility, male staff said they made individual decisions about whether they would go out with girls alone, on the basis of their own risk assessment which consisted of seeking the views of their colleagues about whether individual young women had previously made any allegations and whether they were considered to be the 'sort' who would be likely to make allegations. One worker described this practice as 'hypocritical'. Their emphasis was placed on their own safety with apparently little regard for the safety or the dilemma this could present for young women whose option would be to go out on mobility with a male member of staff or not go out.

In the other units female workers were required to accompany girls. However, some female staff complained that although this was a requirement for the girls, there was not the same requirement for male staff in respect of the boys: 'If a young woman is to go out on mobility, you have to have a female to go, but it doesn't seem to work the other way round.' This illustrates the assumptions highlighted by Aymer (1992) that heterosexual women can work with both sexes and that it is the role of women workers to protect girls from predatory men and men from 'dangerous' girls.

One final issue relating to gender differences which merits comment was raised by the staff in the girls' unit and illustrates the intractable nature of gender stereotypes. The staff (although not the girls) were consulted about improvements to the unit and in addition to the development of the education facilities, it was agreed that a gym would provide the greatest benefit. However, the unit was instead provided with a home economics room for the staff 'to teach them to be mothers'.

Age

All the units accommodated young people up to 18 years, although the majority of young people were within the age range 14–16 years. The age range combinations of children in units aroused no strong feelings among staff. This seemed to be partly because their experience was that the chronological ages of young people were frequently not consistent with their emotional ages. More concerns were expressed about the accommodation of young people with learning disabilities, who were felt to be particularly vulnerable.

However, the concerns that were identified related to the positions of younger children under 13 years and older teenagers, particularly those aged 17 who could be accommodated in units where they were the only one in their age group. Their needs were different and staff questioned the ability of the unit to meet them all. There were also concerns about the vulnerability of younger children to bullying and intimidation and criminal contamination by older teenagers, an issue which has also aroused concern in non-secure residential care where there is greater differentiation on the basis of age (Sinclair and Gibbs 1996).

Conclusion

This chapter has continued the examination of the perspectives of staff and managers in the secure units, particularly in relation to the key debates about the population of young people in secure accommodation. A range of views emerged in response to government policy to promote mixed-gender and mixed legal status units in order to facilitate maximum flexibility in the use of the resources.

Concerns were expressed about the risks associated with mixing offenders with non-offenders, particularly in mixed-gender units and whilst some staff justified the practice on the basis that units could manage the situation, others questioned whether either staff or young people should be expected to manage such risks. Whilst there were concerns and doubts expressed about the wisdom of creating a specialized service, there was widespread support for the development of more specialization within and between units to enable more matching of the needs of young people with the expertise available.

Powerful gender stereotypes were operating and evident in the practice, particularly in the mixed-gender units, and the attitudes of staff which emerged in relation to girls were worrying. Marginalization of girls within the units was evident and they were regarded as more difficult and troublesome to work with and subject to a greater level of surveillance and restriction than their male peers. Unequal relationships emerged between male and female staff, particularly those working in the mixed-gender units. Female staff were generally required to take responsibility for working with the girls, protecting the male workers from the 'dangerous' girls and the girls from predatory men, as well as contributing to the work with the boys. In this way, gender stereotypes were reinforced and the opportunity for female staff to provide empowering role models for the girls was lost.

The perspectives of the staff and managers in six secure units provide part of the context to examine the experiences of the young people which will be undertaken later. In the next chapter the context will be broadened by an exploration of social workers' views about the role of local authority secure accommodation in the care and criminal justice systems.

SEVEN

The Roles of Secure Accommodation

The Views of Social Workers

Introduction

The social work profession has traditionally opposed penal custodial provisions for children, while at the same time providing and using local authority secure accommodation (see for example Millham *et al.* 1978; The Children's Society 1993). In the current political and social climate, social workers have supported the development of secure accommodation but opposed the use of penal custody, including secure training centres for children and young people (Crowley 1998; Howard League 1997). This seems to illustrate the prevailing confusion and ambiguity in the profession about whether local authority secure accommodation provides care or custody.

The perspectives of the social workers were sought to fill some of the gaps in our knowledge about social work attitudes to the use of secure accommodation in the care and criminal justice systems. Social workers play a crucial role at every stage in the process, and provide important links for young people with mainstream services, their families and communities. They also have the primary role in facilitating and supporting young people in their transition from secure accommodation back into community life. Their perspectives have been largely absent from the debates on policy and practice in the use of local authority secure accommodation.

The Social Workers

This chapter examines the views of 25 social workers who were responsible for 15 girls and 10 boys in the study. Of these social workers, eight were youth justice workers and one was a social work team manager. For the sake of simplicity, however, they will all be referred to as social workers. Six of them were male and nineteen were female. Two of the male workers were responsible for girls and four for boys, while six of the female workers were responsible for boys and thirteen for girls. Their periods of involvement with the young people varied from two months to three years, as shown in Table 7.1.

Table 7.1 Period of involvement of social workers with young people admitted through welfare and criminal justice routes by gender (n = 25)

Period of time	**Male**		**Female**		**Total**
	Criminal justice	Welfare	Criminal justice	Welfare	
Up to 6 months	3	2	0	2	7
7–12 months	2	0	0	4	6
13–23 months	1	0	1	2	4
> 2 years	2	0	1	5	8

Reasons for Admission

The reasons given by the social workers for seeking the admission of young people to secure accommodation showed similarities within the different legal admission routes.

Unconvicted Offender

All three boys on remand had initially been placed in young offender institutions. One social worker was concerned about the boy's emotional vulnerability and the other two felt the boys would be negatively influenced by more hardened offenders. Two of them had proposed community remand schemes to the courts, which had been rejected. They suggested that the political climate in relation to young offenders meant that some young people, including these two, were locked up unnecessarily and inappropriately. The third social worker applied for a secure accommodation placement to prepare the boy for a custodial sentence. The girl remanded to local authority accommodation was placed in secure accommodation because she was thought likely to run away, although a non-custodial sentence was envisaged.

Convicted Offender

The decision about placement of young people convicted of offences lies with the Home Office. The six social workers with responsibility for the five male and one female convicted offenders applied for places in secure accommodation as an alternative to other forms of custody and made representations to the Home Office on the basis of the young people's age, gender, vulnerability or educational needs.

It is notable that four of the ten criminal justice social workers had opposed custodial placements and recommended community remands or sentences. Social workers for three of the young people on remand were proposing community placements to the courts and the social worker for one of the convicted boys was supporting an appeal against the custodial sentence. In these cases, secure accommodation was considered to be the best option, rather than the recommended disposal.

Welfare

The reasons given by social workers for admission of the 15 young people through the welfare route follow similar themes and in most cases several reasons were given. They are shown in Table 7.2.

Table 7.2 Reasons given by social workers for welfare admissions			
Reason	**Male (n = 2)**	**Female (n = 13)**	**Total**
To control behaviour	2	13	15
For safety/protection from risk of harm	1	10	11
No other appropriate accommodation	0	5	5
For assessment	0	4	4
To provide counselling/other services	0	3	3
To prevent/control deliberate self-harm	1	1	2

In contrast with those responsible for the young people admitted through the criminal justice routes, all these social workers recommended secure placements and made application to the court for secure accommodation orders to detain them. Two of them had unsuccessfully sought placements in the Youth Treatment Centre. Seven girls and one boy had previous admissions to secure accommodation and all but one of the social workers had also been involved in the previous admission(s).

Admission Policies and Practice

Inconsistency in admissions policies was widely reported. A number of important factors emerged which had influenced the decision to seek admissions to secure accommodation through the welfare route. All the social workers commented on the deficit in good quality residential and foster care for teenagers unable to live with their families and the lack of inter-agency co-operation in the provision of services (Berridge and Brodie 1998; Triseliotis *et al.* 1995). The shortage of options, together with restrictions on funding meant that young people were frequently accommodated inappropriately, resulting in placement breakdown. Multiple placements exacerbated the difficulties of young people and when a crisis occurred, secure accommodation was used. However, the opportunity provided by the placement to find a long-term solution was frequently lost and young people returned to the same or similar circumstances on release, increasing the risk of re-admission. In short, it might be argued that the availability of secure accommodation has played a part in inhibiting the development or funding of non-secure alternatives (Harris and Timms 1993).

Many social workers said that young people who were the subjects of care orders or accommodated by the local authority were more likely than others to be placed in secure accommodation. They suggested that this was often to 'protect the backs' of professionals and to prevent negative media coverage. A further contributory factor was pressure from other professionals, particularly residential social workers or foster carers who could not manage the young people, also noted in previous studies to be a factor in admission (see Cawson and Martell 1979). Pressure from families to 'do something' also influenced the likelihood of admission where young people were breaking family codes of behaviour or were considered to be out of control or at risk. The fear of adverse media reports also featured here. It appeared that in some situations this pressure was the factor which most influenced the decision for admission, rather than an assessment of the actual risk of harm to young people.

The final and frequently determining factor influencing admission related to the availability of places. Social workers described long periods trying to identify placements and, in the absence of a central system of admissions and gatekeeping, dealing with the different referral systems for each individual unit. The desired result appeared to be achieved by persistence and pressure. This suggests, as other research has found (for example Cawson and Martell 1979), that the allocation of places may be determined as much by the motivation of social workers for a place as by the needs of the individual young people. The referral system was described as 'mad' and placements as 'hit and miss'. Some local authorities which manage units, and neighbouring authorities which have negotiated contracts with them, expect priority treatment in allocation of places, which may explain why young people living in a local authority that manages a secure unit are more likely to be placed in one (Harris and Timms 1993; National Children's Bureau 1995).

Involvement of Young People

In most cases the decision to place young people in secure accommodation was made by professionals with little or no participation by the young people. Some differences emerged between the criminal justice and welfare routes. The social workers presented the proposal for placement in secure accommodation as a positive option to all the young people admitted through the criminal justice routes and six of them were transferred from young offender institutions. Three young people, living in the community prior to their convictions, were informed of the plan to place them in secure accommodation at court following their conviction or at the hearing for sentence. Only one girl was given no information about the plan for placement in secure accommodation and she was remanded directly from court having been in police custody following arrest. Although the social workers gave these young people little information about secure accommodation, most of them were informed of the plan and viewed it as a positive option.

In contrast, the social workers for young people admitted through the welfare route regarded secure accommodation as the 'last resort' for those whose behaviour was considered unacceptable or dangerous. The social workers themselves were frequently under direct personal pressure from the young people's behaviour and benefited from the respite afforded by their placement in secure accommodation. All the social workers said they had discussed secure accommodation with the young people. However, it was surprising to find that most of them had used it as a threat, even though they acknowledged that such threats were ineffective as a deterrent, even with young people who had previous placements in secure accommodation, and that the threats seemed to exacerbate rather than deter running away. Two social workers said that they had not told young people they were being taken to secure accommodation until they arrived, to prevent them from running away. Social workers described young people's reactions to the threat of secure accommodation as angry, frightened, shocked and resentful and observed that young people saw it as a punishment, rather than a positive option for their care. One exception was a young woman who had been refused funding for a non-secure placement out of her home area to escape pimps, and she was described as relieved.

Choice of Placement

As already mentioned, the Home Office is responsible for the allocation of convicted offenders, although the decision may be influenced by pressure from the social worker or secure unit. The lack of common procedures for obtaining places results in confusion. Several social workers described making multiple applications and then taking the first available placement. It was seen as a bonus if this happened to be in the local unit. Table 7.3 shows the basis on which units were chosen for young people.

Table 7.3 Choice of placements

Choice/Allocation of place	Male	Female	Total	No. %
Own local authority unit	2	8	10	40
Bed availability	4	3	7	28
Home Office allocation	4	1	5	20
SW choice (single-gender unit)	0	2	2	8
Contract with neighbouring authority unit	0	1	1	4

Only two social workers said they had specifically chosen the unit they felt was most appropriate to meet the young people's needs, which in both cases were single-gender units. Furthermore, one of these social workers had refused a place in one girls' unit because she considered the regime to be too regimented and punitive, and waited for a place in an alternative girls' unit. Mixed views emerged about the benefits and disadvantages of single- and mixed-gender units which provide some insights into the importance attached to this issue by those applying for places.

Single- or Mixed-Gender Units

The common experience of all the social workers was of very limited opportunity for matching the needs of young people with the unit most suitable to meet them, and the shortage of places in single-gender units further restricted the choice. Eleven of the fifteen social workers for the girls said that they either favoured mixed-gender units or were ambivalent about the issue, with only four advocating the development of more single-gender provision. However, these general views contrasted sharply with those which emerged based on their assessment of the needs of the individual girls. Nine social workers said that they would have preferred placement in a single-gender unit where the girls' needs would have been more appropriately met, although only four were actually placed in single-gender units. Four social workers said that the girls' needs would be most appropriately met in mixed-gender units, although only two were so placed.

Greater ambivalence was expressed about this issue by the boys' social workers, which was because boys were in the majority even in mixed-gender units. Many of them stressed the importance of choice, although, like their colleagues for the girls, said that in practice it made little difference as other factors such as bed availability took precedence in determining the choice of placement. Three social workers said that single-gender units would have been preferable, yet all three boys were placed in mixed-gender units. In summary, ten, that is two in five of the social workers, suggested that young people were placed in units where the gender make-up of the resident group was inappropriate for them.

The social workers raised a number of issues relevant to the debate about specialization on the basis of gender. The main factor cited in favour of mixed-gender units echoed the popular argument that they provide the opportunity for 'normal' living to prepare young people for a return to the community. This was considered to be especially important for convicted young people serving long sentences, particularly those who would be transferred to segregated prison accommodation to complete their sentences. A number of social workers said that they were ideologically opposed to single-gender education and favoured the opportunity for mixed education in the units. They suggested that many of the young people had had difficulties in relationships with opposite-sex peers and placement together enabled them to learn how to relate to and respect each other.

Difficulties associated with mixed-gender units were also raised. First, in all mixed-gender units girls were in the minority and concerns were expressed about the priority given to the needs of the boys and the marginalization of the girls. The balance of the group and the placement of girls in units where they were alone or in a very small minority in a group of boys aroused particular concern. Girls were regarded as more vulnerable than boys, both because of their generally younger age and the nature of their previous experiences. General concerns were expressed about the different treatment of girls, such as the more prescriptive dress requirements and more intensive surveillance by staff.

Second, young people in mixed-gender units were reported to be distracted by each other from focusing on their problems. In this connection, social workers referred to the problem of the sexualized behaviour of girls, which they argued increased in the presence of boys, to the detriment of both girls and boys. Finally, anxieties about the risks for girls who had been abused or sexually exploited accommodated in units with boys who had committed sexual offences were widely voiced. These will be considered further in examining the social workers' views on the mixing in units of offenders with non-offenders.

Combining Offenders and Non-Offenders

Of the 25 social workers, 10 were involved with young people admitted through the criminal justice routes and 15 with young people admitted through the welfare route. It is interesting that while 7 social workers expressed ambivalent views, 18, that is almost three quarters, favoured some degree of specialization within and between units. Several social workers critically observed that because of the prevailing ideology even where the design of the building provided the facility to do so, there was no separation of offenders and non-offenders in secure units. While none of the social workers was in favour of the existing policy they acknowledged some of the difficulties involved in separating offenders from non-offenders, such as the vulnerability of some very young convicted offenders. Several social workers expressed concern about mixing younger children with older teenagers in units which accommodated offenders and non-offenders. Their concerns mirrored those expressed by some of the secure unit staff which are contrary to the policies of government and the local authorities managing the units.

Some of their concerns merit more detailed examination. Social workers observed that secure units were designed and catered primarily for offenders and the regimes focused on control. They argued that young people had different reasons for admission and needs, which could not all be met in the same unit at the same time. These differences were compounded in mixed-gender units where abused and exploited girls were accommodated with offending young men. They argued that the combination of care and custody resulted in regimes based on the lowest common denominator, that is containment. With this focus on control, they argued that the needs of those admitted for care and therapeutic intervention were neglected and any potential value for them was minimized.

Many social workers expressed the view that the risk factors associated with being locked up were increased as a result of this combination. Some of the most vulnerable and damaged young people were placed in the same units as some of the most violent and aggressive. Some social workers observed that young people could be exposed to a greater level of risk of sexual, physical and emotional harm in the secure unit than they had been exposed to in the community. Furthermore, they suggested that secure units do not provide sufficient information to enable social workers to assess the potential risk to the young people they are seeking to place. One social worker described her anxiety when the young person she had placed was described by secure unit staff as 'just a little pussycat compared with all the others we have in here'. Another expressed concern at the level of violence suffered by one vulnerable young woman who she noted had 'had to harden up in order to survive'.

The potential for criminal contamination was regarded as very high. Social workers described how young people admitted through the welfare route found themselves in 'an academy of crime' where the likelihood of contamination was increased by the nature of the total institution. They expressed concern about vulnerable young people and those with minor offences who were becoming more sophisticated criminals. One social worker described a girl who was initially very shocked by the behaviour of the offenders, but came to regard their behaviour and the offences they had committed as acceptable, even normal. The social worker said that the risk of her offending had increased because of the criminal contamination which had changed her attitudes to violence and offending (see Cawson and Martell 1979; Harris and Timms 1993; Millham *et al.* 1978).

Regimes in the Units

All the social workers described the regimes in the units as predominantly about control and one social worker observed of one unit, 'it is geared as a prison'. They were critical of the functioning of the units, even where they felt young people were gaining some benefit from the placement. Important recurring themes related to the failure of secure units to provide anything apart from containment and control. Concerns were particularly expressed about the newly developed units which had the appearance of and functioned more like small prisons than children's homes.

Many social workers talked about the closed nature of the institutions, which created their own bureaucracies. They found that the emphasis on the procedures, timetables and structures of the institutions dominated over the needs of young people. One social worker commented on the admissions procedure for a vulnerable girl which included a full body search and the confiscation of shoes and clothes, giving a punitive message and some insight into the strictness of the regime. She said, 'I really didn't want to leave her there'. The behavioural systems operating in the units appeared to be poorly understood and were described as pointless at best and unnecessarily punitive at worst. The system in one unit was described as 'garbage, nothing to do with the real world and a completely outdated way of working with young people'. The use of the behavioural systems and sanctions 'across the board' was widely criticized and social workers repeatedly referred to this as illustrating the inability of secure units to differentiate and address the individual needs of young people.

Several social workers commented on the cultures in the units which they said were 'like prison', 'oppressive', 'over the top' and on the excessive levels of surveillance of some young people who presented no risk. At the same time, it was suggested that the failure of units to differentiate between young people sometimes resulted in inadequate surveillance of those who *did* present a risk. Inconsistency in surveillance was also seen as a problem. For example it was noted in one unit that while individual surveillance was excessive for most of the time, the unit had failed to protect a young woman from harassment by her pimp who had made repeated telephone calls to her without any intervention by staff.

Many social workers said that the young people had needed a therapeutic environment, and one said that ethically it was difficult enough locking up young people who had not committed serious offences, but it became impossible to justify when no therapeutic intervention was provided. This brings into sharp focus the wide gap between the expectations professionals have of secure accommodation and the reality of what it provides. In the light of this, why do social workers continue to admit and re-admit young people?

The Secure Unit Staff

The relationships between residential and field social workers have traditionally been contentious and a recent study observed no improvement in relationships which continue to be 'beset with differences in ideology and status' (Berridge and Brodie 1998, p.116). The views expressed by the secure unit staff and the social workers in this study demonstrated the persistence of these differences. Four broad areas of difficulty emerged from the perspectives of the social workers.

The issue of information sharing was a matter of widespread concern, but appeared to be a particularly contentious issue in three units where social workers said that any problems or concerns they raised were met with a defensive, closed and dismissive response. Social workers observed that it was difficult to know what was actually going on in the units, to obtain information about the young people with whom they were involved and one suggested that more frequent and better quality inspections were needed to identify the occurrence of abuse. The difficulties in information sharing were compounded when young people were placed in units run by different local authorities. A number of social workers commented on the poor quality of written reports and record keeping, which resulted in muddled or inaccurate information. In short, many social workers said they thought that the secure units saw them as interfering and preferred them to stay away.

The second issue related to what was regarded as a lack of professionalism by staff, which included their lack of experience, training and expertise. A general observation by social workers was that some, although not all, of the staff were 'good enough basic residential social workers' but that young people in secure accommodation needed more, and one social worker asked, 'what are we paying for apart from locks and keys?' In addition, concern was expressed about the resistance in some units to the involvement of other professionals who could provide the expertise which was deficient. One social worker described 'regular run-ins' with staff who thought they had the most insight into how the young people functioned and were 'jealous and niggly' about the involvement of field social workers or other professionals. Social workers suggested that the lack of experience of some staff contributed to difficulties in their relationships. One reported that the allocated keyworker was new to residential social work and 'didn't have a clue what to do'. In situations where the social worker was also inexperienced, the difficulties appear to have been compounded. One observed that the needs of a girl had 'got lost' in the confusion and 'fumbling around' which resulted from her own inexperience of secure accommodation coupled with the lack of expertise of the staff in the unit. However, a positive exception reported by social workers for young people placed in one unit was that several members of staff had counselling skills which were better than those of mainstream residential social workers.

The third issue concerned the inconsistency in the treatment of young people. Social workers commented on inconsistency in the practice and attitudes of individual workers and inconsistency between members of staff working in the same unit. These inconsistencies were considered to present significant problems for young people and for social workers and appeared to be an issue of ongoing dispute. In addition, some social workers observed that at times staff avoided difficult issues, withheld information and were dishonest with young people as a means of controlling them.

This linked with the fourth area of concern, that is the attitudes of staff to young people. Social workers observed that negative attitudes were frequently openly expressed by staff to young people who did not want to be in secure accommodation and pushed the boundaries. Moreover, they reported concerns about staff who expressed negative, punitive attitudes to young people they did not feel should be in secure accommodation and whose behaviour they found difficult to understand and handle, such as those deliberately self-harming and with complex histories of abuse. One social worker reported that the keyworker allocated to a young woman didn't like her, failed to arrange meetings with her and was punitive in her treatment, using sanctions excessively. It is of note that this reflects the experiences described by the girl herself.

Social workers' concerns about the lack of flexibility in the regimes to respond to the individual needs of young people have already been mentioned and they complained about the attitudes of staff to young people with individual needs which were different from the rest of the group arising from their race, religion, sexual orientation or other factors. Differences were widely treated as problems and resentment at the need to provide individual treatment was often openly expressed. Several social workers commented on the irony of this in units which claimed to focus on the individual needs of young people. For example, one social worker described the conflict between staff which followed a request to provide for the religious and cultural needs of a Muslim boy. This made him a target for bullying by other young people who, picking up the attitudes of staff also became resentful of what they regarded as his special treatment.

In contrast, five social workers expressed positive views about their relationships with members of staff in three different units. They identified three elements which contributed to their positive relationships: positive impressions of the commitment of the secure unit staff to the young people, the willingness of staff to share information and their ability to work co-operatively with the social workers.

Therapeutic Interventions

The importance attached to the provision of therapeutic services for young people varied between social workers, and was influenced by the young people's reason for admission. However, there was widespread criticism of the failure of secure units to provide therapeutic services and of the difficulties which were almost always encountered in identifying and arranging services. This emerged as a significant issue of dispute between secure units and social workers.

Social workers were critical both of the lack of expertise within the units and the unwillingness of the units to take responsibility for establishing links with other agencies and arranging services. The isolation of secure accommodation from mainstream services was regarded as a significant problem which resulted in an absence of multi-professional working on behalf of young people. A majority of the social workers had expected that when the individual needs of young people had been identified the secure unit would provide the necessary services, from within their own resources or by engaging them from outside the unit. They complained of working in isolation in their efforts to arrange services to meet the needs of young people and of undertaking work with young people themselves. While this was regarded as difficult enough when young people were placed locally, there were additional problems when young people were placed at a geographical distance. Social workers expressed frustration, particularly in respect of four units where they were expected to arrange and secure funding for specialist services. They said that this included appointments for medical treatment and several complained that they were even required to arrange transport and escorts for young people. In the other two units the social workers indicated that the arrangement and provision of services was generally undertaken on a partnership basis, between the social worker and the unit.

Regular conflicts and battles about funding were reported which delayed the provision of any services, particularly where health service or other agency involvement was required. This frequently meant that young people, particularly those who were the subjects of short orders, were not provided with services they needed. More than half the social workers questioned the cost-effectiveness of secure accommodation which they suggested provided containment and control but in the main offered little else by way of specialist expertise in the units or the provision of therapeutic services.

Education Provision

The social workers compared the education provision in the secure units favourably with the provision in other forms of custody such as young offender institutions but extremely unfavourably with mainstream and special education, and criticisms were expressed of the education provided in all the secure units. They cited the educational needs of many young people as a factor in their admission to secure accommodation. Indeed, it was a primary reason for the admission of several convicted offenders who would otherwise have served their sentences in young offender institutions. All the social workers said they had expected that the young people's educational needs would be met by their placement.

A commonly occurring view was that comparison of the education provision in secure units with that in other forms of custody and for children in care, rather than with mainstream education, had resulted in a misleading impression of adequacy. Some social workers observed that expectations were lower for young people in custody or care which resulted in minimum standards in the quality of assessment of their educational ability and achievement. The opportunity existed in some units for young people placed on a long-term basis to take public examinations and whilst the social workers acknowledged that this was more than they would have achieved in young offender institutions, they argued that it was less than they could have achieved in mainstream education.

Many social workers argued that the isolation from mainstream education resulted in non-existent or unsatisfactory links and a curriculum described as 'contrived' and inadequate, equivalent at best to less than half of the national curriculum. In many units an over-emphasis on art work was reported. They contended that the level of education barely occupied the day and failed to educate, stimulate or challenge the young people and that the provision was not consistent with their ages, needs or levels of ability. Furthermore, it was argued that the education provision did not take sufficient account of the special educational needs of young people who were 'statemented'. Many social workers observed that it would be unlikely to have any impact at all on the young people, particularly those who were placed on a short- or medium-term basis. The social workers complained that the education of young people in secure units took place in a vacuum, and lacked continuity with their education prior to admission and with the education planned following their release.

Exit Planning and Preparation

The process of planning for the release of young people from secure accommodation was widely regarded as the responsibility of the social worker rather than the secure unit, although in the case of convicted offenders the exit programme required the approval of the Home Office and the involvement in implementation of secure unit staff. While staff in the units complained about the lack of social work planning, particularly for those admitted through the welfare route, several social workers criticized the lack of involvement of the units in preparation for leaving.

Social workers said that the preparation for exit for convicted offenders would begin approximately six months prior to their release date and would include increasing levels of mobility and home leave. Some young people attended education or training courses outside the unit as part of this preparation. The social workers of five young people in this study said that they would return to live with their families and two would be found supported lodgings in their home communities. The preparation for leaving of the young people on remand was closely related to the court proceedings dealing with their offences. Two social workers had undertaken work with the young men to prepare them for custodial sentences while the other two proposed community sentences and placement with specialist foster carers.

The issue of preparation for the exit of young people admitted through the welfare route was the most contentious for social workers as well as secure unit staff. The difficulties involved in identifying and obtaining funding for community placements have already been mentioned. One of the serious consequences is that orders can run their full term before an alternative placement is identified, leaving young people in a state of uncertainty and with little or no opportunity for preparation for leaving. Moreover, the failure to identify suitable alternative placements can be a factor in the decision to apply for further secure accommodation orders. In this study, three social workers planned to make applications for further six-month orders. One social worker was seeking a therapeutic placement, but nothing had been identified and there was no exit plan or programme of preparation for release in place. Seven social workers had decided that the young people would return to their previous residential placements. While this could be seen as a positive choice for some, it signified the lack of any other better alternative for the majority. All the social workers acknowledged that there were likely to be problems for the young people but said that the placements were either the only ones or the best that were available. Preparation for most of them included a visit to the proposed placement prior to their release from secure accommodation. Four social workers had arranged alternative residential or foster placements for young people and pre-placement meetings had been arranged.

Benefits from the Placement

Differences emerged in the social workers' assessments of what young people gained from their placements according to their admission route. All the young people admitted through the criminal justice routes were thought to have benefited by placement in secure accommodation in so far as it offered a preferable alternative to custody in a young offender institution or remand centre. Furthermore, the social workers identified a number of additional benefits, related to educational opportunities, drug/alcohol/anger management counselling and improvements in health. Social workers for two young people serving sentences observed that one was 'the exception in secure' as she was benefiting from the stability it provided while the other was 'the rare case where everything has worked out'.

Although social workers could identify some benefit for many of the young people, it emerged that most of them had not gained as much from their placements as the social workers had expected and there were significant concerns about whether short-term improvements could be sustained following release. This was particularly evident in respect of young people admitted through the welfare route. Ten social workers said that safety or containment from risk of harm for the period of the placement was the main benefit for young people. However, it is notable that they did not consider the placement had increased the longer-term safety for the young people or increased their ability to protect themselves. Three of them reported additional benefits such as education, anger management work and the safety within which to disclose sexual abuse. However, seven of the ten concluded that the young people had gained nothing from the placement apart from short-term safety, and three also said that they had gained no benefit from their previous placements in secure accommodation either. One of them observed that the professionals had gained more from the respite it had provided and two argued that the harm the young people had suffered from the placement far outweighed the benefit. One social worker said she felt the young woman was now 'lost', that she had been hardened by the placement and now considered drug use and crime more acceptable, that she would be likely to go downhill rapidly but there was no way for professionals to get her 'back on line'. Three social workers reported that young people had gained from individual counselling, one considered a young woman had gained some insight although still thought it likely she would return to her previous lifestyle and one thought a young man had benefited from being 'forced to face up to his unacceptable behaviour', although she too was pessimistic that positive change would result or be sustained following his release.

This summary of the social workers' perceptions of the benefits for young people, some of whom had experienced more than one admission to secure accommodation is not encouraging. The social workers' evaluations of the young people's placements overall will be examined further later.

Conclusions

This chapter has examined the perspectives of 25 social workers on the use of secure accommodation in the care and criminal justice systems. The views of social workers involved in the admission of young people to local authority secure accommodation have been largely absent from the debates about its role and function. A high level of disillusionment and dissatisfaction with secure accommodation provision emerged, and social workers complained that with its emphasis on containment and control it failed to meet many of the needs of the majority of young people. However, confusion was evident in the ambivalent relationship between social workers and secure accommodation which was reflected in contradictions in their practice.

Secure accommodation was seen by the majority of social workers as provision for offenders, and a preferable alternative to other forms of custody. Those involved in the criminal justice system said that the expansion of secure accommodation without an equivalent investment in community provision had resulted in an increasing preference by the courts for custodial remands and sentences. The lack of appropriate community provision and funding for specialist resources also emerged as a key factor in the admission and re-admission of young people through the welfare route. This *faute de mieux* situation might explain one of the striking contradictions which emerged in social work practice, that is the repeated admission of young people to secure accommodation, even though many social workers did not feel that young people had benefited from their placements and some even thought they had been harmful and increased the risk young people would face following release. Similarly, social workers repeatedly used the threat of secure accommodation even though they acknowledged that it was ineffective as a deterrent, and frequently exacerbated running away. Although critical of secure accommodation and its failure to meet young people's needs, in practice the harmful effects and dangers were minimized or ignored by social workers who maintained the illusion that secure accommodation provided the solution to behaviours such as running away and its associated risks.

The failure of units to meet young people's individual needs was partly attributed to the wide range of their needs, problems and reasons for admission. The development of mixed-gender units which combined offenders and non-offenders aroused a range of views, and almost three quarters of the social workers favoured some degree of specialization within and between units, contrary to the policies adopted by government and implemented in the units.

These perspectives on secure accommodation illustrate some similarities and many differences between the secure unit staff and the social workers, and highlight contradictions in social work practice. They provide the broad context for the examination of the experiences of the young people who were placed in secure accommodation, which follows.

Part IV

Children in Security

EIGHT

Life Before Placement in Secure Accommodation

Introduction

This chapter will examine the circumstances which resulted in the young people's admission to secure accommodation, and their views on the appropriateness of the placement. The gender differences in the young people's care pre-secure accommodation have already been described. In summary, 17 of the girls had been living in public care and 10 were the subjects of interim or care orders while 4 of the boys had been living in care, and only 1 was the subject of a care order. Seven of the boys but none of the girls had been transferred to their placement in secure accommodation from young offender institutions.

Circumstances Resulting in Admission to Secure Accommodation

Running Away

Running away is the key element in the legal criteria for admission to secure accommodation through the welfare route, which are set out in the Children Act 1989. It is the behaviour most likely to trigger placement in secure accommodation and is one of the most important factors that differentiates children in open care from those in secure units (Harris and Timms 1993). Nearly three quarters of the young people in this study had histories of running away. Seventeen young people were admitted to secure accommodation through the welfare route and running away was the primary factor in all these admissions, while four of the young people admitted through the criminal justice routes also had histories of running away.

Running away by young people is a significant social issue. There is no formal or legal definition of absconding or of what constitutes a history of absconding, so different interpretations are applied in different contexts. The lack of definition is important in terms of discussion of the issue and the development of effective services. The terminology used includes runaways, absconders, street children and thrownaways, that is children told to leave by their parents or carers (Ringwalt *et al.* 1998). It has been estimated that as many as 1 in 7 under-16-year-olds run away overnight or longer (Rees 1993). Young people under 16 have no legal means to support themselves, they are not entitled to welfare benefits and are unable to obtain accommodation on their own behalf. They risk becoming isolated, losing contact with and access to the welfare systems, education, training and employment opportunities and legal means of self-support and there is an increased possibility of further victimization and criminality. As already suggested, in this study a complex relationship emerged between running away to escape abuse and victimization, admission to care, revictimization and running away from care. Placement in secure accommodation was used as the ultimate solution to running away. This theme will be examined further.

RUNNING AWAY FROM HOME

Most running away begins in the family and 'the family is therefore central to any theoretical analysis of running away' (Stein *et al.* 1994, p.63). As many as 1 in 7 young people run away from their parental home (Wade *et al.* 1998). The relationship between family violence, physical and sexual abuse and running away, identified in the previous chapter, has been reported in studies in the UK and USA, which found aspects of family relationships including physical violence, sexual abuse, marital conflict and parental remoteness from the child to be significantly more common for runaways than non-runaways (Brennan *et al.* 1978; Farber 1984; Janus *et al.* 1987; Whitbeck and Simons 1990). In addition, Roberts (1982) found a significant level of alcohol-related problems in the parents of young people who ran away.

RUNNING AWAY FROM CARE

Children from care are over represented among those who run away (Millham *et al.* 1986; Rowe *et al.* 1989). In comparison with young people who have never been in care, they are more likely to run away, more frequently and from an earlier age (Rees 1993; Stein *et al.* 1994). It has been found that 4 in 10 children in residential homes run away (Wade *et al.* 1998). In this study, the young people's problems and running away appear to have been increased by their placements in care. Their reasons for running away are important as the peer culture in some residential units has been found to compound children's difficulties, inducing them to run away as well as to engage in criminal activity, prostitution and drug use (Millham *et al.* 1978). Other factors relate to young people's powerlessness and lack of involvement in the care system (Newman 1989; Rees 1993) and the quality of care and prevalence of abuse in the placement (Abrahams and Mungall 1992; Hodgkin 1993; Stein *et al.* 1994).

The Reasons for Running Away

Running away can be seen as a positive act, to escape an abusive situation in the home, in care or at school or as an act of assertion by young people who perceive themselves as having no power or control over their lives. Most young people run away from rather than to somebody or something and do not feel that running away provides a resolution of their problems (Stein *et al.* 1994), but regard the problems of street life as preferable to those from which they have run away. In addition to these young people described as 'endangered' runners, a minority of runaways have been identified as 'social pleasure seekers' or 'explorers' who put themselves at risk of victimization (Roberts 1982). In running away, young people are frequently regarded by the public and by professionals simultaneously as victim and villain.

In this study, family violence and physical or sexual abuse emerged as the primary reasons for young people running away. As a result of running away, family relationships broke down and many young people were placed in substitute care, where they continued to run away. For example, the violence between her parents and her father's threats were the precipitating factors for Vicki:

> My dad was always beating my mum up and he used to get drunk and cut his wrists and his neck … My mum left him and then one day he was hiding in the loft with an axe ready to kill us and he beat my mum up again and the police came and took my dad … then my mum got back together with my dad but he started hitting her again … I was about ten and I started running away all the time then.

Several young people saw running away as their only means of escape from physical abuse within their families. This was due in most circumstances to the failure of the non-abusing parent, usually their mother, to provide protection. For example, although the violence suffered by Jamila was perpetrated predominantly by her half-brother, her father joined in the abuse and her mother was unable to protect her. She described how the violence and running away led to a repeating pattern of admissions and discharges from care:

> I've had loads of beatings in my life and my parents wouldn't do anything about it … I was only about four when he started beating us up. My parents couldn't do anything … because they were scared of him. If they'd say something he'd start getting violent towards my dad and swearing at my mum … My brother told my dad to beat up my sister so he did … me and my sister, we'd go to school in the morning with our bus fare and we'd run away … we were scared to go home because we knew we'd get beaten up so we continued running away then we got took into care. After a couple of weeks mum and dad would sign us out and then we'd get beaten up again so we'd run away, we'd get put into care and run away from care … then we just continued running away.

Other young people lived with only one parent, in most circumstances their mother, and when they were abused there was no-one else to provide protection. For example, Karen suffered persistent abuse by her mother and ran away after she was assaulted in front of her friends. When she was eventually found by the police, she was placed in care:

> One day my mum comes over to me with my friends, she pulls my hair and puts me on the floor and tells me to fuck off and live with my dad and I said to my mum I would if I knew who he was, then she started beating me up in front of all my friends so I ran away and I ran away for about two months and then the police found me and that's when I went into care.

Powerlessness and lack of involvement in the care system (Newman 1989; Rees 1993) emerged as other important themes in the young people's reasons for running away from care. For example, Sarah described her lack of participation in decision-making about her placements in care, and the powerlessness she felt to influence what happened to her, other than by running away:

> I was placed in a residential home and I was there for about nine months and it worked all right and then a foster placement turned up and I said I didn't want to go there but social services said it was an appropriate placement for me so they put me there. And I started absconding and the placement broke down about two weeks later. I was placed in another foster home and I started to abscond because I felt it wasn't working and then that broke down as well.

Multiple Placements

All the young people in the study who were in care had experience of multiple residential and foster placements and they described a cycle of unhappy placements, running away and disruption. For example, Roberta was first accommodated aged seven years. By her 11th birthday she had been placed in 22 residential and foster homes and between age 13 and 15 she was admitted to secure accommodation more than six times. She described the stigma associated with being in care:

> It's horrible because you feel like you're the odd one out all the time, you know when friends have got nice clothes, you haven't because you're in care, you don't get as much as the others do ... [it was] rough, I missed my mum and I was homesick and all the other children at school and in the streets used to take the micky out of me

> because I was in care … the teachers treated you different and the kids treated you different as well, like you're not the same as them, you're not human … I felt like nobody cared … I kept running off, I can't remember all the times.

NEW RISKS

All the young people were exposed to new risks when they ran away from home and care. These risks included serious physical injury, involvement in offending and criminalization, drug use and sexual exploitation. The risk of them losing their liberty by placement in secure accommodation was also significantly increased. Several young people described situations in which they had put themselves at risk of physical injury. For example, one girl suffered a major physical injury whilst running away:

> I was put in emergency foster care for three days because I'd run away from home … then I went to one children's home and then I got moved to another and when I was in there I used to run away because I didn't like it in care … I ran away and I got run over and I had to have my leg amputated.

Many young people found that involvement in offending and criminality was an inevitable consequence of running away. For example, Aziz described the risk of offending he associated with running away: 'Once you run away you will keep running away and when you have no food, no money, then you will commit offences to get something to eat.'

One of the girls became involved in offending, shoplifting, begging to survive and was sexually exploited while living on the streets:

> When I was 11 I got adopted with my sister, we stayed with my adoptive parents until I was 13 and then I started going in and out of care, I kept running away … I hitch-hiked to my parents but when I turned up they phoned the police and I got took back … I began to stay out all hours of the night. I used to run to mates' houses or just sleep on the street, on park benches, anywhere I could find. The most I slept out was for a month but other times I kept getting caught by the police … I didn't know what the streets were like, I thought they were all safe but I found out they weren't … I saw a lot

> of strange people ... Occasionally I would get given money but not all that often. I used to have to shoplift and do other things for food.

The connection between running away and the risk of sexual exploitation and prostitution was illustrated by other girls in this study. For example, Vicki began running away because of violence at home. She was then sexually abused and, as a means of survival, began working as a prostitute, suffering further sexual exploitation:

> I ran away with the fair ... I got beat up and raped ... after that I ran away for longer and I got put with foster parents but I ran away ... then I got put in a children's home but I absconded so I got moved to another place ... I was running away a lot there ... I was working all the time at prostitution.

THE PROFESSIONAL RESPONSE

These young people provide compelling evidence to support the view that the major problem faced by those who run away is other people's reaction to it (Millham *et al.* 1978). The professional response to the young people in the study was to lock them up in secure accommodation as the ultimate solution to their running away. Those who ran away from their secure placements faced the imposition of punitive sanctions on their return. The young people clearly articulated their reasons for running away, in most cases demonstrating positive action to escape abusive situations. It is clear that running away in itself did not provide a solution to their problems and they were all exposed to new risks and problems (Stein *et al.* 1994). However, they all experienced the professional response to their running away as punitive and felt that it did not provide what they needed or help them to address the reasons for their running away. For example, Christina articulated the problem: 'I think I needed to talk about why I was running away because until I talk about why I was running away I know I will have to carry on doing it.'

The use of secure accommodation as a response to young people who run away is contentious. If absconding was not specifically included in the criteria for locking up children other approaches to runaway children might be sought and adopted by care authorities (National Children's Bureau 1995). Innovative projects such as the provision of safe houses and streetwork projects have highlighted the vulnerability of young people who run away and by offering alternative, more appropriate models of prevention and support have challenged care authorities to consider alternatives to locking up or ignoring runaway children (Stein *et al.* 1994). Intensive support has been recommended to young people in the family home and those who are looked after, to break the development of a persistent pattern (Wade *et al.* 1998). Intervention has been proposed with young people at liberty on the streets in the form of outreach work and counselling to address their victimization. This approach recognizes that that the forced return of young people to home, care or secure accommodation only results in them running away again and that counselling which focuses on young people's delinquent behaviour rather than their experiences of victimization is likely to achieve only short-term, unsustainable change (Browne and Falshaw 1998).

Prostitution

As already noted, UK Government guidance on safeguarding children involved in prostitution (DH 2000a) has been issued in response to the increasing national and international concerns about child prostitution and the practice which has criminalized children while absolving those adults who use them (Lee and O'Brien 1995; The Children's Society 1997). The guidance recommends the changes which have been repeatedly called for so that children involved in prostitution will be treated as the victims of abuse in need of welfare services rather than criminals, and the adults who abuse them will be prosecuted under the criminal law.

THE REASONS FOR PROSTITUTION

Young people get involved in prostitution for a number of reasons, arguably none of them to do with free choice (Lee and O'Brien 1995; The Children's Society 1997), and the UK Government guidance recognizes that most children are 'coerced, enticed or are utterly desperate'. Several explanations for involvement in prostitution have been offered from different professional perspectives (Jesson 1993). Sereny (1984) regarded child prostitutes as victims who craved love and affection and who believed that the pimp could provide the relationship and stability they needed. She found that most of the young people in her international sample were drawn into prostitution as a survival strategy. Similarly, Jesson (1993) suggested that running away and prostitution were the only means of survival for some young people who had been sexually abused. Weisberg (1985) proposed a number of characteristics which provided a stereotype of the adolescent prostitute: the child has come from an unstable family, is likely to have experienced physical, emotional and sexual abuse, has poor school attendance and has run away from home and care institutions. A more recent study (Stein *et al.* 1994) also found young people providing sex for money as a means of survival to be a significant issue.

In view of the research findings on child prostitution and the experiences of the young people in this study, it should not be surprising that some of them got involved in prostitution. In fact, eight girls reported that they had been working as prostitutes or had received money for sex. Four girls described themselves as working as prostitutes, three from age 12 and one from age 13 years. A further four girls suggested that at times they had received money for sex while on the run from home or care, although they did not describe themselves as prostitutes. Two girls had older sisters who were involved in prostitution and one of them had introduced into prostitution her younger sisters, one of them only 12 years old, as well as other children in her children's home. The mother of one girl also worked as a prostitute. None of the boys talked about being paid for sex, although as there was considerably less focus on the sexuality and sexual activities of the boys it would be unsafe to assume that none of them had experienced sexual exploitation.

The four girls who described themselves as prostitutes explained how and why they had begun working on the streets. They were all in the care of their local authorities and provide evidence of the risk that residential care presents of initiation into prostitution (Farmer and Pollock 1998; Shaw and Butler 1998). For example, Roberta was only 13 and in residential care when she started working as a prostitute:

> I just didn't have no money and I needed money and I stood on the corner thinking who shall I ask to lend me some money not

> thinking about starting to work, then a punter pulled up and he said how much so I just got in the car and it started from there ... and every time I ran out of money I would go down the area to get some and then when I was 14 I started going to London, I met different people and made new friends, it was all right, I felt cared for, just like I was really wanted ... everybody knew I was working. I didn't mind that lifestyle, I didn't like working but I liked doing the things that I did and the places I went.

The risks of initiation into prostitution which being in care presented to all these girls were well illustrated by Karen who started working for a pimp from age 12, even though she was living in a children's home. It is interesting that being in care appeared to afford Karen, as well as the other girls, so little protection or safety:

> He was treating me nice as though I was something special ... and then one day I didn't make enough money and he beat me up so I tried getting away from him and that didn't get me nowhere, everywhere I went he just kept finding me... I moved from one children's home to another but he found me again and I was working on the street ... I went to secure for about two days, it was just a warning and then I went to another children's home but he got hold of me again and then I went to London and started hanging round on the streets again. This time I was earning big money ... and then my social worker got fed up with me and locked me in secure.

Karen said that prostitution provided her with some of the affection and care that she lacked in her relationships with other adults:

> When you're on the streets people are nice to you. I want to be loved and things and because I don't get it from no-one else, I get it from my punters and I get paid for it ... when they're only close to you for a few seconds you can use them and chuck them away.

Although all the girls started working as prostitutes and continued to do so as a means of survival, it was clear that it also endangered their lives. For example, Vicki began working as a prostitute aged 12 as a means of survival but began to deliberately self-harm and attempted suicide. She said:

> I was running away a lot, staying away and going to clubs … I met up with a girl and I started working all the time with her at prostitution … then I just got used to the money but I was unhappy and I started taking overdoses.

THE PROFESSIONAL RESPONSE

Social work responses to young people involved in prostitution have been shown to lack a coherent strategy and to be punitive, controlling young people's social freedom and moving them between children's homes and often into secure accommodation (Jesson 1991, 1993). All the girls in this study who were involved in prostitution had been living in care, they had experienced a range of negative childhood experiences which had eroded their sense of self-worth and they felt punished rather than protected by the professional response.

Girls under 16 are particularly vulnerable when on the run because their 'protector' may threaten to hand them over to the police (Jesson 1993). Girls who run away from care are even more vulnerable because they fear being caught by the police, referred to social workers and being put into local authority secure accommodation. Three of the four girls who described themselves as prostitutes had had more than one previous admission to secure accommodation, as had three of those suspected of working as prostitutes. This provides some evidence of the persistent use of secure accommodation as a response to young people involved in prostitution, even though prison and secure accommodation have been shown to reinforce the deviant role and to be inappropriate (Davis 1978; Jesson 1991). The legal criteria for placement for these young women disappear as soon as they are admitted, yet notwithstanding the permissive nature of secure accommodation orders, they continue to be detained. Hodgkin (National Children's Bureau 1995) found that secure unit staff considered them difficult to work with, that there were concerns about the dangers of recruitment into prostitution of children in the unit who were not prostitutes and a high likelihood that they would return to prostitution as soon as they were released. The repeated admissions to secure accommodation of the girls in this study provide further evidence of the ineffectiveness of this response in addressing their needs.

The moves to decriminalize young people involved in prostitution and respond to them under child protection procedures were supported in the review of the safeguards for children living away from home (DH 1997a, pp.103–4) and recommended in the new Government guidance (DH 2000a). However, these documents make no mention of the use of local authority secure accommodation for young people involved in prostitution, which has not been reviewed. Even with the changes which will mean that young people involved in prostitution are no longer convicted under the criminal law, they will continue to be vulnerable to control and 'punishment' under the civil law and to placement in local authority secure accommodation, alongside those who have been convicted of other offences, including sexual assault under the criminal law. The inherent confusion for the young people concerned will be evident and a review of the use of secure accommodation for young people involved in prostitution is needed.

Offending

Twelve young people were admitted to secure accommodation through the criminal justice routes because they had been charged with or convicted of criminal offences. Six boys and two girls were convicted under section 53 of the Children and Young Persons Act 1933. It was the first and only offence committed by two of the boys and the previous offences of a number of the others were not related to the current conviction. The two boys convicted of sexual offences denied that they had committed them. The four young people on remand had all committed one or more previous offences, although the offences of two of them were unrelated to their current charges.

THE REASONS FOR OFFENDING

The reasons for offending were diverse and although not all the young people could explain their offending behaviour several themes emerged. Some of them talked about offending as part of their way of life rather than as a discrete event. For example, one boy on remand for an offence of attempted murder said he started offending when he was

12, and that criminality was inevitable in the area in which he had lived. He identified himself as a criminal and appeared to gain some self-esteem from this self-concept. He was dismissive of the response from the police and professional agencies to his offending:

> It's just because of the place I'm from, everybody does it to get some money to buy some draw ... I didn't really care ... when I was getting arrested they weren't doing nothing about it, they weren't even giving me cautions, they was just telling me, 'Don't do it again, If you do it again, we'll have to take you to court' ... Only some things go down on my record. If they charged me with everything I've done I'd have a big long record but I've only got about six crimes on there.

Other young people regarded their offending behaviour to be a consequence of their use of drugs and alcohol and yet others described it as a result of peer pressure and the need for social acceptance. For example, Adrian said:

> I got in with the wrong crowd, stealing motorbikes and cars and all that, drinking and smoking drugs and then the police got involved, I was getting arrested, I wanted to be the same as the others, I didn't want to be an individual.

THE RELATIONSHIP BETWEEN OFFENDING AND BEING IN CARE

Concerns have been raised about the criminalization of children in care, particularly those in residential care (Sinclair and Gibbs 1998). In addition to those admitted through the criminal justice routes, 11 of the young people admitted through the welfare route (nine girls and both the boys) reported that they had committed offences. Most of them said that their offending behaviour had commenced following their admission to care and that their criminal record was a direct consequence of being in care. It is interesting to note that the offending behaviour and convictions of the three girls admitted through the criminal justice routes were also attributed by them to their placements in care. The two boys had committed mainly drug- and car-related offences which started prior to and increased following their admission to care. Seven of the nine girls also gained or compounded their criminal records whilst in care. Some of them had committed offences as a means of survival whilst on the run, for example shoplifting and aggressive begging although none of the girls had been charged with soliciting for prostitution. Furthermore, four girls had been cautioned or convicted of offences committed in their children's homes including criminal damage, affray and theft. For example, Sarah's offending began after her placement in a children's home and she had convictions for criminal damage, assault and theft, all committed in the residential unit:

> I got in with the wrong crowd and started sleeping around and taking drugs. I used to go out nicking cars a lot and breaking into other people's houses. I got a bad name for myself and things started getting back to my mum which was giving my mum a bad name as well ... I think my life's gone downhill a lot since I left home ... I started breaking the law and taking drugs whereas at home I don't think I would have been so bad.

Violence

Eleven young people (38%), three girls and eight boys, were placed in secure accommodation on remand or following conviction for offences of violence, rape or sexual assault. Five of them had experienced violence during childhood, both becoming involved in violence between their parents and suffering physical abuse. It is interesting to note that in addition to these five, several girls who had experienced family violence in childhood were placed in secure accommodation to protect them from serious violence and abuse perpetrated on them by male partners.

It can be argued that the nature of power relationships provides a more appropriate explanation for violence than a cycle of violence and abuse which proposes that those who grow up in violent families will necessarily engage in violent adult family relationships, as perpetrator or victim and/or abuse their children. Mullender and Morley (1994) and Kelly (1994) contend that no study has adequately demonstrated that such a cycle exists although they refer to two reviews of existing research which conclude that experiencing violence in childhood may increase the risk of violence in adulthood (Kaufman and Zigler 1987;

Widom, 1989). While accepting that violence does occur in generations of families, the emotional and behavioural consequences for individuals are different and it is clear that many children survive violence in childhood without themselves becoming violent. Children can recover from the effects of family violence, if the violence is stopped and appropriate support provided (Wolfe *et al.* 1986). This reinforces the crucial importance of therapeutic intervention with children, not just as an appropriate response to their distress but also to enhance their resilience to future psycho-social stress and reduce the risk of continuing violence.

Having considered some of the circumstances which resulted in their admission to secure accommodation, the young people's experiences of the process of admission will be examined, although this will not include the court process which is outside the remit of this study.

Admission to Secure Accommodation

Although placement in secure accommodation was proposed by professionals as an alternative to custody or threatened as a deterrent, none of the young people in the study said they felt that they had been given adequate information about secure accommodation. Some young people were given no information about the plan for their placement and at its extreme, several girls were not told they were being taken to a secure unit until they arrived. This is one of the most obvious dangers of the power afforded to local authorities to place young people in secure accommodation for up to 72 hours without the authorization of a court. For example, Jamila described what happened to her:

> When I got there the woman asked me when I went to court for a secure order. At first I didn't understand what she meant by that and she told me it was a secure unit and that's when I got really upset and angry with my social worker … I said to her, 'you said to me that I was going to an open unit' and she said if she had told me I was going to a secure unit you would have run away and I said I wouldn't.

Secure Accommodation As a Deterrent

Most of the young people admitted through the welfare route had been threatened with placement in secure accommodation with the objective of deterrence. Social workers using the threat of secure accommodation emphasized the negative, punitive aspects particularly the loss of freedom. Anna's experience is an example shared by some other girls:

> I was told by the social workers that if I didn't follow the rules I would be put in a secure unit ... so that night there was a knock on the door and the CID and social services and my social worker came, they walked in and said we're taking you to the secure unit now ... I was really frightened and crying, pleading with them but they all said it wasn't a punishment, it was for my own good and safety ... I thought a secure unit was just for murderers and people who had committed crimes and I didn't see it as a sanctuary for girls who was in there needing help.

The threat of placement in secure accommodation for young people considered to be at risk of significant harm is not only ineffective as a deterrent, but counterproductive as it exacerbates running away. It raises some important policy and practice issues. The UN Convention on the Rights of the Child (Article 13) and the Children Act 1989 emphasize the importance of involving young people in decisions on matters which concern them, and the regulations and guidance accompanying the Children Act 1989 (DH 1991c) state that young people should never be placed in secure accommodation through the welfare route as a punishment. Young people who have been threatened with the worst that professionals suggest can happen to them if they do not 'behave', are unlikely to feel good about themselves and perceive placement in a secure unit as a positive strategy for their care. These issues will be explored further in the next chapter.

Secure Accommodation As an Alternative to Custody

The opportunities for pre-placement planning for young people admitted through the criminal routes might appear to be greater than for those admitted in a crisis through the welfare route. However, it emerged that the involvement of the young people in this group in the planning and decision-making process and the level of the information given to them about secure accommodation prior to placement were only marginally better than for those admitted through the welfare route.

A Suitable or Unsuitable Placement?

All the young people expressed their views about whether secure accommodation was an appropriate placement for them. The reason for their placement and the alternatives available to them influenced their views and some of them differentiated between the appropriateness of their current placement and previous admissions to secure accommodation. The views of the young people admitted through the different legal routes will be examined separately.

Convicted Offender

The attitudes of these eight young people to the offences for which they had been placed in secure accommodation inevitably affected their views on the appropriateness of their placement. Two boys had been convicted of offences which they denied. The sense of injustice they expressed about their convictions extended to their placement in secure accommodation. However, one had been on remand in the community while the other had been remanded to a young offender institution and their attitudes to secure accommodation were influenced by their different pre-placement experiences. While the second saw it as a preferable alternative to the young offender institution, the first was resentful at the placement:

> I'm really angry at being here ... being found guilty of the charges against me ... changed everything in my life and with my family ... I've been found guilty of one of the most serious crimes and I haven't done it and I've had to forfeit my education that I was doing when I was going to mainstream school.

The two girls admitted the offences for which they had been convicted but neither of them felt that the secure placement was appropriate, or that it would meet their needs.

For example, Mandy acknowledged the effectiveness of secure accommodation as a means of punishment but was adamant that it was not the way to help her:

> I do think I should be locked up as a punishment. What I want to know though is what it's going to do for me? They say I'll see a psychiatrist or a psychologist ... but how is that helping me? Fair enough, I'm talking about my crime to get it out of me and to have a better chance later on in life but I was doing all that in the open unit anyway. I just don't see in what way it's different except for all the privileges being taken away.

In short, all the young people convicted of offences regarded the primary purpose of their placement in secure accommodation as punishment. Those who felt they should be punished for the offences they had committed appeared more easily to accept their placement whilst those who denied their offences or who had expected non-custodial sentences expressed anger and resentment. However, all of them expressed doubts that their needs would be met by the placement.

Unconvicted Offender

The three boys on remand had been transferred to secure accommodation from young offender institutions while the girl on remand had been admitted directly from court. The attitudes of these young people to placement in secure accommodation varied. For example, while Cathy, on remand for child abduction, felt that her placement was justified 'because I think I would have run away and I wouldn't have gone to court', the others expressed resentment at their placements and felt that they were being punished before they had been convicted and sentenced. It is of note that if convicted, young people remanded to custody in a young offender institution or secure unit are more likely to receive a custodial sentence than if they had been on remand in the community, because they have already been assessed as sufficiently high risk to require containment (Boswell 1996).

Welfare Admissions

The 17 young people admitted through this route were considered to be at risk of significant harm or to present a risk of harm to others. Almost half of them said they recognized that their behaviour had put them at some risk of harm although few thought that secure accommodation was an appropriate response to their needs and those that did, regarded its only benefit to be the short-term safety it provided in a crisis.

The issue of punishment was crucial for all of them. Even where they felt that the placement could provide something positive, such as protection from risk of harm, they regarded its primary purpose as punishment. They were all aware that they were placed alongside young people who had been admitted to secure accommodation explicitly for punishment, some of them for offences of which they had themselves been victims, and that they were being treated in the same way. This issue will be examined further in the next chapter.

LENGTH OF PLACEMENT

The important issue of length of placement and the harmful psychological and social effects of placements were discussed. The length of placement in secure accommodation was important for all the young people and the concerns they expressed related to over-long placements, the uncertainty surrounding the likelihood of placement extension and the absence of positive future plans. Even some of those who accepted that there was some justification for their initial admission had become discouraged as their placements had been extended and uncertainty about future plans prevailed. For example, Charlotte had recognized that she was in need of help and that her life was at risk:

> I was at high risk of killing myself, every time I took an overdose … I always refused treatment … I didn't want to come to a secure unit … and at first it was hard accepting it because I was mixing with other people who had done things wrong and being punished, like we get the same rules and everything.

She said she accepted that placement in secure accommodation might initially have been necessary. However, she expressed resentment at the extension of the placement which she felt was not about her needs but due to the lack of alternative provision: 'Last time they went to court they got another order for two months just because they had nowhere else for me to go.'

A SUITABLE PLACEMENT

Most of those who felt that secure accommodation was an appropriate placement based their view on the immediate or short-term safety it afforded them. For example, Vicki had recognized that she was at risk from violent pimps and she had requested a placement out of her home area which had been refused by the local authority responsible for her because funding was not available. Vicki accepted the placement in secure accommodation as an escape from the risk she faced:

> I realized that it was for the best, that they was doing it for my own good … if I hadn't come in I probably would have ended up dead from working, I'd either have killed myself with drugs or someone would have killed me … I think the thing I needed was to be away from the circle I was in.

And yet, ironically, it emerged that many of those who identified safety as the main benefit of secure accommodation, continued to be at risk of harm in the secure units. Some of the dangers faced by young people in secure units have already been examined from the perspectives of secure unit staff and social workers. The young people's perspectives on this issue will be explored in the following chapters.

AN UNSUITABLE PLACEMENT

The young people who felt the placement was unsuitable either did not accept that they were at risk or accepted they were at risk but regarded placement in secure accommodation as an inappropriate response to their needs. Jamila was one of those who did not accept that she was at risk of harm. She had been admitted to secure accommodation on three occasions and regarded all the admissions as unwarranted. She said:

> I don't think I was at risk because I was with my older brother, that is family, so I don't think I was at risk. They say I was at risk … When I first went to a secure unit I thought I don't need to be in secure accommodation … and I still think the same.

Jane was among the young people who accepted that they were at risk but did not feel that secure accommodation was the right placement for them. She said: 'I think I needed help but I don't think I need to be locked up.'

MULTIPLE SECURE PLACEMENTS

Accommodation by a local authority presents a high risk factor in the likelihood of admission to secure accommodation for young people (Harris and Timms 1993; National Children's Bureau 1995). In addition it appears that placement in secure accommodation itself significantly increases the risk of re-admission. Eleven girls and two boys, that is two in five of those in the study, and almost two thirds of those admitted through the welfare route, had experienced multiple admissions to secure accommodation. They were all aware of the increased risk of re-admission and most of them felt that repeated admissions were inappropriate. For example, Sarah said:

> I think if you've got a background of being in secure accommodation then social services have got more chances of getting another secure order on you … as has been proved with me… This placement didn't work for me last time and I strongly believe that it won't work for me this time … I think a lot of things need to be sorted out in my life … but I don't believe that secure accommodation is the right place to be doing it.

Some of them differentiated between the appropriateness of their various admissions. Roberta had had repeated admissions to secure accommodation since age 13 when she became involved in prostitution, and she accepted that admission might initially have been necessary, but felt it was no longer appropriate. It merits comment that Roberta had spent 340 out of 450 days between January 1996 and March 1997 in local authority secure accommodation in addition to repeated placements between 1994 and 1996. Similarly, Karen articulated her strong sense of injustice that she was in a secure unit only because of the lack of alternative non-secure provision available for her:

> Yes I did need to be locked up before ... If I hadn't been locked up I'd still be on the streets now ... but not this time ... Before, I was on the streets, I was taking drugs, I was doing this and I was doing that. But I've stopped all that this time and the only reason they put me here was because ... they had nowhere else to put me.

Conclusion

This chapter has examined the views of the young people on the circumstances resulting in their admission to secure accommodation, and on the suitability of the placement as a response to their needs. The difficulties in the backgrounds of the young people ultimately resulted in their placement in secure accommodation. The experiences of those in this sample who had been living in the care system confirm findings from other studies that being in care itself constitutes a risk factor increasing the chance of involvement in crime and prostitution and of admission to secure accommodation or other forms of custody (DH 1997a; Rowe *et al.* 1989; Stein *et al.* 1994). Furthermore, placement in secure accommodation increased the risk of re-admission for those in this sample, 45 per cent of whom had experienced multiple admissions to secure accommodation, reinforcing their powerlessness and lack of control in their lives.

Running away was an important issue in the lives of almost three quarters of the young people. A complex relationship emerged between running away from violence and abuse, placement in care, revictimization and running away from care, with professionals using imprisonment in secure accommodation as the ultimate solution to running away. The findings from this small sample study add weight to those from other studies which suggest that placement in secure accommodation is not the most effective response to running away, or the problems and risks associated with it, such as prostitution (Browne and Falshaw 1998; Jesson 1993; National Children's Bureau 1995; Stein *et al.* 1994). Its limited effectiveness might be partly explained by the inadequate therapeutic intervention provided in secure accommodation to help young people address the reasons behind their running away, which will be explored further.

Some serious concerns have emerged from the experiences of the young people in this sample which raise doubts about whether placement in secure accommodation was the most appropriate response to the needs of many of them. In the next chapter, their experiences in the secure units will be examined. Of particular interest is whether their needs were met, how far their rights were respected and whether priority was given to their interests or to those of the institutions.

NINE

Living in Secure Accommodation

Introduction

This chapter will examine the young people's perspectives on life in secure accommodation. The emphasis on control in residential institutions for children is explicated in recent research which shows that surveillance and discipline dominate over meeting children's needs for support and therapeutic help (Parkin and Green 1997). It therefore seems likely that in secure accommodation where 'the first essential of the arrangements is continuous and effective control' (DHSS 1977) care will be subordinated to the interests of security, and the needs of the institutions will be given priority over solving children's personal problems, even though the deprivation of liberty is frequently justified on the basis of their need for treatment (Kelly. 1992; Millham *et al.* 1978). These questions will be investigated in this chapter.

Impressions of the Regimes

The six units in the study implemented different regimes which were all based on behavioural principles. Many of the young people were aware of differences between units. They compared the explicitly punitive regimes in some units, which imposed severe restrictions in all aspects of living, prescribed the clothing which could be worn and allowed only minimal personal possessions, with others in which the controls were less stringent. The different behavioural regimes in two units were described:

> We've got a colour system here, when you first come you automatically start on a red and it takes about two weeks of good behaviour

> to get on a yellow and it's harder to get on a green and even much harder to get on a gold. These colours give you privileges like going on mobility when you're on a yellow and on a green you get the same privileges but you're allowed to have more mobility and to have more things in your room.
>
> In this place you have a level system, you get marked each day from Friday to Friday from 0–4, then only if you get a 3 or a 4 as average for the week then you'll make a level.

Care or Punishment?

Young people admitted through the criminal justice routes regarded the primary purpose of their placement as punishment. Most of those who had been in young offender institutions saw secure accommodation as a positive alternative. For example, Nathan compared secure accommodation with his placement in a young offender institution (Feltham):

> It's like a hotel compared to Feltham, it's just easy ... I see a lot of boys abusing the place, the things they've got in here ... I don't think they really know what it's like to be in prison ... it's no holds barred, it's just prison, no-one cares, you're on your own, you're always getting into fights ... they're lucky to be in here rather than there.

In contrast, many of the young people who had been admitted to secure accommodation for welfare reasons expressed confusion. While the stated purpose of the placement was for their care and protection, they experienced it as a punishment. As the prevailing culture in all the units was one of control, even some of these young people talked about 'doing their time'. For example, Jamila articulated her experience of the inherent contradictions between care and punishment:

> The staff keep telling me that it's not a punishment, it's to give me a break ... it feels like a punishment because you are permanently watched, the staff listen carefully to everything you say, waiting for you to slip up on everything, and this can lead to being jeopardized as to when you get out ... I never wish to come back to a place like this.

There were some marked gender differences in young people's reactions to the regimes, with more of the girls than the boys suffering adversely from the deprivation of their liberty and the level of control and surveillance exercised over them. For example, Anna described her experience on admission:

> On the first night I couldn't get used to being locked in the room ... if you need the toilet at night you have to ring your buzzer... The next day I was given a uniform and a pair of shoes that I had to wear ... being in a secure unit hits you really hard as you can't do anything without permission or anything for yourself ... A lot of people say it's not a punishment to put you in here but it feels like it.

Confinement of the sort exercised in secure accommodation forces young people to confront their past experiences and difficulties, often without support and therapeutic services in an environment which deprives them of their usual coping mechanisms. For example, Mandy experienced the loss of freedom and privileges as punishment, but her main problem was having to face what she had done, without being able to use her usual coping mechanisms:

> I can't smoke, I can't go out ... before I used to go out whenever I felt like it, but now I can't and sometimes when you get upset and go outside and have a fag, that's what calms me down and I can't do that any more ... I can't walk into the kitchen and make a hot drink when I want one and I really miss that ... I can't get away from the fact that I've done what I've done because I only have to think secure and I think what I've done again and again and again.

Other girls described how their previous experiences and problems became more intense and painful because they were forced to focus on them constantly and were unable to get any respite. For example, Jessica said:

> Being in secure makes you think about things more because whereas if you're in an open unit you can run away from your problems, you can get drunk, you can take drugs and your problems have gone, in here you've got to think about your problems all the time.

DELIBERATE SELF-HARM

Young people may self-harm because of distress at past experiences or memories. It is a coping mechanism and makes young people's lives more bearable or manageable (Bristol Crisis Service for Women 1994; Coleman *et al.* 1995). In all the secure units young people who self-harmed were restrained and kept under surveillance to prevent or control their self-destructive behaviour. Indeed, the rationale for placement of some self-harming young people in secure accommodation is the provision of surveillance to contain the behaviour. The young people who had been self-harming before their admission to secure accommodation expressed surprise at the punitive controls which were imposed on them. For example, Charlotte described a system of surveillance which maintained her in a room, stripped of all her belongings, dressed in cut-down pyjamas, with two or three members of staff in attendance. When she attempted to self-harm, she was physically restrained, on occasions by as many as four members of staff and confined under supervision to her stripped room.

Many young people in this study reported that they became more depressed during their placements and their self-harming increased. Charlotte's experience illustrates the issues and is typical:

> You sit down and think about things all the time, so you get more and more depressed and then you self-harm ... I feel worse about myself now, I've self-harmed myself more times in here than I did outside.

There are complex issues involved in caring for young people who deliberately self-harm and the attitudes of professionals often become polarized between a sympathetic understanding of the needs and distress behind the behaviour and a punitive resentment of the power the young person appears to wield over the adults by their threats of suicide and self-harm, which cannot be ignored (Reder *et al.* 1991). Many professionals in the care and health services fail to understand self-harming behaviour. As already shown, the attitudes of many of the staff in the units lacked understanding. This may be partly explained in that there is anxiety among staff in the units that self-harming behaviour, particularly cutting, is contagious, and one young person engaging in such behaviour, unless restrained and punished, will induce others who have not previously deliberately self-harmed.

The use of restraint on young people who self-harm which reinforces their sense of worthlessness and self-destructive intent can be profoundly harmful. It does nothing to meet the young people's needs which is the only effective way to help them to reduce their self-harming behaviour and to facilitate their long-term recovery. The experiences of these young people raise a number of important issues and support findings from earlier research that some young people, particularly girls, react badly to being locked up and the experience increases their vulnerability, self-harming behaviour and aggression (Hoghughi 1978). In short, secure accommodation makes them *more* rather than less vulnerable. The argument is powerful that such young people should not be placed in local authority secure accommodation at all, but as long as they are, the importance of the provision of specialist therapeutic services cannot be overstated.

Sanctions

Sanctions were imposed on young people as a standard part of the discipline and control in all the units. Sarah explained the system in one unit:

> You can get any sanction from a jewellery ban or a tape ban which can last for however long the staff want it to, you can get a yard ban ... you can get a red square which means you have to go to bed at 9.30 pm or you can get a twenty-four hour no colour which means that you lose all your privileges ... basically you can lose all privileges even down to silly things like watching TV or listening to a music tape and you have to be in bed by 8.30 pm ...

Sanctions are frequently imposed on young people on their return to secure units after running away, despite cautions that such responses can compound running away and recommendations that such children should be welcomed back (Millham *et al.* 1978). For example, Jamila described the sanctions imposed on her after she ran away from the secure unit:

> I got took to the police station … the police rang the unit but they said they didn't have enough staff to pick me up, so I stayed there in the police cell and it was horrible, disgusting. I asked if they could bring me one of my cigarettes but they wouldn't because they said I was only 14. Then in the morning three members of staff came to pick me up and when I came back I got sanctioned, four nights early bed and then three weeks on admission [no privileges or mobility] … I asked if I could see my sister but they said 'No'.

The arbitrary use of sanctions was an important issue which all the young people complained about. For example, Adrian said:

> If you get in a fight then you're going to lose something, it could be anything from your power [electricity] to mobility, home leave, if you've got any, not going down to the gym, anything, they can just stop until further notice and if you swear at staff that will immediately take your power ….

The ultimate sanction imposed in all the units was to confine young people in isolation in their rooms, with or without electricity. All the young people complained about this sanction, and many of them regarded it as the worst thing that could happen to them. The isolation of young people in their rooms, within the maximum security of secure units provides an explicit example of the conflict between care and custody, particularly in its use as a response to self-harming behaviour. Children who have been deprived of their liberty for care and treatment, instead find themselves contained in isolation in their rooms for punishment.

Mobility

Mobility within and outside the secure unit is of critical importance to young people and is a key part of the behavioural systems. The arrangements for mobility, including levels of supervision, differ on the basis of legal status. Young people are highly sensitive to these differences and many of those in this study raised this issue as one of the disadvantages of accommodating together young people admitted through different legal routes. Although plans for mobility should form part of individual care plans, mobility depends upon young people 'earning' it by good behaviour and compliance with staff expectations. The withdrawal of mobility is widely used in secure units as a sanction (see Boswell 1996; Kelly 1992). Mobility is also dependent on staff availability and many young people in this study complained that staffing and other institutional problems restricted their mobility. For example, Christina said:

> You can't go out when you want to go out, even when you've got unlimited mobility you can't use it because there's always other people who's got to go out first or there's not the staff available.

Self-Control

An important aspect of a treatment-oriented approach is that it allows young people to develop their own controls, rather than subjecting them to purely external controls (Street *et al.* 1966). Although, as already noted, a treatment-oriented approach is not implemented in secure accommodation, it has been suggested that one of the purposes of locking up children is to teach them self-control (Kelly 1992). A crucial question therefore is whether young people are helped to develop their own controls by attaining a greater level of understanding of themselves and their feelings or just deterred from expressing their emotions by the use of external control such as the threat of restraint and sanctions, and learn to conform without achieving any real change.

Many young people referred to the difficulty of controlling emotions such as anger, sadness and frustration and some described their sense of helplessness to exercise any control in their lives, in an environment where they were subject to a high level of external control. For example, Sarah said:

> People's expectations are too high and people want too much from young people in secure accommodation … They expect us to be well behaved, they expect us not to shout and swear at them if we're upset, they expect us to speak to them calmly if we're upset but they don't understand that sometimes we can't … in a place like this there's no end to it until social services says there is … you haven't got control of your life, you haven't got to think for yourself, you

> don't have to do anything for yourself ... you get locked up for 12 hours a day and you haven't got a life at all.

On the whole, on the basis of the young people's and the social workers' accounts, it did not appear that young people in this study were helped successfully to develop their own controls. Anger, frustration and other emotions expressed in a way regarded as unacceptable by staff were met with external controls, even where the deterioration in behaviour was a consequence of therapeutic work on painful issues. Young people were aware of the serious implications of expressing their feelings inappropriately, which included the imposition of sanctions, the possibility of an extension of their placement or their transfer to penal custody. However, there were six young people who said they thought that they had learned to exercise more self-control during their placement in secure accommodation. All of these were either convicted offenders who had served long sentences or young people who had spent long periods in secure accommodation because of multiple admissions through the welfare route. For example, Karen said: 'I'm not violent so much no more, I can control myself, I can take myself off. I've learnt to cry, I've learnt to talk about my problems.'

Privacy, Confidentiality and Surveillance

The psychological effects of public living have been explored and four states of privacy distinguished, all of which are considered essential for psychological health (Cohen and Taylor 1981). Solitude is the state of being alone or unobserved; intimacy is the type of privacy sought by two or more people who wish to achieve a maximum personal affinity; anonymity is the seeking and achievement of freedom from identification and observation in public places and reserve is a person's ability not to reveal certain aspects of her/himself that are intimate or shameful. The demands of security within a secure unit will prevent young people achieving any of these states of privacy.

Privacy and confidentiality for children are contentious issues. Young people's rights to privacy and confidentiality are particularly vulnerable to violation on the basis of what is judged to be in their best interests (NCCL 1991) and in practice these rights are not afforded to young people in secure accommodation.

PRIVACY

It emerged that many young people in this study found the lack of privacy oppressive. It was interesting to note that all the girls but fewer of the boys emphasized the importance of privacy and that there was less privacy afforded to the girls who were subject to greater surveillance, particularly in the mixed-gender units, because of concerns about their sexual behaviour. For example, Anna described the lack of privacy which shocked and left her with little trust in the integrity of the adults:

> I wrote many letters and gave them to staff to post, but I have now found out none of these letters were posted, but they still took them off me and didn't tell me they weren't going to post them ... In my review meeting the staff brought in a bag of letters which I had tried to send out and a load of letters which had been sent in to me which I had never received because they had opened them without my permission ... They had also opened and read all the letters I had tried to send out. It's humiliating and embarrassing ... They never even told me they weren't going to send the letters out because they wanted me to write them and give them to them so they could read them ... I felt very, very angry and humiliated and embarrassed ... I thought they were very sly the way they just, each day, took the letters I wrote off me and didn't explain in any way that they would not be posted and also every day to look me in the eye and say no when I asked if there was any mail for me ... they even kept Valentines cards which came in for me.

CONFIDENTIALITY

The lack of confidentiality was an issue for almost all the young people, not least with regard to the reason for their admission to secure accommodation. For example, Julie said that she had been told by members of staff the reasons why all the other young people were in the unit and realized that personal information about her would also be widely shared. She felt such practice was wrong:

> They shouldn't tell you someone else's private life, it makes me think of what they're doing with my life … they talk about things in front of all the other kids and all the other staff, things that I wouldn't want people knowing about … When I came in here I wouldn't have a strip search and so they locked me in my room, they took everything off me and the other kids said 'Why isn't she allowed out of her room, what has she done?' and they said 'It's because she won't have a strip search, she's not complying' … I didn't want them knowing my personal things and why I was in my room … nothing you tell them is treated as personal.

SURVEILLANCE

In all the units, high-level surveillance was intrinsic to the regimes and, as already noted in the mixed-gender units, there was higher surveillance of the girls than the boys. Some of the practical implications of this were described:

> Obviously you can't just go where you want, you've got to have a member of staff with you to open doors and shut doors behind you, after a meal the cutlery gets counted which makes you feel like a child.

As already noted, many young people, particularly the girls felt oppressed and even persecuted by the high levels of surveillance. This gender difference might be partly explained by the higher level of surveillance of the girls, by the greater importance attached to privacy by the girls than the boys and by possible differences in expectation as many of the boys but none of the girls had experienced placement in penal custody. For example, Julie said:

> It does my head in being here. If I knew I was coming in and I knew what it was like I would have killed myself or run … They watch over you all the time, like yesterday I was sitting at the dinner table and I said 'Can I leave the table please to go to the toilet?' and they said 'No' and I was upset and I said 'It's not up to you' but they said 'Yes it is', they said 'At the end of the day we're the ones that control you while you're in here' and other things like that and I think there's no need for it … They make you want to commit suicide,

> that's what it's got to ... I'd rather be in a prison, at least I'd be left alone, not watched over 24 hours a day.

Another girl admitted because of suicidal behaviour following a disclosure that she had been sexually abused by both her parents, said she found that the constant surveillance left her no private space to deal with her feelings:

> I had a really bad day yesterday, I got upset because I don't get any visits, all the others have visits from their parents who buy them things and I'm the only one in the unit that doesn't get visits from friends or parents ... I cried a lot, got angry, swore at staff, so then the staff came in and took all the things out of my room ... It helps if people will leave me alone and let me get upset but I never get that.

These young people's experiences of surveillance and the lack of privacy and confidentiality afforded to them are of concern, especially in the context of the levels of privacy necessary for them to maintain their psychological health, and the provisions of the UN Convention on the Rights of the Child, particularly Article 16. Many aspects of the regimes are like prison and have been described as degrading and unnecessary, such as frequent body and room searches, the use of rooms for isolation and the scrutiny of mail and literature, and recommendations have been made for them to be discontinued (Millham *et al.* 1978). Yet it is clear from the experiences of these young people that this practice continues.

Relationships with Peers

Many of the problems of making friends in maximum security where there is little choice of companions apply to children and between children and staff in secure units (Cohen and Taylor 1981; Millham *et al.* 1978). Relationships remain superficial as a protection against the uncertainties in the length of placements and the likelihood of the relationship being ended suddenly by an unplanned or unexpected move. Difficulties in relationships with peers emerged as a common theme. The young people said that peer confidentiality as well as staff confidentiality was important. However, the majority of them expressed a lack of trust in their peers. For example, Julie's experience was of being unable to trust her peers because 'they grass you up left, right and centre and they let all your private life out.' A second aspect of the difficulties in peer relationships concerned the pressure to conform from other young people. Jenny said she had tried unsuccessfully to be accepted by the other young people:

> People like certain things and you change what you like so you're not different from them. You think that's how it should be but in the end you go back to being who you are and that's when the arguments start ... When I first came here I went out of my way to be like everyone else and on occasions I was actually threatened by some people.

Several young people described how the behaviour of one or more members of the group could result in the whole group being punished. This exemplified how the regime and needs of the institution took priority over individual needs. Whilst this practice had implications for the whole group, the position of the individual whose behaviour resulted in the punishment could be jeopardized by the consequent increase in hostility and even bullying from others in the group. In this regard the issue of accommodating in units young people across the age range was raised as a problem by a number of the older teenagers. For example, Nathan complained: 'Most of them are younger than you and they've got all the mouth, they're little kids and they try to wind you up.'

A further aspect of the difficulties in peer relationships emerged in the narratives of the girls who talked about the emotional demands made on them by other distressed young people. They found it difficult to cope with other people's difficulties in addition to their own. Karen explained how she coped:

> I stay away from them ... there's one girl particularly who has similar problems to me and she kept coming to talk to me about her problems and I couldn't cope with it ... I can't cope with my own problems never mind hers, so I told her I didn't like her and that I wasn't her friend ... That's not true, it isn't that I don't like her it's just that I don't want to listen to her problems, it hurts too much.

Only one girl described a close friendship she had made with another girl in the unit. However, professional staff disapproved of the friendship because the girls were considered to have a detrimental effect on each other and the other girl was moved to an alternative placement.

Bullying and Intimidation

An important issue in any discussion of relationships between young people concerns bullying and intimidation. Almost all the young people had experience of bullying in the units. While some young people felt that staff were in control, the majority view in all the units was that staff did not know the extent of bullying or deal with it to ensure adequate protection, so they had to find ways of protecting themselves. It emerged that many young people, particularly those who had been the victims of prior abuse, felt unable to complain to staff about ill-treatment by their peers. Several young people complained that staff did not treat the issue seriously and protect them, and then punished them when they tried to protect themselves. It has already been shown that this issue was generally minimized by staff in the units. For example, Aziz described how he retaliated to bullying which resulted in the imposition of sanctions by staff:

> I started getting bullied and one day I thought I ain't having this no more so I started sticking up for myself and then I got into fights, but then I got in more trouble from the staff … I used to get bullied for money and cigarettes.

Name-calling was reported as a common occurrence in all the units and it emerged that some of this was racially motivated. For example Nathan said: 'You'll get kids calling you names. Sometimes they'll make racist remarks as well to try to provoke you.'

Many of the girls talked about bullying in the context of considering the disadvantages of mixed-gender units, which will be examined later. Some of them had experience of bullying by girls as well as boys and a few girls acknowledged that they bullied others. For example, Vicki said:

> When I am in a mood I have got a very bad attitude, I am nasty … I am trying to sort my temper and my attitude out and to speak to people rather than to argue and fight.

Several girls saw themselves as particularly vulnerable and easy targets for bullies. For example, Jane expressed her fear of assault:

> I'm easy to be bullied, like people just pick me out and say 'oh, we'll bully her' … I'm weak, I don't stick up for myself … I'm scared of them hitting me.

Many young people found the violent language, attitudes and behaviour of their peers difficult to cope with. For example, Anna admitted to feeling afraid and suggested that she had several times given in to demands from her peers, for example to give away a pair of her jeans. She said that staff were unaware of what was going on and that complaining about it would have made matters much worse:

> A lot of the girls in here are violent. I don't think they realize that calling them names, actually hurts them. A lot of girls bully other girls in the unit and the staff don't seem to do much about it a lot of the time … I just try to stay out of their way and stay friends on all sides although there have been incidents when I thought things were going to resort into fights. I have never been a violent person and I don't know how to react when people talk to me the way they do as I don't like to shout back or argue … A lot of things happen without the staff realizing, a lot of things go unnoticed … some of the other girls in here feel the same way that I do but they are too afraid to say.

Furthermore, evidence of sexual victimization and intimidation emerged. As already noted, the lack of confidentiality in the units meant that most of the young people were aware of the reasons for admission of their peers and some of their personal information was also public knowledge. Some of the girls who had been sexually abused or had worked as prostitutes, or who on the basis of previous experiences had been ascribed negative labels based on sexuality such as 'slag' were subject to verbal, physical and sexual assaults. This was particularly evident in the mixed-gender units. However, most of the girls were reluctant to discuss these experiences. One girl who did talk about them became very distressed, while at the same time claiming not to care about the effect on her of insults and assaults in the unit, which she said were inevitable when people learned that she had worked as a prostitute.

Education Provision

As already shown, the education careers of most of the young people in this study had been disrupted, some from as early as primary school. Thirteen, more than two in five, had been permanently excluded from mainstream school, one boy had been excluded from a residential special school and one in five of the young people were the subjects of Statements under the Education Act. Three young people were above the school leaving age, one went out to college locally as part of his exit plan and the other two were required to attend school in the units.

The views of the young people about the education provision in the units varied and there were some gender differences. Half of the girls (nine) and nearly three quarters of the boys (eight) expressed an interest in the education they were receiving in the secure unit and educational aspirations. The school experiences of many of them were negative and few of them expressed any positive hopes or expectation of returning to mainstream school following their release from secure accommodation. Almost all of them felt they would be disadvantaged in the future as a result of their lack of education and only a few felt that the education provided in the units would make any positive difference. Perhaps unsurprisingly these were long-stay young people. Some of these favourably compared the education in the secure unit with their previous education. For example, Adrian said:

> It's not like normal school, the teachers are not like normal teachers, they're trained to deal with people who have learning problems, who haven't been to school. They can sit down and talk to you about anything, explain everything in detail.

Two other boys who had been placed in secure accommodation rather than other forms of custody primarily because of the better educational opportunities expressed positive views about the education in the units, and one boy found that although the educational opportunities in the secure unit were poorer than those in mainstream school, they were better than those in many of the other secure units to which he could have been sent:

> When I started school here I was told by our teacher that I would only be able to do four GCSEs here but I was quite happy at that because I'd been told that if I'd gone to any other secure unit I probably wouldn't have got any GCSEs at all.

However, the social workers expressed significant criticisms about the quality of the education provision in secure accommodation, related to its isolation from mainstream education, the inadequacy of provision in comparison with the national curriculum and the emphasis on subjects such as art which did not adequately prepare young people for a return to mainstream, or even special education. The isolation of secure accommodation from mainstream services has a significant impact not only on the quality and range of education provision within the units but also on the education plans for young people leaving secure accommodation.

Single- or Mixed-Gender Units

As already shown, three boys and eight girls were accommodated in single-gender units and eight boys and ten girls were placed in mixed-gender units. Some of the young people had experience of previous placements in other units with a different gender make-up, enabling them to make some comparison between single- and mixed-gender placements. For example, one boy placed in a mixed unit had previously been in a boys' unit and six girls placed in mixed units had previously been in girls' units. The young people raised issues in favour of and against single- and mixed-gender units. The girls expressed stronger views than the boys about the benefits of single-gender units and the disadvantages of mixed units with ten girls, that is more than half, but only three boys stating a preference for placement in single-gender units. It must be noted that most of the remaining eight girls said they favoured a mixed unit primarily because the facilities were significantly better than those in the girls' units. Only five young people expressed a clear preference for placement in mixed-gender units. The analysis of the young people's views confirms the findings from the staff and social workers that the benefits of mixed-gender units are benefits for the boys, whilst the disadvantages predominantly affect the girls.

Disadvantages of Mixed-Gender / Benefits of Single-Gender Units

The different treatment of girls and boys in mixed-gender units was widely commented on by the young people. Girls placed in mixed-gender units were thought to be disadvantaged because the needs and interests of the boys who were in the majority were always given priority. For example, Jackie described how the boys were given priority in the use of facilities:

> The boys get more advantages than us. Because there's more boys than girls, they get to go down the gym whenever they want but we have to wait until they're not in there or there's only a few of them in there or there's enough staff around to take us down there.

Most of the girls in mixed-gender units complained about the attitudes of the boys which they experienced as sexist and hurtful. For example, Charlotte said she would have preferred placement in a girls' unit:

> I'd like it to be just girls because I feel a lot safer with girls than boys ... sometimes I mix with the other girls and we always get on but the boys are really horrible to you ... When I wear tee shirts they always comment on the scars on my arms and call me a suicidal and that I should ring the Samaritans but then, like today we had a talk from some people from the Samaritans and the boys shouted at me why don't you kill yourself instead of talking to the Samaritans, you only waste the telephone bill.

Anna was placed in a girls' unit and expressed concerns about the potential for increased conflict in a mixed unit:

> I feel more comfortable around just girls but if boys were there I would feel a lot more self-conscious ... When it is girls only it's

> better in a lot of ways because girls being around boys can cause a lot of girls to show off and have cat-fights over boys and getting involved in relationships in the unit.

The quality of relationships between girls was reported to be better in the girls' units than in the mixed-gender units. For example, Sarah said 'I think the girls pull together and stick together more than if it was mixed' while Karen said she felt more isolated in a mixed-gender unit:

> In the all-girls units we used to have girl talks and we used to talk about things we can't talk about in here with boys around, like relationships outside, what we've done with other people ... now there's always boys in the room, I wouldn't want to have those conversations with boys around.

Advantages of Mixed-Gender Units

One girl had a different perspective on this issue from her female peers. She was the only girl convicted under section 53 placed in a mixed-gender unit and the opportunity to build friendships was her main priority. As all the other girls in the unit had been admitted through the welfare route and the length of their stays were shorter and uncertain, she had established relationships with the boys:

> I get on better with the boys ... they class you as a friend and every one of them looks after me, no-one would let anything happen to me. If a new boy came in and he hit me he'd have all the rest of them to answer to.

It is interesting that the most positive comments about mixed units from the boys, also came from some of those convicted under section 53. For example, one said 'I think it's good because it makes it more realistic to the real world when you're with girls' while another said:

> I think it's good training for when you eventually get out, it's not just boys, boys, boys all the time, you do see a girl's face ... the girls seem to be more sympathetic than the boys, the girls will say if you ever need to talk I'm here and I appreciate that.

Offender/Non-Offender Mix

The mix of offenders and non-offenders was a major issue of concern for the majority of young people with only eight who said they did not have a view. Two thirds (19) of those in the study felt that young people of different legal status should be accommodated separately. This group comprised 5 young people admitted through the criminal justice route (4 boys and 1 girl: 42 per cent of those admitted through both criminal routes but 62 per cent of those convicted) and 14 young people admitted through the welfare route (12 girls, 2 boys: 82 per cent of those admitted through welfare route). Their concerns can be grouped around a number of themes, which will be examined below.

Everyone is treated the same and all those in secure units are labelled as criminal, even if they are not.

This issue was predictably of especial concern to those admitted through the welfare route. For example, Christina said:

> I just reckon it's stupid mixing those who run away with offenders because we're getting treated just the same as if we've done a crime and we haven't ... I think secure units should be just for criminals. There should be different types of units for people who run away.

The issue of stigma was raised by many of the girls. For example, Karen was worried about the label she would carry as a result of her placement in secure accommodation:

> People outside here don't like me ... they think all young people in secure have done bad things and are hard and that's a bad thing for my reputation in the future.

The misperception that everyone in secure accommodation is criminal was actually expressed by some of the young people. For example, Lawrence said:

> Most people in here are here for crime even if they're here for protection because you can't just come in here for protection, there's got to be another reason as well ... you've got to have done a crime as well.

It is interesting that some of those admitted through the criminal routes also thought that locking up young people in need of protection together with those convicted of offences was inappropriate. One of these said:

> You speak to them and I've learnt a bit about what the girls have to cope with from their pimps, the pressures, getting beaten up … some of the things I've talked to them about make me really sad … they're here for their own protection but they shouldn't be locked up like this, there should be another way of coping with them.

There is insufficient protection from the risks of harm within the units.

Almost all the girls and one of the boys admitted through the welfare route complained about the risks and harmful emotional and physical effects on them of living with young people who had committed offences, particularly where they themselves had been the victims of such offences. One girl described the difficulty:

> I really don't like it because one of the boys is here because of rape and I just can't deal with that and another is here for setting fire to someone and it was manslaughter … having been burnt as a child it really hurts me … I think it would be better if they were in their own unit.

Another girl articulated a widely shared anxiety about the inadequate recognition given to the risks of violence and sexual assault within units:

> If you get somebody who is a section 53 in here who has been placed in here for assaults and there's a section 25 who has been assaulted then it makes the section 53 out of place because of what they've done and the section 25 is obviously going to feel pretty strongly about being in the same unit as somebody who has assaulted someone … I know how it feels because I was assaulted … I think it should be separate units for the section 25s and the section 53s or at least they should be separate within the unit … I think there's got to be more of a risk assessment done on the section 53s and the section 25s being together because we're locked up

> together 24 hours a day and stuff does happen ... I think the risks in here need to be taken seriously.

Some girls argued that the risks in the secure units were greater than those they had been exposed to in the community. For example, Anna said:

> There's a girl in here who tried to stab another girl ... it was a real shock as she was sat right next to me ... she had a knife and she started arguing, then she picked up the knife and went for this girl ... I don't think that girls with those sort of problems who have committed criminal offences should be in the same sorts of units as girls who have been put in here because they are at risk outside ... we are also at risk in here as it is very lucky that no-one was hurt.

Those convicted of serious offences may be a target for bullying.

Research in remand centres (Godsland and Fielding 1985) has shown that offenders may be targeted when the nature of their offence is discovered. Many of the offenders in this study complained about the judgmental attitude of some young people admitted for welfare reasons to those convicted or remanded for serious offences. One boy said:

> Everybody's advised not to tell other people why they're here ... but they find out and when they do you can be ditched straight away if you're in for a crime people don't like and if you have an argument they bring it up and throw it in your face.

This view was shared by the girls who said they felt it would be better if section 53s were accommodated together because then they would be more 'equal'. One girl said:

> First of all I didn't mind mixing with the section 25s but one of the girls got a hint of why I was here in here and gave me a hard time ... it was as if I was a completely different person ... I think that if it was just one unit for section 53s and one unit for section 25s it would be better for everyone because no-one would be able to give you a hard time because they'd obviously have done something wrong and been caught for it and sentenced for them to be here.

Many of the non-offenders did in fact express a critical attitude toward the serious offenders, illustrating that there was some substance to the offenders' fears. For example, one boy said:

> It depends what people are in for … if someone's on a section 53 for rape or for something to do with little kids, then I feel sorry for them if people find out because if I found out and I knew about it and I see that person sitting next to me and he's done something to a little kid or something, then that little kid could have been my little brother or sister, I'd just want to kill him or her … I reckon people on a section 53 who are doing a long time should be in one unit and section 25s should be in another unit.

One convicted offender who withdrew from the study after the first interview, described his experience of being treated differently from the other young people:

> I got 3½ years for manslaughter. It was just a prank that went very seriously wrong, I didn't mean him no harm or pain or death. When I got admitted here, I didn't feel welcomed by the staff, they didn't want me here …I don't like this place, people get treated different ways to me … the staff treat me different to the other children.

Young people in secure units for welfare reasons jeopardize the position of convicted offenders, leaving them vulnerable to transfer to penal custody.

Many young people reported a difference in the attitude and behaviour between the offenders and those admitted for welfare reasons, which the offenders argued presented problems for them. Two of the offenders described the problems:

> When people are here for welfare reasons for short stays they don't mind about messing up or messing other people up because they know that in a couple of months they are going to be out anyway … they're only going to be here for three to six months and they're not really bothered about their education because they're going to be out soon and they try to distract the class and stop others learning so that everyone will be just like them.

> Well you've got care orders and section 53s who don't like it when the care orders run off … they get caught and they come back … If section 53s run off they don't come back, they go to prison … now I understand that care orders are different, like most of them haven't done a crime, they're in here for their own protection, but for some boys it really gets up their nose, like they can mouth off at staff and nothing happens but if a section 53 does that then they lose their power [electricity], their mobility and their home leaves. So, I think it's a really bad move putting care orders and section 53s together.

The opportunity for young people serving long sentences to make friendships are limited when they are placed in units where most young people are admitted for short placements.

The difficulties of living in a group of people that is frequently changing was an issue particularly for those on section 53 orders who remained on a long-stay basis. One boy's view reflected the general feeling:

> I'd prefer it if it was just people here who'd committed offences and who are here for a long time rather than loads of people being here for a short time because you can learn to live with them better and get on with them and make friends better.

Mobility arrangements for visits outside the units are different for those admitted through the different legal routes, leading to conflict.

Mobility outside the unit was a crucial issue for everyone. Different rules applied to mobility for those admitted for different reasons, which the young people complained resulted in problems for everyone. The different arrangements were problematic from the offenders' perspective:

> The section 25s get mobility faster than the section 53s and that's when it really reminds you that you've done something wrong and you're being punished for it … if we were on a unit of just section 53s we would all get mobility at the same time so everyone would know what you're feeling and what it's like to have to wait six months for mobility.

However, the different arrangements were also regarded as problematic from the non-offenders' perspective. They felt aggrieved as they saw those on section 53 going out unsupervised and having home leave, whilst their mobility was heavily controlled and supervised and they were not allowed to have home leave. Jackie summed up the dissatisfaction:

> You get so frustrated when everyone else gets mobility and you're still locked up, just left watching them go.

Conclusion

This chapter has begun the examination of the young people's experiences of life in secure accommodation. These young people have described some of the difficulties they experienced in a system which whilst notionally committed to the interests of the child, implements strict measures of control and surveillance and has security as its primary objective. In the experiences of the young people, the need for security and control took precedence over everything else, including their rights to privacy, confidentiality and participation in matters of concern to them. The emotional and psychological health of the young people was also shown to be at risk from the lack of privacy afforded to them.

Most of the young people expressed strong views on the key issues of debate, particularly the specialization debate. There were gender differences in their views on specialization on the basis of gender, with over half the girls but only a quarter of the boys favouring single-gender units. However, two thirds of them felt disadvantaged by current practice and felt that there should be specialization on the basis of legal status, with offenders and non-offenders accommodated separately. Whilst it might be predictable that young people admitted through the welfare route would hold this view, it emerged that two thirds of those convicted of criminal offences also favoured separate placements. These views are contrary to the policies promoted by the government, but consistent with the views on these issues held by the majority of the staff in the units and the social workers who participated in the study.

The next chapter will continue the examination of life in secure accommodation from the perspectives of the young people. It will focus on the treatment interventions and specialist services provided to meet the needs of young people who are regarded as among the most troubled or troublesome in society.

TEN

Therapeutic Interventions

Introduction

This chapter will examine the ways in which the young people were helped with their difficulties and the therapeutic specialist interventions provided. Although secure accommodation does not constitute a therapeutic environment, there is the expectation that it will provide skilled care and specialist therapeutic interventions for young people whose complex needs are considered to be beyond the ability of other types of care or custody. It has been shown in this and other studies that the placement of many young people is justified on the basis of their need for treatment (Brogi and Bagley 1998; Harris and Timms 1993; Kelly 1992). It has also been shown that in addition to the problems which led to their admission to secure accommodation, all the young people in this study had unmet needs and required a high quality of care. Kelly's (1992) argument that the idea of therapeutic intervention in secure accommodation amounts to little more than official rhetoric in a context of control will be investigated.

The Nature of the Services Provided

Services to young people may be provided directly by their social workers, by specialists arranged by their social workers or the secure unit and by secure unit staff, particularly the key/link workers allocated to them.

Social Worker

All the young people in this study had an allocated social worker from their home local authority who maintained contact with them during their placement in secure accommodation although the nature and frequency of their involvement varied. The most frequent contact was twice per week while the least frequent was three-monthly. Eighty per cent visited at least once per month and a quarter had weekly contact with young people. Even where social workers were not engaged in any direct work, this contact was important in maintaining links for young people with their families and communities.

The factors which appeared to influence the work undertaken with young people by social workers included the reason for young people's admission, the quality of the relationship between social workers and the young people, the geographical location of the unit and the provision of services in the secure unit. As illustrated earlier, the quality of relationships between social workers and the secure units was variable and in many cases social workers said that they undertook direct work with young people to compensate for deficits in the secure unit provision and the lack of expertise of secure unit staff. An important role for social workers lay in co-ordinating the professional involvement with young people.

Specialist Assessments and Ongoing Therapeutic Intervention

The importance of an integrated, multi-agency approach to the needs of young people in residential care has been demonstrated (Berridge and Brodie 1998; Sinclair and Gibbs 1998) and it is arguable that the multiple needs of young people in secure accommodation cannot be tackled by secure units in isolation from other professional agencies. However, there was little evidence of a multi-agency approach in the units which participated in this study and, as already shown, they operated in isolation from the wider child-welfare services.

There was an absence of clear policies in the units regarding the provision of therapeutic services. Although placement in secure accommodation is one of the most expensive residential resources for children, it emerged that therapeutic services were not included in the 'package' of care. There are a number of factors which, it is suggested, militate against the provision of specialist, therapeutic services. These include the length of time involved in arranging and waiting for specialist assessments and services in relation to the length of placement, particularly where they involve other agencies such as health; the frequently uncertain length of the placement; the additional costs involved for the placing authority; the isolation of secure units from mainstream services; and the confusion and time taken in sorting out where the responsibility lies for arranging and funding the services. The lack of policies resulted in confusion and protracted discussions between the professionals and delayed the provision of services for several young people in this study. When young people's placements are short- or even medium-term, delay can in effect mean non-provision.

The assessments which had been undertaken with young people in this study were either completed prior to admission as part of court proceedings, during in-patient hospital treatment, following referral to child and adolescent psychiatric teams, following admission by psychologists attached to the unit or as part of ongoing court proceedings. A number of issues of concern emerged in relation to the assessment of young people. First, the formal assessment of young people appeared to be accorded low priority. The nature of assessments undertaken by the units varied but appeared to relate mainly to young people's behaviour. This meant that care plans constructed in the absence of a comprehensive assessment of need contained only generalized objectives. Some young people were provided with services by the secure unit in the absence of a clear assessment. While some of these services were provided appropriately, in other cases services were included in the care plan on the basis of what the secure unit could arrange rather than the needs of the young people and sometimes proved to be inappropriate.

Second, the information provided to secure units about some young people was incomplete or delayed. It appeared that some assessments that had been undertaken prior to the admission of young people were not made available to the secure units. This highlights the issue of information-sharing between field and residential social workers, which has already been shown to be a matter of concern (see Berridge and Brodie 1998; Farmer and Pollock 1998). Third, the assessments which had been undertaken prior to admission varied on the basis of multiple factors including the young people's reason for admission, the professional discipline of the person undertaking the assessment and the comprehensiveness of the assessment. Some assessments of young people had been undertaken by their social worker with no other specialist input. Where young people had been known to professional agencies over an extended period of time, assessments could be out of date. Finally, it emerged that even where assessments had been undertaken, there was no certainty that the recommendations would be followed or therapeutic interventions would be provided to meet the identified needs.

It might reasonably be expected that even if the emotional and psychological needs arising from the young people's adverse childhood experiences were not met, the problems which resulted in their admission would be given priority. However, it appeared that the focus for intervention with young people was not necessarily determined by the reason for their admission and decisions were sometimes taken not to address issues which were felt to be beyond the abilities of the unit or could not be resolved in the time available. These were then left in abeyance to be addressed at a future, unspecified time when and if the young people moved somewhere considered to be more appropriate. This meant that some of the young people's most serious problems were left untreated and unresolved.

Table 10.1 details the young people for whom specialist assessments had been undertaken before or following their admission to secure accommodation and therapeutic interventions provided in the secure unit. The nature of these assessments and interventions will be described and the young people's views of the services they received will be examined.

Table 10.1 Specialist assessments and therapeutic interventions provided for young people before or during their placements in secure accommodation by legal status

Assessments and interventions	Welfare	Convicted offender	Unconvicted offender	No.	%
Specialist assessment	4	3	0	7	24
Specialist assessment and intervention	5	1*	1*	7	24
Therapeutic intervention	3	3	0	6	21
No assessment or intervention	5	1	3	9	31
Total	17	8	4	29	100

*Referred for therapy although no work had started at the time of the study.

Welfare Admissions

ASSESSMENT

Specialist psychiatric or psychological assessments were undertaken with nine young people, five of whom also received ongoing therapeutic interventions. Assessments were undertaken with four young people following their admission to secure accommodation by the psychologist attached to the unit, with two young people by psychiatrists during earlier hospital in-patient treatment and with three young people prior to admission by psychiatrists attached to child and family psychiatric units.

SPECIALIST SERVICES

In addition to the above five, specialist services were provided for a further three young people. These eight young people, placed in four units, were provided with one or more services described as individual therapy (for five), rape crisis counselling (for two), drug and alcohol counselling (for three), domestic violence counselling (for one). The focus of the individual therapy was not clear in most cases, and there appeared to be a lack of information about the work available to staff providing the day-to-day care. Five young people admitted through this route on the basis of their need for treatment had not engaged in specialist assessments or been provided with any therapeutic intervention.

CRITIQUE

From this examination of the interventions provided to the young people it is evident that the problems which led to the admission of most of them, such as sexual and physical abuse, running away, prostitution, deliberate self-harm, drug and alcohol use, were only partly addressed by their placement. Arguably, such problems cannot be resolved by placement in secure accommodation, although it appears that the needs which lay behind these problems were also hardly addressed. Furthermore, it has already been shown that the self-harming behaviour of some young people increased because they were forced to confront past experiences or memories without therapeutic support in an environment which deprived them of their usual coping mechanisms and reinforced their sense of guilt and shame. This must be a matter of particular concern when part of the justification for the placement of many of those who had histories of running away and self-harm was that they needed to be stabilized in order that work could be undertaken with them.

Of the 17 young people admitted through this route, 13 had previous admissions to secure accommodation. Many of them felt that the harm they suffered from the placement in secure accommodation outweighed the benefit they may have gained and some felt that they had gained nothing. Some of the eight young people who received specialist interventions were able to identify some positive benefits, but these were generally seen as benefits from the therapeutic intervention, rather than from the placement. Some young people benefited from individual therapy. For example, Jenny had sessions with a counsellor arranged by her social worker, which were planned to continue following her release from the unit. Jenny felt that apart from this counselling she had gained nothing from her placements and that the experiences had been harmful to her. Her social worker was equally pessimistic that her needs had been addressed by her placements in secure accommodation.

Convicted Offender

ASSESSMENT

Two girls were convicted of violent offences. Only one had had a psychiatric assessment which was undertaken for the court. Specialist assessments had been undertaken with two boys convicted of sexual offences, one by the psychiatrist attached to a young offender institution and the other following admission by the psychologist attached to the secure unit. No specialist intervention was planned with either of them, because of their denial of the offences. A psychiatric assessment had also been undertaken with a boy convicted of armed robbery prior to the offence for which he was convicted. It was unclear whether the secure unit had access to this assessment, which in any event was out of date. No specialist assessments were undertaken with the other boys who had been convicted of offences.

SPECIALIST SERVICES

Individual therapy had been arranged for one girl by her social worker and a referral had been made for the other girl, although no work had begun. Specialist drug and alcohol counselling was arranged for two boys and one of them was also provided with anger management and bereavement counselling as his father died during his stay in the unit. Another boy, who had been convicted of arson, had been referred to an arson project run by the local fire service and his social worker was supporting an appeal against sentence and aiming to engage him in family therapy with his mother and siblings.

CRITIQUE

Eight young people had been admitted through this route and were at different stages of their sentences. Four of them were receiving specialist services. For example, Adrian said he had benefited from drug and alcohol counselling but acknowledged that he would be returning to a lifestyle in which he would resume using alcohol and drugs.

The girl who had been provided with individual therapy said that the work had helped her. However, she had not addressed many of the issues related to her offence and she had become depressed and her deliberate self-harming had increased. She expressed suicidal and violent feelings which she felt had increased during her time in secure accommodation. The other girl who had not begun any therapeutic work said that all her needs could have been more appropriately met in an open unit and that the need for her to be punished had taken precedence over all her other needs. She felt that her placement in secure accommodation had compounded her sense of loss, and the trauma of the offence she had committed.

In summary, while the requirements for security and punishment were met by the placement it appears that from the perspectives of the young people, their other needs arising from their offences and their childhood experiences were addressed in a limited way (for four young people) or not at all.

Unconvicted Offender

ASSESSMENT/SPECIALIST SERVICES

No specialist psychiatric or psychological assessments were arranged with the three boys on remand and no work was undertaken in relation to their offending behaviour, even though two of them were charged with serious violent offences and one with arson. The focus of the work which was undertaken by their social workers related to their preparation for court, and the prospect of further custody. A psychiatric assessment was arranged for the young woman on remand by her social worker as part of the legal proceedings.

CRITIQUE

No therapeutic intervention was offered to the three boys. The requirement of custody pending their trials was met and work was undertaken by their social workers in relation to the preparation of reports for court and preparation for custody. The primary benefit of the secure accommodation placement was seen in it providing an alternative to custody in a young offender institution. None of them felt they should be locked up and two of them found the regime and level of surveillance in the unit oppressive. The needs of the girl on remand were addressed by her social worker who arranged a psychiatric assessment and proposed a care plan which included a specialist community foster placement and arrangements for individual therapy. She felt that she had benefited from this work and that the placement in secure accommodation had provided her with safety.

In summary, the primary reason for admission, to provide containment pending trial of their alleged offences, was met by the secure unit. Other needs were addressed by the social workers or not focused on at all during the placement.

Critique of Specialist Services and Therapeutic Interventions

What is striking from this review of the specialist services provided to the young people, is the limited nature of the work undertaken and the lack of attention given to the problems which resulted in their admission to secure accommodation and to the needs arising from their adverse experiences in childhood. It emerged that therapeutic or specialist services were mostly regarded by secure unit staff and placing local authorities as an optional extra to the main work in secure accommodation, that is the work undertaken by the staff, particularly the key/link workers.

It is notable that this state of affairs is not substantially different from that which pertains to the provision of therapeutic services for children in non-secure residential care (Berridge and Brodie 1998; Sinclair *et al.* 1995). However, while the difficulties in the provision of therapeutic services may be similar in secure and non-secure care, professionals and the courts have higher expectations of secure accommodation, which as already suggested presents itself as offering excellence in residential care and custody. As already noted, it is an expensive resource and its cost effectiveness should be a matter of debate. These findings call into question one of the justifications for placement in secure accommodation of many young people, particularly those admitted through the welfare route, which is so they can be 'available' for treatment they had been unreceptive to in the community. Furthermore, Farmer and Pollock (1998) found that therapeutic input did not in itself ensure good behavioural outcomes and the context in which the therapeutic help was offered was of considerable importance. The best outcome in terms of behaviour was for those who had been helped to explore their difficult experiences both in a therapeutic relationship and with caregivers in their everyday lives. It is therefore important to examine the staff and particularly the key workers' intervention with the young people, both in terms of the direct work undertaken by them with young people in the absence of therapeutic intervention, and in supporting young people in dealing with the difficulties in their everyday lives.

Staff and Key/Link Worker Intervention

All the units emphasized the importance of their behaviour programmes and regarded these as providing the primary focus for work with the young people. As already shown, in all the units one or two key/link workers were allocated to young people. They were expected to construct the young people's individual care plans and take a key role in decision-making about them, have a greater level of contact and awareness of their needs and problems and work with young people to resolve them. Variation emerged in the role and the practice of the key/link workers. There were differences in the levels of their knowledge of the young people, in the frequency of their contact with them and in their training and expertise which would equip them to meet the young people's needs. There were also differences in the work they undertook with young people which ranged from watching television programmes with them to more focused work and individual meetings. It seemed to be generally accepted among the professionals involved with young people that the quality of the keyworker was the main determining factor in whether young people would be engaged in any effective work. However, keyworker allocation appeared to be arbitrary without any 'matching' on the basis of needs or relationship. The only guiding principle which was evident in two mixed-gender units was that where possible female keyworkers should be allocated to girls. Many of the young people were not clear what they could expect of their keyworkers and the significant level of mistrust of staff which emerged extended to keyworkers. There appeared to be little if any formal evaluation of the quality of the work that was undertaken by keyworkers.

The quality of relationships between young people and staff were influenced by factors such as the reasons for young people's admission, their length of stay in the secure unit and the attitudes of staff towards enforcing control and the use of sanctions, as well as individual personalities. A number of important and overlapping themes emerged from the examination of the young people's views of the staff and their keyworkers which will be examined below.

INADEQUATE STAFFING

The first emergent theme related to the constraints and additional restrictions suffered by young people when there were insufficient staff on duty. This had implications for keyworker availability, restrictions on activities and on arrangements and opportunities for mobility. Many young people talked about these problems and identified additional difficulties when there were insufficient female staff on duty in mixed-gender units, which has already been examined from the perspectives of the staff.

LACK OF TRUST IN STAFF

An important theme related to the young people's lack of trust in staff. This mistrust appears to have inhibited many young people in their engagement with keyworkers. Young people expressed concern about the level of expertise and understanding of the staff, they voiced doubts about whether the staff had the ability to help them and also whether their personal difficulties would be accorded confidentiality and respect. This is a matter of concern. First, keyworkers provide the only opportunity for many young people in secure units who are not provided with specialist therapeutic intervention to have help with their difficulties, and second, for those who are receiving therapeutic intervention, it is important that they are able to explore their difficulties with caregivers in their everyday lives as well as in a therapeutic relationship (Farmer and Pollock 1998).

One of the young people who felt let down by the two keyworkers allocated to her explained her problem. She experienced difficulty in gaining their time and attention and expressed concerns about whether she could trust them to understand her problems:

> I would prefer to have a full-time female keyworker as my keyworkers at the moment work part time and they're never available and I don't think the people here are trained or experienced enough and I don't think they understand.

Another girl expressed helplessness at the lack of interest of staff. She complained about their lack of understanding of her distress at being locked up, and their power to punish, which she felt was exercised too freely:

> They don't listen to me, like I'm meant to have a key session with a keyworker but I've only had one in all the time I've been here and then she was talking about her kids ... I try to talk to them and they don't listen and then when they don't listen I get angry and then they punish me for it, they sanction me, they say, 'Right, that's it, you're going to your room' and restrain me and put me in my room ... it got to the extent that I wanted to kill myself ... one time I was really upset and I said I needed to talk to someone about something and they said 'yeah, yeah' and it got later and later and then it was time for bed ... but then nothing's kept personal that you tell them anyway.

The integrity and honesty of staff was questioned by some young people. For example, one girl was shocked by what she regarded as staff hypocrisy:

> Although it's the staff's job to be nice to people, I now realize that it's not real ... for instance the two girls who went [absconded] the other day, the staff were normal with them when they were here, the same as everyone else but now that one of those girls has gone they can't express how much they're glad she's gone and they hope she doesn't come back ... They say in conversation about where the

> girls are and some will say, 'well I'm not really bothered because they're never going to learn' and other comments like that ... I think, oh God, I wonder what they're going to say about me when I have gone.

CONFIDENTIALITY

The third, related issue concerned the lack of confidentiality afforded to young people and the likelihood that any information that they shared would be shared in the unit or used in future court proceedings or an equivalent forum, to their own detriment or incrimination. Young people's concerns about the lack of staff and peer confidentiality in the units were described in the last chapter.

UNEQUAL POWER RELATIONSHIPS

The final issue concerned the power relationships between staff and young people and the inconsistent way in which power was exercised and punishments imposed. Several young people felt that some staff would even seek opportunities to make life more difficult for them. For example, one boy who was serving a long sentence highlighted the differences in attitude and inconsistencies in practice between individual members of staff and described the way in which some members of staff abused their power:

> Some of the staff have got different opinions about certain things, some of them will let you get away with some things and when you say something to another they will immediately room you ... One of the members of staff said to me 'We can call you an idiot but if you say something to us, we can just lock you up in your room', I thought that was just taking the piss out of us ... They think they're better than us and it makes you feel angry because they think they can get away with saying things ... The staff swear at you all the time and if you swear back at them, they'll room you.

Although a majority of young people expressed negative views about staff there were some who felt that they had gained most from their relationship with their keyworkers or other members of staff. The most positive views were expressed by some of the convicted offenders who were serving long sentences, although a few of those admitted through the welfare route were also positive about individual members of staff. For example, Adrian talked to his keyworkers about the difficulties he experienced in the unit, to avoid getting himself into trouble with his peers and other members of staff, and Mandy said:

> [They] are like second parents to me and they're only the second adults I've ever trusted in children's homes ... I get to talk about things and not build them up inside so much, although I still do.

Conclusion

This chapter has continued the exploration of the young people's experiences in secure accommodation and examined the therapeutic interventions and support provided to meet their needs. In this study, it emerged that the problems which led to young people's admission to secure accommodation were addressed to only a very limited extent, if at all, in the secure units. Moreover, the difficulties already faced by some young people were compounded by their placement in secure accommodation. Almost one third of the young people received *no* specialist assessment or therapeutic intervention to help them with their difficulties, while a specialist assessment and ongoing therapeutic intervention had been provided for less than a quarter of them. The provision of therapeutic interventions to young people in secure accommodation is a matter of considerable concern and the findings from this small sample suggest that a review is needed of the existing structures and arrangements for services to ensure that young people receive the help which they need.

Furthermore, it has been shown that therapeutic input in itself does not ensure good behavioural outcomes. The context within which therapeutic help is provided is also important and young people need good care-giver support to explore their difficulties in their everyday lives, as well as in therapeutic relationships (Farmer and Pollock 1998). In this respect, the secure units emphasized the importance of the key/link workers. However, many young people in this study expressed a high level of mistrust in staff and keyworkers which prevented them from engaging in relationships or work in the units, even where staff had the expertise to provide it. This might be explained by the conflict which was evident in the units between the philosophies of care and control. Control and security appeared to dominate over therapeutic relationships and over good care-giver support, suggesting that the language of treatment and welfare which is used may not represent the reality of practice in the units.

The inadequacy of therapeutic services and relationships for young people observed in this study might partly explain the poor outcomes for young people leaving secure accommodation which have been noted in other studies (for example Kelly 1992; Millham *et al.* 1978). The next chapter will examine the social workers' and the young people's evaluations of their placements in secure accommodation and of their prospects for the future.

ELEVEN

Evaluation and Outcomes

Introduction

In previous chapters, the young people's lives before and during their placements in secure accommodation have been explored and their multiple needs and problems examined. In this chapter, young people's views of themselves will be considered through an examination of their self-concepts and levels of self-esteem. Second, the young people's and the social workers' evaluations of the placement in secure accommodation will be summarized and finally the social workers' assessments of the future prospects for the young people will be considered. Although it was not the aim of this study to examine the longer-term outcomes for young people, the short-term outcomes of almost a third of them are known and will be examined.

Self-Concept and Self-Esteem

The importance of the developing self-concept and positive self-esteem for young people has already been discussed. In the interviews with young people, their self-concepts were explored and the self-perception profile for adolescents (Harter 1988) was administered with all but one of them. This profile was chosen because it contains nine separate subscales, addressing eight specific domains as well as global self-worth (the extent to which one likes oneself as a person, is generally happy with the way one is and the way one is leading one's life). Assessing global self-worth separately from the specific domains enables an examination of the relationship between global self-worth and the domain-specific perceptions of competence. It is predicted that where young people feel competent in specific domains which they judge to be important, they will have an accompanying self-worth that is high. In contrast, where young people feel that certain areas are important but their competence in these areas is low, that will result in low self-worth. The scores are rated from 1 (low) to 4 (high).

Harter (1988) designed this profile for young people aged 13–16 years and she administered it with eight sample groups living in neighbourhoods ranging from lower to upper middle class in Colorado, USA. The sample sizes ranged from 35 to 180 and 90 per cent of her subjects were Caucasian. The small sample group in this study is clearly not directly comparable with Harter's samples, but nonetheless it is interesting to compare the pattern of findings within the different samples.

Gender differences in self-esteem have consistently been reported with lower self-worth in girls, both globally and in specific domains (Block and Robbins 1993; Bolognini *et al.* 1996; Harter 1985) and these will be explored as a matter of particular interest. In addition, as the majority of the boys had committed criminal offences while most of the girls had experience in the care system, differences on the basis of admission route and the type of behaviour which led to their admission will be examined.

Self-Perception Profile

Harter (1988) suggests that the global self-worth of young people who feel competent in the areas they judge to be important and who have good social support will be about 3.5 on the scale. In contrast, the global self-worth of young people who rate themselves as having low competence in areas judged to be important and who have low social support will be around 2.0. In this study, it is noteworthy that nine girls but none of the boys scored 2.0 or below, two of whom scored the lowest possible, that is 1.0.

The findings from the self-perception profile revealed differences on the basis of gender, legal admission route and the type of behaviour. The mean scores generally fluctuate around 2.8, which is above the mid-point on the scale but lower than the mean scores found by Harter. It is also of note that the behavioural conduct sub-scale is notably lower than the other domains for both boys and girls, which might be predicted for young people who have been locked up as a consequence of their behaviour. Harter found that close friendship was invariably rated the highest, which is also the case in this group. However, while Harter consistently found that girls see themselves as more adequate than boys in the domain of close friendship with an average difference of 0.2, in this sample the opposite finding emerged with the boys rating themselves more highly (average difference of 0.2). The results from this study also demonstrate other gender differences with the boys rating themselves higher in each specific domain, with the single exception of scholastic competence, where the girls rated themselves higher (average difference of 0.2). While Harter found that girls consistently rate their athletic competence lower than do boys with an average difference of 0.5 as well as their physical appearance with an average difference of 0.4, in this study the differences were greater at 0.8 and 1.3 respectively. With regard to global self-worth, she found that girls see themselves as less adequate than boys with an average difference of 0.2. In this study the difference was again greater at 1.0. In summary, while the pattern of gender differences identified by Harter was generally reflected here, the degree of the difference between boys and girls was greater.

The differences between young people on the basis of their admission routes are also of interest. The global self-worth of those admitted through the criminal justice routes was higher than those admitted through the welfare route. This finding is perhaps predictable given the gender differences in admission routes which have already been established. However, the analysis also shows differences between the two criminal justice routes with those convicted of serious offences rating themselves more highly than those on remand awaiting trial. The global self-worth and domain mean scores can be found in the appendices.

CORRELATIONS BETWEEN SUB-SCALES

As already noted, Harter (1987,1988) designed this scale for adolescents aged 13–16 years and she administered it with school children in the USA. She found correlations between specific domains and global self-worth, most notably that physical appearance is consistently and highly related to self-worth. This means that the discrepancy between the importance ascribed to being good looking and one's actual evaluation of one's appearance has a major impact on overall sense of self-worth. This may be predictable in the Western cultural context, which lays emphasis on physical appearance and dress code, particularly for adolescents, and Harter's finding was replicated in this study. To examine the correlations in this study bivariate analysis was undertaken using Microsoft Excel and SPSS (Bryman and Cramer 1990). In respect of the 28 subjects in the study who completed self-perception profile questionnaires, the correlation (Pearson coefficient) between physical appearance and global self-worth was statistically significant ($p<0.01$).

Harter found that scholastic competence, social acceptance, close friendship, romantic appeal and behavioural conduct bear moderate relationship to self-worth whereas athletic and job competence are less highly related to self-worth. In this study, correlations were also found between global self-worth and other domains which were statistically significant at lower levels. These were behavioural conduct ($p<0.03$) and athletic competence ($p<0.09$). An examination of gender differences revealed a stronger correlation between behavioural conduct and global self-worth for the boys ($p<0.01$) while the correlation between social acceptance and global self-worth was significant only for the girls and at a lower level ($p<0.04$).

Behaviours and Self-Worth

It has been shown that while diverse behaviours and problems resulted in the admission of young people through the different legal routes, the differences between them were subsumed following their placement in secure accommodation. Although it has been shown that such aggregation is unhelpful because different 'career routes' mean that needs, outcomes and likely long-term life chances are different (Bullock *et al.* 1998; Farmer and Pollock 1998) young people continue to be treated the same, irrespective of their legal status or the reason for admission (Harris and Timms 1993). Disaggregation is important so that individual needs and problems can be identified, appropriate care and therapeutic interventions can be provided in the units and suitable alternatives to secure accommodation can be found. Analysis was undertaken of the differences in the self-concept of young people on the basis of their behaviours, disaggregating the categories of offender and non-offender into sexual offenders, violent offenders, non-violent offenders, those at risk, prostitutes and those deliberately self-harming. Although there are overlaps, for example some of those in the prostitutes group were also self-harming, they were grouped on the basis of the primary problem, apart from running away, which resulted in their admission. The sexual and violent offenders had the highest mean global self-worth scores while the prostitutes and those who were self-harming had the lowest scores. The young people's self-perception profile ratings were highly consistent with their descriptions of themselves. Some examples illustrate some of the factors which contributed to enhance or diminish their level of self-esteem.

SEXUAL OFFENDERS

The self-worth scores of the two boys convicted of sexual offences produced the highest mean score on the self-perception profile. Both these boys denied the offences, they did not see themselves as offenders, they were not engaged in any offence-related work and they talked about appeals against their convictions and of the possibility of early release. Both of them achieved high global self-worth by promoting the importance of domains in which they were successful (scholastic and athletic) and discounting those domains in which their achievement was low (Harter 1987). For example, although Rory said that his sense of himself had been changed by his conviction and placement in secure accommodation, he expressed confidence in himself and his ability, emotionally and educationally, to come through his experience:

> Before this I wouldn't care what people around were saying about me but now if people are saying lies about me I get really wound up because I'm in here for people saying lies about me ... I've been found guilty of one of the most serious crimes and I haven't done it ... and unless I can find new evidence for an appeal against conviction I'm going to have this conviction on my back for the rest

> of my life … people are always trying to put you down so when I get out I'm going to make sure I'm my own person and do well … I'm going to do everything I can in the future to make sure that my life is good.

VIOLENT OFFENDERS

Some of the boys in this group appeared to have taken on a criminal identity and actually described themselves as criminals. They appear to have gained some self-esteem from this identity, which is reflected in relatively high mean scores on the profile. In contrast, one girl was struggling to hold on to her concept of herself as separate from the offence she had committed of which she was ashamed, reflected in her self-worth score on the profile which was way below the mid point at 1.2. She said:

> I'm stupid and I hate myself … how could I have been so sick as to have been there … There's two sides to me, there isn't just one of me. I'm here, I'm one person and people sometimes don't see both of me, they see what they want to see and forget what else there is to see … it's like people look at me in here, especially the staff because they know what I've done, and they don't see me as the person who's getting her life sorted out, they see me as the one who's committed the offence. So just by looking at me you can see there's two sides, the offence isn't me, there's more to me, look inside before you think what you want to think of me.

Several young people appeared to have gained in self-esteem as a consequence of the positive changes they perceived in themselves during their placement. For example, Adrian said:

> When I started drinking …, I would get very aggressive and violent … maybe being locked up … is the best thing that could ever happen to me, not the part that I've killed someone and I'll never forgive myself for that … I'm not so violent, I have feelings for other people and not just myself … It has helped me a great deal … My attitude has got a lot better… I understand that you've got to have respect for people out in the world, not just yourself.

DELIBERATE SELF-HARM

Three of the five young people in this group had self-worth scores at or below 2.0 on the self-perception profile, and these low scores were reflected in their negative descriptions of themselves. Most of them expressed feelings of worthlessness which seem to have been reinforced by a strong sense of isolation. A consistent theme which emerged related to their need to have someone to talk to, someone who they felt would really listen and care and understand the difficulties they were experiencing. This was illustrated by Jane who expressed feelings of worthlessness and talked about how let down she felt by the adults who were caring for her:

> I wanted to kill myself … my friends at school tried to help but they couldn't do much and my mum weren't no good … I just wanted someone to talk to, I did need help but nobody would help me … when I told the staff I was depressed they said 'Oh you don't know the meaning of the word, we're depressed' … I feel like killing myself, I feel like the world was going to swallow me up, I still feel like that.

PROSTITUTES

Two of the girls in this group had the lowest possible scores on the self-perception profile. Their descriptions of themselves were similar and consistent with these scores. For example, Karen said:

> I feel as though I'm not worth nothing … I would describe myself as a no-hoper really, I'm selfish, I think I'm dirty and it just hurts to think that's how it really is … I don't like nothing about myself, that's why I cut myself, I cut myself all the time when I get depressed.

However, the girl who had the highest score in this group which was above the mid point, said that placement in secure accommodation had made her angry, which had helped to change her view of herself. She felt that in being locked up, she had been treated with a lack of respect which had made her realize that she was worth respect:

> I'm a person and I deserve respect and I respect myself also and that I can be a somebody ... I'll make sure that I never get myself in a situation where I'm going to have to come back into secure.

Evaluation of the Placement

In earlier chapters, the young people's experiences in the secure units were explored and the social workers' perspectives on the gains for young people from their placements considered. Their evaluations of the placements will now be examined to identify whether young people and their social workers felt that secure accommodation had improved their circumstances. Thirteen young people had previous admissions to secure accommodation which may be seen as evidence that it had failed to meet their needs, change their behaviour and protect them from the risks which had led to their admission, other than by containment on a short-term basis. Bullock and his colleagues (1998) found that the strategy most likely to achieve improvement for young people was the treatment regime together with interventions matched to individual needs and that those who gained little or nothing from their secure placements fared relatively badly in the long term. Similarly, Farmer and Pollock (1998) found that the best outcome in terms of behaviour was for those who had been helped to explore their difficult experiences both in a therapeutic relationship and in their everyday lives.

The young people and their social workers were asked to evaluate the placements on the basis of whether young people had benefited from the behavioural regime in the unit and keyworker input or therapeutic interventions provided to meet their needs, and whether things had improved or were improving as a consequence of their stay in secure accommodation. As there were notable gender differences, boys and girls will be considered separately first. Analysis of the groups of behaviours which led to admission and the secure units in which young people were placed will then be examined.

Boys

Five of the eleven boys felt they had gained some benefit from the work they had undertaken to address their problems during their stay in secure accommodation and that things had improved or were improving for them. Four of their social workers agreed with their evaluations. The social worker of the fifth boy thought that he was benefiting only in so far as secure accommodation provided a less harsh regime than a young offender institution. One social worker felt that a boy was benefiting from the work he was undertaking in the placement, although the boy himself did not share this view. The remaining four boys and their social workers did not feel they had benefited from the placement in secure accommodation. In summary, four boys (36%) and their social workers agreed on their evaluation of the placement as beneficial.

Girls

Of the eighteen girls, 5 (27%) felt that they had gained or were gaining some benefit from their placement and that things had improved or were improving for them. Their social workers also felt that they were benefiting in some way from their placement. Thirteen girls did not assess their placements as beneficial in terms of the regimes or interventions provided and did not feel that things had improved or were improving for them. Ten of the social workers agreed with their assessments while the views of three social workers were not known.

In summary, in the assessment of their social workers and themselves, 9 of the 29 young people, that is less than a third (31%) were benefiting from the regime, keyworker input and/or from therapeutic interventions and their circumstances had improved or were improving as a consequence of their placement in secure accommodation.

Types of Behaviour

An analysis of the social workers' and young people's evaluations of the secure placements on the basis of the types of behaviour which led to their admission reveals some clear differences. While the placement was considered to be beneficial for 42 per cent of convicted and unconvicted offenders, only 23 per cent of those admitted through the welfare route were considered to have gained any benefit from their placement. This may be seen to confirm the view of secure accommodation as a facility catering primarily for offenders. A breakdown of those for whom placements were considered to be beneficial by type of behaviour is shown in Table 11.1.

Table 11.1 Positive evaluation of placement by type of behaviour and gender

Category and number	Male	Female	Total
Sexual offender (n = 2)	1	0	1
Violent offender (n = 8)	2	1	3
Non-Violent offender (n = 2)	0	1	1
Total offenders (n = 12)	3	2	5
At risk (n = 8)	0	2	2
Deliberate self-harm (n = 5)	1	0	1
Prostitutes (n = 4)	0	1	1
Total non-offenders (n = 17)	1	3	4

Secure Units

An examination of the relationship between the six secure units and the nine young people for whom the placement was considered to be beneficial reveals an interesting pattern which may illustrate the differences between units. It emerged that two thirds of the young people who participated in the study placed in one unit were considered to have benefited and their circumstances to have improved compared with just over one third in another unit, a quarter in two units and none in two units. An alternative interpretation is that nearly half of the young people in the study who were considered to have benefited from the placement or from therapeutic interventions were accommodated in one unit.

Prospects for the Future

There are many personal, family and social factors which influence the quality of outcome and future prospects for young people apart from whether their placement in secure accommodation was helpful and improved their circumstances. There are also questions about appropriate time-scales for assessing outcomes for children (DH 1991b; Parker *et al.* 1991). The need to focus on intermediate as well as long-term or final outcomes has been established and the importance has been highlighted of 'micro-outcomes' which are synonymous with daily interventions which influence, positively or negatively, longer-term outcomes. In essence, then, the everyday experiences of the young people of the regimes and interventions provided in the secure units can be seen as a kind of outcome, which influences intermediate and longer-term outcomes. It is not the intention here to try to predict the outcomes for these young people as others have done (Bullock *et al.* 1998). The focus of interest is the young people's own feelings about their future prospects, together with those of their social workers whose evaluations were based on their knowledge of the young people, their families and communities and the resources and therapeutic interventions available for them. The factors which they noted as important in whether young people would achieve or sustain the change in behaviour necessary for them to live safely and happily were family (or substitute family) support, educational or employment opportunities, the provision of therapeutic intervention and the individual's determination and ability to withstand peer pressures.

There were striking gender differences in the social workers' evaluations of the young people's future prospects. Six of the eleven boys were judged to have good or relatively good prospects. All of these had been admitted through criminal justice routes. Five were violent offenders and one was a non-violent offender. It is interesting to note that the secure accommodation placements had been assessed as beneficial for only two of these boys, both of them violent offenders. The prospects for a further three boys were thought to be uncertain, as they rested on the provision of appropriate therapeutic intervention and substitute family placements. Two of these were sexual offenders and the third was in the at risk group. The placements were judged to be beneficial for two of them. Two boys were thought by their social workers to have very poor prospects in that they were likely to be isolated from family support, to have little or no educational prospects and to drift into criminality. One of these was a violent offender and the other was in the self-harming group. The placement in secure accommodation had been assessed as beneficial in respect of the second of these boys.

In contrast, only two of the fifteen girls about whom social workers expressed a view were thought to have good prospects for the future. These two girls, one a violent offender and the other a non-violent offender, were admitted to secure accommodation through criminal justice routes and their placements were assessed as beneficial. The prospects for a third girl who was in the at risk group were considered to be in the balance as she was to be placed with a substitute family. Her placement had also been assessed as beneficial. The other twelve girls were all thought by their social workers to have very poor prospects for the future although the placements in secure accommodation had been assessed as beneficial for two of them. Four girls were in the prostitutes group, five were at risk of sexual harm, exploitation or offending and three girls were in the deliberate self-harm group. All these girls were thought likely to return to prostitution, to other living situations considered unsafe or unsuitable, to continue running away, to become involved in criminal activity and be placed in custody or to require in-patient psychiatric care.

It is interesting to contrast these findings with those of Bullock and his colleagues (1998) that outcomes for girls leaving secure treatment centres are generally better than for boys, although it is of note that their indicators of the best outcomes for girls are marriage and children.

The young people's evaluations of their future prospects were mixed, reflecting the diversity in the group. Some of them could not see beyond the current placement in secure accommodation and expressed great anxiety about what would happen in the future. Most of them felt that their lives would be severely affected by the behaviour, both criminal and non-criminal, which had led to them being in secure accommodation and the majority of them expressed their awareness of their stigmatization and 'otherness'. Only a small minority expressed positive feelings about the future and a sense that they had some control and power to exercise choice and determine what would happen to them.

Some common concerns emerged which related to: the difficulties and fears of returning to living in the community after lengthy stays in institutional care; the difficulty of achieving or sustaining change particularly for those who were anticipating a return to the same situations from which they had been admitted; limited employment opportunities as a consequence both of their poor educational achievements and their criminal convictions; lack of social support and isolation; and problems in relationships with family and friends. Many young people voiced serious doubts about their ability to lead a 'normal' life with people to love and care for, to stay out of trouble and be happy. Several of them expressed suicidal feelings and a sense of powerlessness to achieve change and hopelessness about the future. Some of them talked in terms of their life being 'ruined' and a number of young people said that they wished that they could start their life over again. For example, Adrian said 'I'd go back to my childhood and change every bit of it' and Jenny said 'I wish I could start the whole thing all over again'.

Short-Term Outcomes

What happens to young people following their release from secure accommodation may provide some indication of the effectiveness of the placement in meeting their needs, helping them to change their behaviour and improve their circumstances and life-chances. Whilst no formal follow-up of young people was undertaken following their release from the secure units, information was obtained about what happened to nine, that is almost a third of them, who were transferred to other custodial provision, released or ran away. Two were boys who had been admitted to secure accommodation on remand who were convicted at trial, given custodial sentences and transferred to young offender institutions. Neither of them were judged to have benefited from their placement in secure accommodation. Their social workers assessed the future prospects of one of them as good in spite of his custodial sentence and the other as poor.

The other seven were girls who had been admitted through the welfare route, five of whom had previous admissions to secure accommodation. As already discussed, the exit plans for many of those admitted through the welfare route are often inadequate, frequently returning young people to the same situations, risks and problems from which they were admitted. This can result in a 'revolving door' in and out of secure accommodation. Only one of the girls was thought to have gained any benefit from the secure accommodation placement and the social workers assessed all the girls' future prospects as very poor. Their circumstances will be summarized.

Jamila ran away from the secure unit a week before the secure order ended. This was her third admission to secure accommodation and she had run away from all three placements. It seems likely that she would have returned to live with her brother or sisters, two of whom were working as prostitutes. Anna was admitted to secure accommodation following an overdose of heroin. She returned to live with her boyfriend and it was thought likely that she would have resumed her drug use and be at risk of sexual exploitation. Jane also returned to live with her boyfriend, an older man who was thought to sexually exploit her and encourage her drug use. Both girls had been admitted to secure accommodation with the aim of separating them from these men.

The remaining four were young women who had been admitted to secure accommodation because of their involvement in prostitution. Vicki returned to the same children's home in which she had previously lived, despite her expressed wish to move to a different area away from the influence of pimps. She resumed working as a prostitute, in the company of her two sisters. She was also reported to have taken another girl from the children's home with her working on the streets. Karen also resumed working as a prostitute and her social worker was considering making application for a placement in the Youth Treatment Centre. Immediately after her release from secure accommodation Roberta ran away. Her social worker felt that after multiple placements in secure accommodation, none of which had met her needs, no further applications could be made. Jessica also ran away from the children's home in which she was placed, a week after release from secure accommodation. Jessica's needs had not been met by placement in secure accommodation and her social worker said no further secure placement would be sought.

The short-term outcomes for these young people following their release from secure accommodation are not encouraging. It appears that the placements were ineffective in terms of achieving change in the behaviour which had directly led to the girls' admission and that they failed to provide the interventions to meet the girls' emotional needs. It might be argued that the use of secure accommodation as a crisis response for non-offenders is only justifiable if it provides a basis from which to set up therapeutic intervention to achieve meaningful change. Caution has been expressed against seeing secure accommodation as the 'solution' rather than a temporary opportunity within which solutions can be sought (Harris and Timms 1993). All these young women were back where they started. It could be argued that, at best, placement in secure accommodation was an extremely expensive but pointless intervention which interrupted the pattern of their lives but achieved nothing. But it may be even worse than that, because for many young people the placement not only did not help them, it may have caused them further harm by compounding their difficulties. Due weight must be given to the oppressive and stigmatizing effect of placement in secure accommodation described by some of these young people, for whom 'protection' became punishment and whose trust in professionals was undermined rather than strengthened.

Conclusion

This chapter has examined the self-concepts of the young people through their narratives and a formal measure of domain specific and global self-worth. The self-worth of the girls was lower than the boys, replicating the findings of previous studies. The global self-worth mean scores of the offenders were higher than those of young people admitted for welfare reasons, which partly reflected the gender differences in the groups.

Young people and their social workers evaluated the placements in terms of whether they felt there had been improvements for young people as a consequence of the behavioural regime or the therapeutic interventions provided for them. Nine young people, that is less than one third, were thought to have gained some benefit from the placement. There were marked differences between offenders and non-offenders, with the placements assessed as beneficial for 42 per cent of offenders in contrast with only 23 per cent of non-offenders.

There were also gender differences as 36 per cent of boys but only 27 per cent of girls (18 per cent of whom were offenders) were thought to have benefited from their placements. There were even more striking gender differences in the social workers' assessments of the future prospects for young people, which were judged to be good or relatively good for 54 per cent of the boys but for only 11 per cent of the girls. The short-term outcomes that are known show young people returning to the problems and lifestyles which led to their admission/s to secure accommodation, and support the findings of other studies that secure accommodation generally fails to treat or change behaviour (Harris and Timms 1993; Kelly 1992; Millham *et al.* 1978).

The findings from this small study add weight to the argument that it is extremely difficult, if not impossible, for secure units to create a regime and provide therapeutic interventions that can meet the diverse needs and problems of boys and girls admitted through different legal routes and accommodated together. They support the findings from other studies which have recommended that offenders should be separated from non-offenders and that abused, self-harming and suicidal young people, the majority of whom are girls, should be in specialized health or foster care rather than in secure accommodation (Brogi and Bagley 1998; Littlewood 1996; Millham *et al.* 1978; National Children's Bureau 1995).

Part V
Conclusions

TWELVE

Summary and Conclusions

Introduction

This research was undertaken to provide information about the circumstances of young people in trouble who are imprisoned in secure accommodation through the care and criminal justice systems. The key findings as they relate to the young people, the social workers and the secure units will be summarized and the emerging themes which are of interest for practice, policy and planning will be examined.

The Young People

Of the 29 young people who participated in the study, 41 per cent (12) were admitted because they had been charged with or convicted of serious criminal offences and 59 per cent (17) were admitted because they were considered to be at risk of significant harm. The national gender differences in admission route were reflected in this sample with 83 per cent (15) of the girls admitted for welfare reasons and 81 per cent (9) of the boys admitted through the criminal justice routes. Eleven were placed in single-gender and eighteen in mixed-gender units. Although the numbers are small and so have only limited meaning, there were some other notable gender differences: 94 per cent (17) of the girls but only 36 per cent (4) of the boys had been in state care; 55 per cent (10) of the girls were the subject of interim or care orders in contrast with only 9 per cent (1) of the boys; and 61 per cent (11) of the girls but only 18 per cent (2) of the boys had one or more previous admissions to secure accommodation. Prior to admission to custody or secure accommodation 88 per cent (16) of the girls but only 27 per cent (3) of the boys had been living in residential or foster care. The placement histories in care of the girls were also longer and more complex than those of the boys. On the other hand, 63 per cent (7) of the boys had been on remand in young offender institutions or remand centres.

The pattern of family relationships was also more complex for the girls than the boys: 45 per cent (5) of the boys maintained relationships with both parents and 55 per cent (6) with their mothers only, in contrast with 33 per cent (6) of the girls who maintained contact with both parents and 44 per cent (8) who maintained contact with one parent. The real difference perhaps, is that 22 per cent (4) of the girls had no contact with either parent.

Most of the young people had experienced problems in their education careers. One in five were the subjects of statements under the Education Act, 41 per cent (12) had been permanently excluded from mainstream school, only 10 per cent (3) of whom had received alternative educational provision. This had implications for their social contacts and normal peer relationships as well as their educational development, particularly in the light of research findings that contacts made at school can improve the life chances of children from disadvantaged backgrounds (Quinton and Rutter 1988). There were also significant health issues for the majority: all the girls and 91 per cent (10) of the boys smoked cigarettes; 79 per cent (23) of them used alcohol and 76 per cent (22) used illegal drugs. At least 41 per cent (12) of them also had mental-health needs and had engaged in suicidal behaviour, including deliberate self-harm, a figure comparable with that found among young people in non-secure residential care (for example, Sinclair and Gibbs 1996, 1998).

The adverse childhood experiences of the majority of these young people were severe: 51 per cent (15) of them had witnessed and become involved in serious violence between their parents; 65 per cent (19) reported physical abuse or ill-treatment by their parents and 50 per cent

(9) of the girls although none of the boys reported sexual abuse, rape or sexual exploitation. Many of them had also suffered the loss of significant relationships with parents, grandparents, siblings and others through death or loss of contact, and at least two girls had miscarried or terminated a pregnancy. Furthermore, many of their parents had experienced adversity in childhood and adulthood which might have affected the quality of their parenting (Quinton and Rutter 1988). Moreover, it is likely that this is an incomplete picture, as information about the young people's adverse experiences emerged in their narratives rather than in response to specific questions about adversity.

The experiences of the young people in this study support findings from previous research which show that admission to care may compound children's adverse experiences and itself constitutes a risk factor increasing the chance of running away, involvement in crime and prostitution and admission to secure accommodation or custody (DH 1997a; Farmer and Pollock 1998; Millham *et al.* 1978; Rowe *et al.* 1989; Sinclair and Gibbs 1998; Stein 1993).

Circumstances Resulting in Admission

Eight young people (27%) were admitted to secure accommodation following convictions for serious non-violent, violent or sexual offences. The two girls, but none of the boys, had committed their offences whilst living in local authority residential care and one was the subject of a care order. Four young people (14%) were placed in secure accommodation on remand; the three boys had been living with their families and the girl had run away from local authority accommodation.

Running away was the main factor in the admission of the 17 young people admitted through the welfare route, which would be expected as it is the main criteria for welfare admissions. Additional factors related to risk of sexual harm and prostitution (for the girls), violence, alcohol and drug use, suicidal behaviour including deliberate self-harm and taking cars (for the boys). Eleven of these (65%) were the subjects of interim or care orders and sixteen (94%) had been living in state care. It emerged that prostitution and the risk of sexual harm were factors in the admission of almost all the 15 girls, while there were no equivalent concerns expressed about any of the boys.

A striking theme which emerged in this study was young people running away from homes and institutions to escape abuse or violence, facing new risks and being revictimized in care or on the streets, and incarceration in secure accommodation being used by professionals as the ultimate solution to running away and its associated risks. Important questions to investigate were whether placement in secure accommodation provided an appropriate and effective response to these young people, whether it provided the required protection and whether it helped to resolve running away and change behaviour such as prostitution and deliberate self harm.

Experiences in Secure Accommodation

The emphasis on security and control in the secure units meant that all the young people experienced their placement as a punishment. Those admitted through the criminal justice routes generally regarded secure accommodation as a preferable alternative to other forms of custody but confusion was evident among those admitted through the welfare route about the purpose of their placements. While they were told they were there for care and protection, they experienced the loss of their freedom, the high levels of control and surveillance and the imposition of sanctions as punitive. They were also aware that they were accommodated with and treated the same as young people convicted of serious offences, some of which such as rape and violent assault they had previously been the victims. Ironically, this resulted in those admitted through the welfare route generally feeling *more* punished and stigmatized by their placement than those admitted through the criminal justice routes for whom punishment was an explicit objective of the placement.

Two thirds of the young people thought that offenders and non-offenders should be accommodated separately in units, or in different units. It is perhaps to be expected that those admitted through the welfare route would have views about this issue, but almost two thirds of the convicted offenders also favoured separate placements and there were significant ways in which they, as well as those admitted through the welfare route, felt disadvantaged by current practice. The conflict between the philosophies of care and custody appeared to leave all the young people feeling aggrieved, contributing to the difficulties in peer relationships, including bullying and intimidation, which were evident in all the units and reflecting the wider conflict found in secure units between 'care cases' and 'criminal cases' (Howard League 1995).

The mix of boys and girls in units also aroused strong feelings, although more of the girls than the boys favoured single-gender units. This is understandable in that boys are almost always in the majority in mixed-gender units and the benefits of mixed-gender units identified by the young people emerged primarily as benefits for the boys. Furthermore, vulnerable girls admitted because they were at risk were exposed to the risk of further significant harm as a consequence of their accommodation with violent or sexually abusive young men. As young people were aware of the reason for admission of their peers, the difficulties faced by some girls were compounded by the anxiety and fear they felt of their male peers, from whom they felt they had no escape.

The control, high levels of surveillance and lack of privacy and confidentiality were experienced by many young people, but most notably the girls in this study, as oppressive and in some cases even persecutory. Furthermore, it emerged that the girls in mixed-gender units were subjected to a higher level of surveillance than the boys because of concerns about their sexual behaviour, which illustrated the sexual double standard and reinforced the stereotype of predatory, 'dangerous' girls. Different attitudes to girls and boys, both generally and specifically in relation to their sexuality, emerged as an important issue among the staff in the units which will be summarized later.

A related, important emergent theme concerned the difficulty young people experienced in having to confront their past experiences, memories and reason for admission without any respite or relief in an environment of control, which deprived them of their usual defence and coping mechanisms and largely failed to provide adequate support or therapeutic intervention. This was a problem for almost all the girls but fewer of the boys. More than a third of the young people had attempted suicide or deliberately self-harmed prior to their placement in secure accommodation, and it is arguable that they should have been in some form of health care rather than imprisoned in secure accommodation (National Children's Bureau 1995). Deliberate self-harm may occur because of distress at past experiences and is also a way of young people exercising some control. It emerged that staff in the secure units had little understanding of suicidal and self-harming behaviour and it was responded to by confinement and increasing levels of restraint which reinforced the young people's sense of worthlessness and self-destructive intent, and would be likely negatively to affect their prospects of longer-term recovery. In the units it seems that their needs and the underlying causes of the behaviour were generally unknown or ignored in the focus on control of the behaviour.

Therapeutic Interventions

All the young people in this study had substantial needs arising from their adverse childhood experiences and the complex reasons for their admission. A paradox which emerged was that while a function of secure accommodation was seen as to contain and control young people in order to provide treatment for those who are out of control or not receptive to help in the community, relatively little therapeutic intervention was actually provided. Control was the dominant philosophy in all the units, and the regimes were institution rather than treatment oriented. Less than a quarter of the young people had participated in a formal, specialist assessment prior to or during their placement and on the basis of their identified needs were receiving or had been referred for ongoing therapeutic intervention. Two in five had been provided with specialist services such as drug or alcohol counselling from a 'menu' of services and while some of these were appropriate and based on identified needs, others were not directly relevant to the young people. Almost a third of the young people had no specialist assessment and had been provided with no therapeutic intervention to help them with their difficulties. While more of the convicted offenders than the unconvicted offenders and non-offenders had been assessed and/or provided with specialist services, it is a matter of concern that little or no therapeutic work was provided for some of those who had committed violent and sexual offences.

Furthermore, it has been shown that therapeutic input does not in itself ensure good outcomes and that children need to explore their difficult experiences in a therapeutic relationship *and* with caregivers in their every day lives (Farmer and Pollock 1998). In all the units emphasis was placed on the role of the key/link workers in working with young people to address their individual problems and needs. However, substantial difficulties emerged in the relationships between young people and their keyworkers. Within the context of control, there was a high level of mistrust of staff for many of the young people. Moreover, it emerged that a minority of keyworkers had the expertise to work with young people themselves or had the information about their needs and histories which would have enabled them to understand the behaviours which were presented. Where young people were involved in therapeutic work with specialists, it appeared that staff did not generally have sufficient information or understanding about the work to be able to support young people and help them to integrate the benefits from their therapeutic work in their everyday lives. As a result, it emerged that when therapeutic work on painful issues increased the behaviour problems of some young people, the behaviour was punished by the imposition of sanctions.

Evaluations

The social workers and the young people evaluated their placements on the basis of whether they had benefited from the regime or the work with keyworkers or therapeutic interventions arranged by the unit or the social worker, and whether things had improved or were improving as a consequence of their stay in secure accommodation. The placements were evaluated as beneficial for only nine young people, that is less than one third. There were marked differences on the basis of gender, admission route and type of behaviour. The placements were assessed as beneficial for 42 per cent of offenders but for only 23 per cent of non-offenders and for 36 per cent of boys but for only 27 per cent of girls (18 per cent of whom were offenders). The differences on the basis of gender and admission route are even more stark in the social workers' assessments of the future prospects for young people, which were judged to be good or reasonably good for more than half of the boys but for only one in five of girls, all of whom had been admitted through the criminal justice routes. Although nearly a quarter of those admitted through the welfare route were thought to have benefited from their placement, the future prospects of all the young people admitted through the welfare route were assessed as poor or very poor. This might suggest that even where the placements had provided some benefits, they were thought to be short-term and unsustainable following the young people's release from the units. These findings add weight to the contention that secure accommodation primarily provides a custodial facility which is a preferable alternative to other forms of custody for offenders who are mainly boys, although an inconsistent pattern emerged in the extent to which their offences and their emotional problems were formally assessed and therapeutic intervention was provided. In this study, secure accommodation was thought to have had very limited effect in meeting the needs or changing the behaviour of most of those admitted through the welfare route and the majority of the girls.

Significant differences on the basis of gender and admission route also emerged in the young people's evaluations of their levels of self-esteem. Consistent with previous studies (Bolognini *et al.* 1996; Harter 1987) the self-esteem of the girls was lower than that of the boys and the mean scores of those admitted through the welfare route were lower than those admitted through the criminal justice routes. This is partly explained by the gender differences in admission route. However, differences also emerged between the two criminal justice routes with those convicted of serious offences rating themselves more highly than those on remand. It is of interest that the mean scores of the sexual offenders were the highest in the study while the lowest were of those who deliberately self-harmed and the prostitutes. These scores were largely consistent with the young people's descriptions of themselves. A sense of helplessness and powerlessness to make changes and to exercise any control in their lives emerged from the descriptions of some of those with the lowest scores, which, on the basis of their accounts, did not appear to have been improved by their placements in secure accommodation.

Short-Term Outcomes

What happens to young people following their release from secure accommodation provides some indication of the effectiveness of their placement in addressing their needs and helping them to improve their life chances. No formal follow-up of young people was undertaken but information was obtained about the short-term outcomes of nine, that is almost a third of those in the study. Two boys were convicted of offences, given custodial sentences and transferred to young offender institutions while six girls admitted through the welfare route were released and one ran away from the unit. Following release all these girls were returned to their previous care placements. Two of them stayed in their placements but resumed working as prostitutes (one of them taking other girls from the home with her), two of them returned to live with men who had sexually exploited them and two of them ran away and were thought to have resumed working as prostitutes. Five of these girls had one or more previous admissions to secure accommodation. Their placements were unsuccessful in meeting their needs or changing their behaviour and they returned to the same risks and problems from which they had been admitted. It emerged that these girls who ran away or were involved in prostitution were incarcerated in secure accommodation as a means of control because of a lack of alternative placements, the will to fund placements at a geographical distance from their networks and the absence of practice ideas about how to engage them and keep them safe. Furthermore, the placement experiences of most of them were negative, compounding their difficulties, reinforcing their determination not to return, if necessary by running away again, and undermining their trust and confidence in the ability of professionals to help them. The experiences of these vulnerable young women reinforce the pressing need for alternative, more effective approaches to be found.

The Social Workers

The social workers' perspectives illustrated the prevailing confusion in the profession about the role and function of secure accommodation. While they were in support of local authority secure accommodation, they opposed other forms of custody including the secure training centres. At the same time, they were very critical of many aspects of the legal and professional systems and the provision of secure accommodation. The social workers regarded secure accommodation as primarily a facility for offenders and concerns were expressed about the marginal position of those admitted for welfare reasons and the girls. Their predominant concern related to the inadequacy of community provision as an alternative to custody in secure accommodation for young people in the care and criminal justice systems.

Social workers in the criminal justice system favoured placement in secure accommodation in preference to other forms of custody. However, it emerged that the increase in provision had widened the net of those likely to be admitted and resulted in more young people being locked up, rather than a reduction in the number of those placed in other custodial provision. In a climate where incarceration is seen as the solution, the social workers found the courts to be increasingly dismissive and sceptical of community remand schemes and sentences and to favour custodial disposals, particularly where these could be served in secure accommodation. While social workers negotiated with the Home Office and the units for placements for young people for whom other forms of custody were considered harmful, the majority of them also expressed dissatisfaction with the provision in the secure units.

Social workers in the care system regarded secure accommodation as a 'last resort', which was hastened for many young people by the lack of alternative placements or effective policies and practice strategies to respond to their needs and behaviours. It emerged that secure accommodation was frequently used by social workers as a crisis response but that the opportunity it provided to find a long-term solution to young people's difficulties was often lost. In the absence of appropriate provision, the placements in secure accommodation were extended or young people returned to the same circumstances on release, which often jeopardized their chances of successful rehabilitation into the community and carried an increased risk of re-admission.

A number of broad themes emerged in the social workers' criticisms of secure accommodation. The first concerned the arbitrary nature of the admissions procedures in both the care and criminal justice systems. The juxtaposition of discretion with legal criteria, the lack of co-ordination of placements and information about units, and inconsistency in practice between units results in a placement lottery for young people in terms of the quality of care they receive and whether their needs are met. Some social workers also complained that the lack of information about the children resident in units prevented them from assessing the potential level of risk for new admissions. All the social workers regarded as urgent the need for more integrated and co-ordinated admissions systems. The second area of complaint concerned the isolation of secure accommodation from mainstream child-care services, the lack of communication between secure unit staff and other child care professionals and structural links with other agencies. Many social workers were ill-informed about the structures and systems within secure accommodation and there was confusion about the demarcation of roles and responsibilities. Difficulties between the secure unit staff and the social workers emerged, with only one in five reporting good working relationships. Widespread complaints concerned the lack of expertise of secure unit staff, their unwillingness to work co-operatively with field social workers and professionals from other agencies and the problems in arranging therapeutic interventions and specialist services for young people in the units.

This relates to the social workers' primary area of dissatisfaction, that is the regimes and the practice in the units. A recurring theme concerned the failure of secure units to provide more than containment and control. The behavioural systems in the units appeared to be poorly understood by the social workers, most of whom regarded them as largely irrelevant, and concern was expressed about the extent of the individual discretion and arbitrary use of sanctions in some units. Although a few social workers thought young people were benefiting educationally, the education provision was widely criticized as inadequate and operating in a 'vacuum', isolated from mainstream education. Major anxieties related to the inability of units to differentiate between young people and to provide the services to meet their individual needs and the marginalization of some young people with different needs arising from their race, religion or sexuality as well as gender. On this theme, it emerged that almost three quarters of the social workers favoured some degree of specialization between offenders and non-offenders and the separation of younger children from older teenagers within and between units. Although there was greater ambivalence about specialization on the basis of gender, the importance of choice was emphasized and concern expressed about the reduction in the number of places in single-gender units, particularly for girls.

Finally, although all the social workers said that they supported the development of secure accommodation, they questioned its cost effectiveness and argued for an equivalent investment in community therapeutic provision and alternatives to custody. Many of them complained that it presented itself as a specialist, even therapeutic resource which justified the high cost, but the reality was that what it primarily provided was containment.

Some striking contradictions emerged in social work practice which suggest there is professional self-delusion in relation to the use of secure accommodation. First, social workers widely used the threat of secure accommodation with young people 'at risk' in the hope that it would act as a deterrent, whilst simultaneously conceding that it had proved to be ineffective as a deterrent even with those young people who had previous admissions. Furthermore, many of them acknowledged that such threats and the experience of placement itself increased the likelihood of young people running away, to the extent that two social workers admitted they had taken young people to secure units without first informing them of the plan to detain them in secure accommodation. In the light of the new risks which face young people running away, illustrated by this study and others, it is extraordinary that social workers continue to implement a practice idea which they acknowledge *increases* rather than reduces the risk of running away, particularly as some alternative practice ideas have been proposed (Browne and Falshaw 1998; Stein *et al.* 1994).

Second, the conflict between care and custody emerged in the wide gap between the social workers' expectations that secure accommodation would provide a therapeutic environment, or at least some therapeutic intervention as part of the 'package of care', and the reality of the custodial, non-therapeutic environment it actually provided. It was the first experience of secure accommodation for six social workers and many of these said they had been disillusioned by the experience, and disappointed at the effect on the young people. However, it was surprising that some more experienced social workers who were critical of secure provision had nonetheless applied for the re-admission of young people in the full knowledge that their previous admissions had been ineffective in meeting their needs, and in some cases had compounded their problems. This might be partly explained by the lack of alternative provision or practice strategies and the personal pressure which the social workers frequently experienced, particularly where young people were in care. And yet the self-delusion and denial of the reality of the experience and effect of secure accommodation illustrates the ambivalent and confused relationship between social workers and secure accommodation. It emerged that placement in secure accommodation was sometimes more beneficial in providing respite for the social workers who were under pressure, than for the young people.

Third, many of the social workers complained about the punitive nature of the regimes and expressed concern about the risks which young people faced in the units from violence, bullying, including sexual intimidation and assault, criminalization and emotional pressures which resulted in an increase in self-harming behaviour. However, it seems that in practice they generally minimized or denied these everyday risks as well as the longer term risks of placement in secure accommodation (Bullock and Little 1991; Millham *et al.* 1978). In their applications for orders where the emphasis was on presenting evidence to meet the legal criteria, it seems that they rarely acknowledged or balanced these risks against the risks young people faced in the community, or presented information to enable the court to do so. This is important in view of the very limited discretion that can be exercised by the court if the criteria for an order are met.

The social workers acknowledged that most of the young people 'at risk' experienced their placements as punitive. Their evaluations reveal how few of them thought young people had benefited from their placements; some of them even thought they had been harmful and increased the risks to young people during their placement and those they would face following their release. There is a pressing need for social workers to develop and implement more effective policies and ways of helping and keeping safe, rather than punishing or ignoring, vulnerable young people such as those with prior histories of abuse who run away, deliberately self-harm and become involved in prostitution. The findings from this study suggest that in many of these cases, secure accommodation does not provide the required solution, and support the argument that social workers need to challenge and free themselves, as well as the young people, from the illusion that it does.

The Secure Units

The six secure units were different in terms of their size, gender make-up, geographical location and type of behavioural regime, although they were all institutionally-oriented with a primary focus on control and security. Substantial inconsistencies emerged in practice between staff in some units and between units, which appeared to be due in part to the lack of clarity or consensus about the purpose and ideology of secure accommodation. Secure units were isolated from one another, as well as from the wider child-care world, severely limiting the opportunities for the development of a shared purpose, greater levels of expertise and mutual support for those providing a 'secure service'. A lack of consensus emerged about this, with some staff advocating greater co-operation and cohesion and others identifying distinct advantages in their isolation from other secure units and from mainstream child care provision. At the same time, many staff were critical of the unrealistic expectations and lack of understanding among social workers and other professionals about the role of secure accommodation and the complexities and difficulties faced by staff working in a secure setting.

There was general agreement that the primary function of secure accommodation was control but confusion emerged about the purpose of the control, the balance to be achieved between care and control and whether and to what extent secure accommodation was used for punishment. Secure accommodation was seen essentially as provision for offenders, as an alternative to other forms of custody and some confusion was evident in some units about where young people fit who are admitted for welfare reasons and whether their needs could be met. Contradictions emerged between the 'official' line and descriptions of practice, and the muddled messages given to young people in some units reflected the confusion of the staff. Although all the units implemented behavioural regimes, the staff who participated in the study were not generally able to describe a theoretical model which informed their practice. The differences in culture which were evident were influenced by factors including the gender make-up of the groups of staff and young people. The nature of the culture in an institution is important and influences the approach to the residents and the morale of the staff. In several units tension resulted in a 'climate of crisis' and a heavy-handed approach by staff, and in those same units sickness rates among staff were described as high.

The debate about mixing offenders with non-offenders in units aroused substantial concerns, particularly about the risks of combining young people who had been abused with those convicted of violent or sexual offences, especially in the mixed-gender units. Some managers and staff suggested that units should not be expected to manage such risks and expressed a preference for more specialization within and between units to allow for more matching of the needs of young people with the expertise available. However, most said that the combination of young people was managed well and that this issue presented more of a dilemma philosophically than in practice. This appeared to be mainly because the similarities between the young people's histories and problems were emphasized and their differences, including the reason for admission and their different needs, were minimized or ignored.

The debate about specialization on the basis of gender aroused diverse views, heightened by the recent change from single-gender to mixed-gender provision experienced by some staff. While the staff in the single-gender units favoured specialization, the majority of those in mixed-gender units argued that they provided a more normal experience for young people. However, the cultures in the mixed-gender units were masculine and male-dominated and the girls were marginalized. Even those staff in favour of mixed-gender provision considered that some single-gender units were essential for some young people.

Some striking gender issues emerged. Girls were widely regarded as more difficult to work with than boys and most of the staff, apart from those in the girls' unit, said they would prefer to work just with boys. Many of the difficulties faced by staff in the mixed-gender units were attributed to the presence of girls, who were in the minority. It emerged that many male staff avoided engaging with the girls because they felt threatened by behaviour such as deliberate self-harm which they did not understand and did not know how to handle, and this increased the pressure on the female staff. However, they also expressed fear of girls they regarded as 'dangerous'. Powerful gender stereotypes operated in the units and a sexual double standard applied, with greater surveillance of the girls than the boys, even though many of the boys had also been sexually active and some of them had been convicted of sexual offences. Female staff who were required to protect their male colleagues from the girls, as well as the girls from predatory males, reinforced the stereotype of 'dangerous' girls and in so-doing they missed the opportunity to provide empowering role models for the girls.

There were also gender issues for the staff, as the women workers in the mixed-gender units were expected both to meet all the needs of the girls and to share the responsibility for work with the boys. While male members of staff were given choice about working with girls, it appears that the same degree of choice was generally not afforded to female workers, who were expected to tolerate intimidation and sexual harassment from the boys as well as male colleagues as an unavoidable part of the job. The unequal power relationships between male and female staff in the mixed-gender units, institutionalized through the maintenance of traditional gender roles, emerged as a significant issue of concern, not only personally for the individual members of staff but also in relation to the role models which were provided for the young people, many of whom experienced difficulties in relationships with opposite-gender peers.

The attitudes of staff to the difficulties in relationships between young people in the units appeared somewhat complacent and they generally minimized the incidence of bullying, intimidation and sexual harassment. This was both surprising as the young people identified it as a substantial problem (exacerbated by the mix of offenders and non-offenders) and worrying because bullying is influenced by the culture in a unit and can more frequently occur when an institution fails to take the issue seriously (Lane and Tattum 1989).

In theory, the units emphasized the focus on young people's individual needs, but it emerged that they experienced considerable difficulty putting this theory into practice, particularly when an individual's needs were different from the rest of the group. Managers and some staff referred to the use of individual care plans as evidence of their focus on the individual, which they suggested justified the accommodation together of young people with different needs and reasons for admission. However, a considerable gap emerged between the claims which were made for individual care plans and the reality of practice in the units. Care plans were rarely constructed in participation with the young people concerned, and (with the exception of the keyworkers) were not generally read by other members of staff, who were therefore unaware of the problems or the nature of any therapeutic work undertaken with young people, and in some units identical care plans were used for everyone. Furthermore, many staff complained that care plans could not be properly completed because of the lack of information provided by social workers about young people's needs and histories. In a context where they were working with young people on a group basis, many staff appeared to find individual care plans irrelevant. Similarly, all the units emphasized the importance of the allocated keyworker in addressing young people's individual needs and problems. However, differences emerged within and between units in the understanding staff had of the role and in their levels of expertise to undertake individual work with young people. This resulted in widespread inconsistencies in the nature, level and the quality of the work undertaken by keyworkers.

An important theme which emerged in this study, echoing findings from previous studies and from inquiries (for example, Levy and Kahan 1991; Waterhouse 2000), concerned the levels of experience and qualifications of staff and their access to supervision, consultation and training. The background experiences, training and qualifications of staff varied, and although no systematic data on this issue was collected it appeared that only a minority had training which would provide them with an understanding of the behaviour of many of the young people or equip them to undertake counselling work with them. Despite the complexity of young people's needs, consultancy for workers with specialists was generally not provided or available and supervision within the units appeared to be inconsistent and, particularly in one unit, provided only in response to problems rather than as part of staff development programmes aimed at achieving and maintaining best practice. This contributed to the inconsistencies which were evident in the practice in the units and in the culture, where some of the staff were 'doing their own thing'. Staff in one unit talked positively about the training opportunities available but staff in all the other units described the opportunities for training as almost non-existent, even though it emerged that two units had in fact provided a training programme for newly-constituted staff groups. Some staff reported that access to professional social work training was deliberately restricted because it was seen as an 'escape route' out of residential care. Furthermore, a negative attitude to training was evident in four units. A pattern emerged of staff recruited with or gaining qualifications and skills becoming disillusioned by the critical or negative attitudes of their managers and peers and leaving to work elsewhere.

None of the units undertook formal evaluation of the work with young people, or of the effectiveness of the placement in meeting their needs or alleviating their problems either during their stay or following their release, even though the importance of developing a culture of evaluation has been emphasized (Ward 1995). Staff in all the units experienced difficulty in describing how they evaluated the effectiveness of their work, which it seems was largely determined on the basis of the 'level' or rating young people achieved in the behaviour programmes and anecdotal, informal feedback from social workers. This lack of effective evaluation of the practice in the secure units results in problems for the units and the young people placed in them. The differences between units are significant and need to be more openly acknowledged. In theory, the substantial increase in the number of places in secure accommodation provides the opportunity for disaggregation and more 'matching' of the individual needs of young people with the units most suitable to meet them. But this can only be achieved if units are able to be clear about their purpose and method of working and evaluate their practice and the outcomes for children. This would enable them to identify the young people they could help and whose needs they could meet, and to be more selective in their admissions rather than taking all-comers in order to fill beds, with little attention to whether the unit has the expertise to alleviate their problems and improve their longer term life-chances.

Many issues of concern emerged about the practice in the secure units in this study which consisted of a cross section of single- and mixed-gender, older and newly developed units in different regions of England. Although they represent only one in five of the secure units in England, it is likely that many of the issues emerging in this study are generalizable to the other units in England and Wales which are operating within the same legal and professional systems and employing similar models of practice.

Some Implications for Policy and Planning

Admissions Policies

The admission of children to secure accommodation has been shown to be an arbitrary process in an incoherent system. As more beds become available, children are admitted who would otherwise have been accommodated in non-secure provision elsewhere and confusion is evident about why some children are admitted, and others with similar needs and problems are not. Following the government review, secure accommodation is included with prison system accommodation such as young offender institutions, as part of the 'secure estate' and the Youth Justice Board for England and Wales has responsibility for commissioning, purchasing and overseeing the placement of all young people on remand and under sentence. Although it is indisputable that secure accommodation provides a preferable alternative to other forms of custody, it has emerged that more young people whose needs could be met by non-custodial placements are remanded and sentenced to custody because of the increased availability of secure accommodation. The change in the criminal justice climate towards young offenders and the shortage of community schemes had resulted in an increase in custodial remands and sentences even before the full implementation in April 2000 of the additional custodial provisons contained in the Crime and Disorder Act 1998. The changes in legislation and policy establish secure accommodation unequivocally as a facility for offenders, operating within a criminal justice philosophy of control which has been shown to be irreconcilable with the welfare philosophy of treatment and care. In the discourse about this change, surprisingly little attention has been given to the implications for young people 'at risk', most of whom are girls, who will continue to be admitted through the welfare route and to occupy a minority, even marginalized position in secure accommodation.

WELFARE ADMISSIONS

As already discussed, running away and its associated risks, particularly of involvement in prostitution and drug and alcohol use is the behaviour most likely to result in admission through this route. The findings from this study, although limited, suggest that secure accommodation is ineffective as a deterrent and confirm earlier findings that it is largely ineffective in meeting young people's needs or changing behaviour such as running away and involvement in prostitution (for example Browne and Falshaw 1998; Jesson 1991, 1993). Secure accommodation did not provide the therapeutic intervention or quality of care that many young people needed and it compounded rather than alleviated the problems of some of them. Less than a quarter of those admitted through the welfare route were thought to have gained any benefit from their placement and the short-term and predicted longer-term outcomes for all of them were poor. Furthermore, almost two thirds of them had one or more previous placements, showing that multiple admissions may constitute a further risk factor which adds to young people's problems.

These findings add weight to the increasing argument for a review of the legal criteria and procedure for admission through the welfare route contained in the Children Act 1989 (Brogi and Bagley 1998; Butler and Hardy 1997; National Children's Bureau 1995). They provide further evidence to support the proposal that the absconding ground should be abandoned because the forced return and containment of young people who run away only results in them running away again. Alternative policies and practice ideas for those who run away are required and some have been developed but need more evaluation and wider implementation (for example Browne and Falshaw 1998; Stein *et al.* 1994). Furthermore, more judicial safeguards for young people in the system are needed, and at the very least when courts are considering the application to lock up young people, the plan for their release should also be considered.

Similarly, it has been argued (Hodgkin 1993; National Children's Bureau 1995) that those who deliberately self-harm should not be placed in an environment of control and restraint but should be in some more appropriate form of health care. The findings from this study endorse this view, particularly as they show that self-harming behaviour frequently *increases* in secure accommodation and that the majority of staff find the task of managing such behaviour threatening, with many reacting punitively because they lack the theoretical or emotional understanding of the behaviour to know how to respond.

Multi-Professional Approach

As already discussed, secure units are isolated from each other and from mainstream child-care provision in social services and they lack structural links with other agencies such as education- and health-providing services for children. This isolation has continued despite evidence of the importance of an integrated, multi-professional approach to work with young people in need and at risk (DH 1996; DH

1999b; Home Office *et al.* 1991). The relationships between the secure units and the social workers were variable but only a minority described them as positive, and a major issue of complaint on both sides related to the poor quality of information-sharing, due mainly it seems to a mutual mistrust. While the difficulties in relationships partly reflect wider historical differences between residential and field workers, the implications of their lack of co-operation were serious for the young people caught in the middle.

A significant problem to have emerged in this study is the inadequate provision in secure accommodation of therapeutic interventions and specialist services for young people. Many of them were emotionally disturbed and had suffered adverse experiences in their lives and some had committed violent or sexual offences which made them a potential danger to others. It is a matter of especial concern that the justification for admission for many of them was their need for therapeutic intervention, which was frequently not provided. The importance for children of joint work between social services and health has been stated (Audit Commission 1994) but it emerged that low priority was generally accorded by local authorities to the provision of therapeutic services which were regarded as 'extra' to the work in the unit. Attempts to obtain therapeutic services were hindered by the lack of clear policies and structural links between secure units, local authorities and other professional agencies which resulted in disputes about funding and timescales. Furthermore, only a minority of staff had access to consultation with specialists or to supervision or training that would provide them with the necessary expertise to undertake the complex therapeutic work required with young people. The focus on young people's 'delinquent' behaviour, rather than their adverse experiences and victimization, means that any change was likely to be short-term and unsustainable (Browne and Falshaw 1998).

The isolation of secure accommodation and the lack of joint professional planning had implications for young people at every stage in the process from admission to release, and jeopardized their chances of successful rehabilitation in the community. The findings from this study reinforce the need for joint planning for children in secure accommodation within and between social services, education and health authorities.

Different Needs

The backgrounds of offenders and non-offenders in custody have been shown to be similar, and the former should as readily be conceptualized as 'children in need' as the latter. However, instead of this, with the current prioritization of punitive and retributive policies, non-offenders in trouble who are accommodated with offenders in secure accommodation are also being criminalized and subject to regimes based on control rather than welfare. An important theme emerging from this study is the importance of the *differences* between young people, including the differences in the reasons for admission, which are being minimized. The differences, particularly the gender differences, are striking, and the backgrounds of the girls are substantially more disadvantaged than those of the boys. The girls were marginalized in the care and criminal justice systems, their needs had been neglected and their placements in secure accommodation were largely due to the lack of alternative practice ideas and community services to meet their needs. These findings support the calls for an increased commitment and higher priority to be given to the needs of girls which may be achieved through a separatist strategy to working with girls in trouble (Hudson, A. 1989).

Although the secure units claimed to meet young people's individual needs through the use of care plans, it emerged that everyone was treated in the same way within the regimes. Fundamental differences in reason for admission, emotional, physical and educational needs, gender, age, race, religion and sexual orientation were minimized or ignored in units which accommodated everyone together, and justified on the basis of the similarities in their background experiences and problems. In practice it emerged that the only way units *could* accommodate together such different young people was by emphasizing the similarities between them. This has been shown not only to be disadvantageous for young people but also to result in ideological confusion and conflict for the workers in the units, who realistically cannot create a viable regime for young people admitted for diverse reasons with such different needs (Millham *et al.* 1978). Legislation and guidance which claims to give priority to the best interests of children has done nothing to prevent this practice and the prevailing 'legislative confusion' (Smith and Gander 1996) urgently needs review and clarification.

The findings from this study reflect those from earlier studies (for example, Brogi and Bagley 1998; Bullock *et al.* 1998; Farmer and Pollock 1998) which stress the importance of differentiation between young people if their needs are to be met and their life-chances improved. Collectively they support the need for a review of the existing policies which reinforce the similarities between young people in the drive to achieve maximum flexibility, that is maximum occupation of beds. Evidence from this study and others of the importance of disaggregation leads to the conclusion that the offenders and non-offenders for whom secure accommodation is considered to be the best or only option generally ought to be accommodated separately in more treatment-oriented regimes which will meet their needs and help them achieve positive outcomes. Findings by Bullock *et al.* (1998) that where there is a greater overlap 'career route' is a stronger predictor of outcome than offender/non-offender provides an additional important dimension to be considered in the assessment process.

Evaluation of Outcomes

It is surprising that despite the increasing focus on evaluation of practice with children and young people and the measurement of outcomes (for example DH 1998a; Ward 1995), there are no formal systems in place by which units evaluate their practice, the outcomes for the young people following their release from secure accommodation or the cost effectiveness of what are very expensive facilities. How far the desired outcomes for young people leaving secure accommodation are realized is not known, and evidence is not available to enable a comparison of the outcomes for young people who have been placed in different units. With the expansion and increased use of secure accommodation, this information is essential to ensure the development of effective practice specifically with those young people whose needs *can* be met and life chances improved by placement in secure accommodation.

Conclusion

In the current social and political climate the trend toward locking up children in trouble seems set to continue. This study has shown that many of those who are deprived of their liberty in secure accommodation are locked up as a consequence of their difficult life experiences and because of the failure of legislation and the professional systems to meet their needs. For many such children, particularly the girls, local authority secure accommodation does not provide the required solution and for some it even makes matters worse. The development and implementation of alternative practice ideas and strategies is needed to help and support them more effectively, and to ensure that only those young people who need to be imprisoned because they present a danger to others are placed in secure accommodation. At the same time, it is important that practice in the units gives a higher priority to meeting the needs, rather than just controlling the behaviour, of the children 'in need' who are deprived of their liberty, and to ensuring that the 'cure' of secure accommodation is no worse than the 'disease' (Harris and Timms 1993).

The inside stories of the incarcerated young people in this study have made visible the diversity and complexity of the needs and problems of some of those labelled 'troubled' and 'troublesome' and the contexts which produced their behaviour and make it understandable. If such disadvantaged young people are to improve their life-chances to be able to look forward to a more positive future, they need effective help from legislative and professional systems which co-ordinate and differentiate in their policies and practice and do not treat all children in trouble who are labelled 'extreme' the same.

Appendix 1

Mean self-worth scores by domain and gender				
Domain	**Boys**	**Girls**	**Total**	**Difference**
Scholastic competence	2.6	2.8	2.7	0.2
Social acceptance	3.2	3.0	3.1	0.2
Athletic competence	3.1	2.3	2.7	0.8
Physical appearance	3.1	1.8	2.4	1.3
Job competence	3.0	2.6	2.8	0.4
Romantic appeal	2.8	2.4	2.6	0.4
Behavioural conduct	2.1	1.8	1.9	0.3
Close friendship	3.3	3.1	3.2	0.2
Global self-worth	2.9	1.9	2.4	1.0

Appendix 2

Mean self-worth scores by domain and legal status			
Domain	**s.25 Welfare**	**s.53 Convicted**	**s.23 Unconvicted**
Scholastic competence	2.6	2.5	2.9
Social acceptance	3.1	3.0	3.3
Athletic competence	2.4	2.9	2.9
Physical appearance	2.2	2.7	2.5
Job competence	2.5	3.0	3.6
Romantic appeal	2.7	2.3	2.4
Behavioural conduct	1.7	2.7	1.6
Close friendship	2.8	3.5	4
Global self-worth	2.1	2.9	2.3

Appendix 3

Global self-worth scores by behaviour group	
Behaviour group (n and gender)	**Global self-worth mean score**
Sexual offenders (n = 2, male)	3.5
Violent offenders (n = 8, 2 female, 6 male)	2.7
Non-violent offenders (n = 2, 1 female,1 male)	1.9
At risk (n = 8, 7 female,1 male)	2.2
Deliberate self-harm (n = 5, 4 female, 1 male)	1.8
Prostitutes (n = 4, female)	1.8

References

Abrahams, G. and Mungall, R. (1992) *Runaways: Exploding the Myths.* London: NCH Action for Children.

Ackland, J. (1982) *Girls in Care.* Aldershot: Gower.

Adams, R. (1986) 'Juvenile Justice and Children's and Young People's Rights'. In B. Franklin (ed) *The Rights of Children.* Oxford: Basil Blackwell.

Alanen, L. (1994) 'Gender and generation: Feminism and the "child question".' In Qvortrup, J. (ed) *Childhood Matters: Social theory, Practice and Politics.* Aldershot: Avebury.

Alderson, P. (1995) *Listening to Children. Children, Ethics and Social Research.* Barkingside: Barnardos.

Allan, G. (1991) 'Qualitative Research', G. Allan & C. Skinner (eds) *Handbook for Research Students in the Social Sciences.* London: Falmer Press.

Apter, T. (1990) *Altered Loves. Mothers and Daughters During Adolescence.* Hertfordshire: Harvester Wheatsheaf.

Archard, D. (1993) *Children: Rights and Childhood.* London: Routledge.

Audit Commission (1994) *Seen but Not Heard: Co-ordinating Community Child Health and Social Services for Children in Need.* London: HMSO.

Audit Commission (1996) *Misspent Youth: Young People and Crime.* London: Audit Commission.

Aymer, C. (1992) 'Women in Residential Work' in Langan, M. and Day, L. (eds) *Women, Oppression and Social Work.* London: Routledge.

Bailey, S. (1997) 'Sadistic and violent acts in the young.' *Child Psychology and Psychiatry Review, 2,* 3, 92–103.

Ball, C. (1992) 'Young Offenders and the Youth Court.' *Criminal Law Review,* 277–87.

Ball, C. (1995) 'Youth justice and the youth court – the end of a separate system?' *Child and Family Law Quarterly, 7,* 4, 196–206.

Barter, C. (1997) 'Who's to Blame: Conceptualising Institutional Abuse by Children.' *Early Child Development and Care, 133,* 101–14.

Barton, L. and Tomlinson, S. (eds) (1981) *Special Education: Policy, Practice and Social Issues.* London: Harper and Row.

Bates, P. (1994) 'Children in secure psychiatric units: Re K, W. and H – "Out of sight, out of mind"?' *Journal of Child Law, 6,* 3, 131–7.

Baum, V. and Walker, S. (1996) 'Locked Up in Care.' *Legal Action,* 6–7.

Bebbington, A. and Miles, J. (1989) 'The background of children who enter Local Authority Care.' *British Journal of Social Work, 19,* 5, 349–68.

Becker, H. (1963) *Outsiders: Studies on the Sociology of Deviance.* New York: Free Press.

Becker, H. (1967) 'Whose side are we on?' *Social Problems, 14,* 239–47.

Bell, S. E. (1988) 'Becoming a political woman: The reconstruction and interpretation of experience through stories.' In D. Todd and S. Fisher (eds) *Gender and Discourse: The power of talk.* Norwood NJ: Ablex.

Berk, R. and Adams, J. (1970) 'Establishing rapport with deviant groups.' *Social Problems, 18,* 102–17.

Berridge, D. (1985) *Children's Homes.* Oxford: Basil Blackwell.

Berridge, D. (1990) 'Residential schools for children with emotional and behavioural difficulties: new research project.' *Young Minds, 6,* 14.

Berridge, D. and Brodie, I. (1996) 'Residential Child Care in England and Wales: The Inquiries and After.' In M. Hill and J. Aldgate (eds) *Child Welfare Services.* London: Jessica Kingsley Publishers.

Berridge, D. and Brodie, I. (1998) *Children's Homes Revisited.* London: Jessica Kingsley Publishers.

Berridge, D. and Cleaver, H. (1987) *Foster Home Breakdown.* Oxford: Basil Blackwell.

Biehal, N., Clayden, J., Stein, M., Wade, J. (1992) *Prepared for Living? A Survey of Young People Leaving the Care of Three Local Authorities.* London: National Children's Bureau.

Biehal, N., Clayden, J., Stein, M., Wade, J. (1995) *Moving On: Young People and Leaving Care Schemes.* London: HMSO.

Block, J. and Robbins, R. (1993) 'A longitudinal study of consistency and change in self-esteem from early adolescence to early adulthood.' *Child Development, 64,* 903–23.

Blos, P. (1967) 'The Second Individuation Process of Adolescence' in A. Freud (ed) *The Psychoanalytic Study of the Child.* New York: International Universities Press.

Blumenthal, G. (1985) *Development of Secure Units in Child Care.* Aldershot: Gower Press.

Bolognini, M., Plancherel, P., Bettschart, W., Halfon, O. (1996) 'Self-esteem and mental health in early adolescence: development and gender differences.' *Journal of Adolescence, 19,* 233–45.

Boswell, G. (1996) *Young and Dangerous: The backgrounds and careers of section 53 offenders.* Aldershot: Avebury.

Bottoms, A. and Pratt, J. (1989) 'Intermediate Treatment for Girls in England and Wales.' In M. Cain (ed) *Growing Up Good.* London: Sage.

Bottoms, A. (1995) *Intensive Community Supervision of Young Offenders: Outcomes, Process and Cost.* Cambridge: University of Cambridge Institute of Criminology.

Bowker, L.H., Arbitell, M. and McFerron, J.R. (1988) 'On the relationship between wife beating and child abuse.' In Yllo, K. and Bograd, M. (eds) *Feminist Perspectives on Wife Abuse.* London: Sage.

Bowlby, J. (1951) *Child Care and the Growth of Love.* Harmondsworth: Penguin.

Brennan, T., Huizinga, D., Elliott, D. (1978) *The Social Psychology of Runaways.* Lexington. MA: Lexington Books.

Bridge Child Care Consultancy (1991) *Sukina: An Evaluation Report of the Circumstances Leading to her Death.* London: Bridge Child Care Consultancy.

Bristol Crisis Service for Women (1994) *Self Help for Self Injury.* Bristol: BCSW.

Brogi, L. and Bagley, C. (1998) 'Abusing Victims: Detention of Child Sexual Abuse Victims in Secure Accommodation.' *Child Abuse Review, 7,* 315–29.

Browne, K. and Falshaw, L. (1996) 'Factors Related to Bullying in Secure Accommodation.' *Child Abuse Review, 5,* 123–27.

Browne, K. and Falshaw, L. (1998) 'Street Children and Crime in the UK: A Case of Abuse and Neglect.' *Child Abuse Review, 7,* 241–53.

Bruner, J. (1990) *Acts of Meaning.* Cambridge, Mass.: Harvard University Press.

Bryman, A. and Cramer, D. (1990) *Qualitative Data Analysis for Social Scientists.* London: Routledge.

Bullock, R. (1996) 'Residential Child Care.' *Research Matters,* October 1996.

Bullock, R. (1997) '*What Does Research Tell Us?*' Conference Paper, Secure Care – Young People, October 1997.

Bullock, R., Hosie, K., Little, M. and Millham, S. (1990) 'Secure Accommodation for Very Difficult Adolescents: some recent research findings.' *Journal of Adolescence, 13,* 205–16.

Bullock, R. and Little, M. (1991) 'Secure Accommodation for Children.' *Highlight,* 103, National Children's Bureau/Barnardos.

Bullock, R. Little, M. and Millham, S. (1998) *Secure Treatment Outcomes: The care careers of very difficult adolescents.* Aldershot: Ashgate Publishing.

Burns, J. (1979) *The Self Concept. Theory, Measurement, Development and Behaviour* London: Longman.

Butler, J. and Hardy, S. (1997) 'Secure Accommodation and Welfare.' *Family Law 27,* 425–8.

Cain, M. (1989) *Growing Up Good: Policing the Behaviour of Girls in Europe.* London: Sage.

Calouste Gulbenkian Foundation (1993) *One Scandal too Many ... the case for comprehensive protection for children in all settings.* London: Calouste Gulbenkian Foundation.

Campbell, A. (1981) *Girl Delinquents.* Oxford: Basil Blackwell.

Caprara, G. and Rutter, M. (1995) 'Individual Development and Social Change.' In M. Rutter and D. Smith (eds), *Psychosocial Disorders in Young People: Time Trends and their Causes.* Chichester: Wiley.

Card, R. and Ward, R. (1994) *The Criminal Justice and Public Order Act 1994.* Bristol: Jordan and Sons.

Carlen, P. (1987) 'Out of Care into Custody.' In Carlen, P. and Worrell, A. (eds) *Gender, Crime and Justice.* Milton Keynes: Open University Press.

Carroll, R. (1998) 'Gangs put boot into old ideas of femininity.' *The Guardian,* 22 July 1998, 5.

Casburn, M. (1979) *Girls will be Girls: Sexism and Juvenile Justice in a London Borough.* London: Women's Research and Resources Centre.

Cawson, P. and Martell, M. (1979) *Children Referred to Closed Units.* DHSS Statistics and Research Division, Research Report No.5, London: HMSO.

Chesney-Lind, M. (1997) *The Female Offender.* London: Sage.

Child Care Act 1980. London: HMSO.

Children Act 1989. London: HMSO.

Children's Legal Centre (1982) *Locked Up in Care: A report on the use of secure accommodation for young people in care.* London: Children's Legal Centre.

Children's Legal Centre (1991) 'Young people, mental health and the law.' *Childright, 78,* 23–5.

Children's Legal Centre (1993) 'Mental health code revisited.' *Childright, 101,* 7–8.

Children's Legal Centre (1998) 'Control and Restraint of Pupils: Section 550A comes into force.' *Childright,* No.149, September 1998, p.8.

Children's Legal Centre (2000) 'Detention and Training Orders.' *Childright, 169,* 5.

Children's Rights Development Unit (1994) *UK Agenda for Children.* London: CRDU.

Children's Rights Office (1995) *Making the Convention Work for Children.* London: CRO.

Children and Young Persons Act 1933. London: HMSO.

Children and Young Persons Act 1969. London: HMSO.

Chodorow, N. (1978) *The reproduction of mothering: Psychoanalysis and the sociology of gender.* Berkeley: University of California Press.

Christopherson, J. (1989) 'Sex Rings.' In A. Hollows and H. Armstrong (eds) *Working with Sexually Abused Boys: An Introduction for Practitioners.* London: National Children's Bureau.

Cohen, R. and Hughes, M. (1994) *School's Out: The Family Perspective on School Exclusion.* London: FSU/Barnardos.

Cohen, S. and Taylor, L. (1981) *Psychological Survival.* Harmondsworth: Penguin.

Cohen, S. (1985) *Visions of Social Control.* Cambridge: Polity Press.

Coleman, J. and Hendry, L. (1980) *The Nature of Adolescence.* London: Routledge.

Coleman, J. (ed) (1987) *Working with Troubled Adolescents: A Handbook.* London: Academic Press.

Coleman, J. Lyon, J and Piper, R.(1995) *Teenage Suicide and Self-Harm,* Brighton Trust for the Study of Adolescence.

Collins, P.H. (1990) *Black Feminist Thought: Knowledge, Consciousness and the Politics of Empowerment.* London: Routledge.

Cooley, C. (1968) 'The Social Self: On the Meanings of "I".' In C. Gordon and K. Gergen (eds) *The Self in Social Interaction, Vol 1: Classic and Contemporary Perspectives.* London: John Wiley.

Commission for Racial Equality (1992) *Submission from the Commission for Racial Equality to the Royal Commission on Criminal Justice.* London: CRE.

Commission for Racial Equality (1996) *Exclusion from School: The Public Cost.* London: CRE.

Coppock, V. (1997) 'Mad, Bad or Misunderstood?' In P. Scraton (ed) *Crisis in Childhood.* London: UCL Press.

CRC (1995) Reports Submitted by States Parties under Article 44 of the Convention: UK and Northern Ireland Committee on the Rights of the Child.

Crime and Disorder Act 1998. London: HMSO.

Criminal Justice Act 1982. London: HMSO.

Criminal Justice Act 1988. London: HMSO.

Criminal Justice Act 1991. London: HMSO.

Criminal Justice Act 1993. London: HMSO.

Criminal Justice and Public Order Act 1994. London: HMSO.

Crowley, A.(1998) *A Criminal Waste: A Study of Child Offenders Eligible for Secure Training Centres.* London: The Children's Society.

Davis, H. and Bourhill, M. (1997) 'Crisis: The Demonization of Children and Young People.' In P. Scraton (ed) *Childhood in Crisis.* London: UCL Press.

Davis, N. (1978) 'Prostitution: identity, career and legal economic enterprise.' In J. Henlin and E. Sagarin (eds) *The Sociology of Sex.* New York: Schocken Books.

Dawson, R. and Stephens, R. (1991) *Family Proceedings Court: A Handbook on the Children Act 1989 and the Rules for Practitioners and Others.* Chichester: Barry Rose/Justice of the Peace.

Denzin, N. (1989) *Interpretive Interactionism.* Newbury Park: Sage.

Denzin, N. and Lincoln, Y. (1994) (eds) *Handbook of Qualitative Research.* London: Sage.

Department of Health (1989) *Secure Accommodation in Community Homes.* London: HMSO.

Department of Health (1991a) *Children in the Public Care: A Review of Residential Care.* London: HMSO.

Department of Heath (1991b) *Patterns and Outcomes in Child Placement.* London: HMSO.

Department of Health (1991c) *The Children Act 1989. Guidance and Regulations: Volume 4 Residential Care.* London: HMSO.

Department of Health (1991d) *The Children Act 1989. Guidance and Regulations: Volume 5 Independent Schools.* London: HMSO.

Department of Health (1992a) *Choosing With Care: The Report of the Committee of Inquiry into the Selection, Development and Management of Staff in Children's Homes.* London: HMSO.

Department of Health (1993) *Children Act Report 1992.* London: HMSO.

Department of Health (1996) *Focus on Teenagers.* London: HMSO.

Department of Health (1997a) *The Review of the Safeguards for Children Living Away from Home.* Sir William Utting, London: HMSO.

Department of Health (1997b) *Children Accommodated in Secure Units Year Ending 31 March 1997.* London: The Government Statistical Service.

Department of Health (1997c) *The Control of Children in the Public Care.* Circular C1(97)6, London: DOH.

Department of Health (1998) *Caring for Children Away from Home: Messages from Research.* Chichester: John Wiley.

Department of Health (1998a) *Quality Protects – Transforming Children's Services.* London: Department of Health.

Department of Health (1999) *Children looked after in England 1998/99.* London: The Governmental Statistical Services.

Department of Health (1999a) *Convention on the Rights of the Child: Second Report to the UN Committee on the Rights of the Child by the United Kingdom 1999.* London: Department of Health.

Department of Health (2000) *Children accommodated in Secure Units Year Ending 31 March 1999.* London: The Government Statistical Service.

Department of Health, Home Office, DfEE, National Assembly for Wales (2000a) *Safeguarding Children Involved in Prostitution.* London: Department of Health.

Department of Health and Social Security (1977) *Community Homes Design Guidance – A Small Secure Unit.* London: HMSO.

Department of Health and Social Security (1979) *Inspection of Secure Accommodation for Children and Young Persons: Guidance for Social Work Services* (Kahan Report). London: DHSS.

Department of Health and Social Security (1981) *Offending by Young People, a Survey of Trends.* London: DHSS.

Department of Health and Social Security (1981a) *Legal and Professional Aspects of the Use of Secure Accommodation for Children in Care.* Report of a DHSS Working Party. London: DHSS.

Donzelot, J. (1980) *The Policing of Families.* London: Hutchinson.

Dworkin, R. (1977) *Taking Rights Seriously.* London: Duckworth.

Eekelaar, J. (1992) 'The Importance of Thinking that Children have Rights.' *International Journal of Law and the Family,* 6, 221–35.

Ely, M., Anzul, M., Friedman, T., Gardner, D. and Steinmetz, A. (1991) *Doing Qualitative Research: Circles within Circles.* London: Falmer Press.

Ely, M., Vinz, R., Downing, M. and Anzul, M. (1997) *On Writing Qualitative Research.* London: Falmer Press.

Ennew, J. (1986) *The Sexual Exploitation of Children.* London: Polity Press.

Erikson, E. (1965) *Children and Society.* Harmondsworth: Penguin.

Farber, E. (1984) 'Violence in families of adolescent runaways.' *Child Abuse and Neglect, 8,* 3, 295–9.

Farmer, E. and Parker, R. (1991) *Trials and Tribulations: Returning Children from Local Authority Care to their Families.* London: HMSO.

Farmer, E. and Owen, M. (1995) *Child Protection Practice: Private Risks and Public Remedies.* London: HMSO.

Farmer, E. and Pollock, S. (1998) *Sexually Abused and Abusing Children in Substitute Care.* Chichester: John Wiley.

Farrington, D. and Morris, A. (1983) 'Sex sentencing and re-conviction.' *British Journal of Criminology, 23,* 3, 229–48.

Farson, R. (1974) *Birthrights.* London: Collier Macmillan.

Ferguson, L. (1978) 'The Competence and Freedom of Children to Make Choices Regarding Participation in Research: A Statement.' *Journal of Social Issues, 34,* 2, 114–21.

Finkelhor, D. and Browne, A. (1985) 'The traumatic impact of child sexual abuse: A conceptualisation.' *American Journal of Orthopsychiatry, 55,* 4, 530–41.

Finkelhor, D. (1983) 'Common Features of Family Abuse.' In D. Finkelhor, D. Gelles, G. Hotaling, M. Straus (eds) *The Dark Side of Families.* London: Sage.

Finkelhor, D. (1984) 'Boys as Victims: review of the evidence.' *Child Sexual Abuse: New Theory and Research.* New York: The Free Press.

Finkelhor, D. (1988) 'The Trauma of Child Sexual Abuse.' In G. Wyatt and G. Powell (eds) *Lasting Effects of Child Sexual Abuse.* London: Sage.

Flax, J. (1997) 'Postmodernism and Gender Relations in Feminist Theory.' In S. Kemp and J. Squires (eds) *Feminisms.* Oxford: Oxford University Press.

Fox Harding, L. (1991) *Perspectives in Child Care Policy.* London: Longman.

Franklin, B. (1986) *The Rights of Children.* Oxford: Basil Blackwell.

Franklin, B. (1995) 'The Case for Children's Rights: A Progress Report.' In B. Franklin (ed), *The Handbook of Children's Rights.* London: Routledge.

Freeman, M. (1983) *The Rights and Wrongs of Children.* London, Frances Pinter.

Freeman, M. (1993) 'Laws, Conventions and Rights.' *Children and Society,* 7, 1, 37–48.

Freeman, M. (1995) 'Children's rights in a land of rites.' In B. Franklin (ed) *The Handbook of Children's Rights.* London: Routledge.

Freud, S. (1905) *Three Essays on the Theory of Sexuality.* London: The Hogarth Press.

Frost, N. and Stein, M. (1989) *The Politics of Child Welfare: Inequality, Power and Change.* London: Harvester Wheatsheaf.

Gabbidon, P. (1994) *Young Women in Secure and Intensive Care: Margins to Mainstream., Proceedings of Day Conference, November 1994.*

Gabbidon, P. and Goldson, B. (1997) *Securing Best Practice. An induction manual for residential staff in secure accommodation.* London: National Children's Bureau.

Gelsthorpe, L. and Morris, A. (1990) *Feminist Perspectives in Criminology.* Buckingham: Open University Press.

Gelsthorpe, L. and Morris, A. (1994) 'Juvenile Justice 1945–1992.' In M. Maguire and R. Reiner (eds) *The Oxford Handbook of Criminology.* Oxford: Clarendon Press.

Gergen, K. and Gergen, M. (1983) 'Narratives of the Self.' In T. Sarbin and K. Scheibe (eds) *Studies in Social Identity.* New York: Praeger Publications.

Gergen, K. and Gergen, M. (1986) 'Narrative Form and the Construction of Psychological Science.' In T. Sarbin (ed) *Narrative Psychology: The Storied Nature of Human Conduct.* London: Praeger.

Gergen, K. and Gergen, M.(1988) 'Narrative and the Self as Relationship.' *Advances in Experimental Psychology, 21,* 17–27.

Giallombardo, R. (1974) *The Social World of Imprisoned Girls.* New York: John Wiley.

Gilligan, C. (1982/1993) *In a Different Voice: Psychological Theory and Women's Development.* Cambridge, Massachusetts: Harvard University Press.

Glaser, D. (1993) 'Sexual Abuse' in Brook, C. (ed) *The Practice of Medicine in Adolescence.* London: Edward Arnold.

Gluck, S. and Patai, D. (eds) *Women's Words: The Feminist Practice of Oral History.* London: Routledge.

Godsland, J. and Fielding, N. (1985) 'Young persons convicted of grave crimes: the 1933 CYPA (s53) and its effects on children's rights.' *Criminal Justice, 24,* 282–97.

Goffman, E. (1961) *Asylums: Essays on the Social Situation of Mental Patients and Other Inmates.* Harmondsworth: Penguin.

Goldson, B. (1995) *A Sense of Security.* London: National Children's Bureau.

Goldson, B. (1997a) 'Childhood: An Introduction to Historical and Theoretical Analyses.' In P. Scraton (ed), *Childhood in Crisis.* London: UCL Press.

Goldson, B. (1997b) 'Children in Trouble: State Responses to Juvenile Crime.' In P. Scraton (ed) *Childhood in Crisis.* London: UCL Press.

Goldson, B. (1997c) 'Children, Crime, Policy and Practice: Neither Justice Nor Welfare.' *Children and Society, 11,* 77–88.

Goldson, B. (1997d) 'Locked Out and Locked Up: State Policy and the Systemic Exclusion of Children "In Need" in England and Wales.' *Representing Children, 10,* 1, 44–55.

Gordon, L. (1988) *Heroes in Their Own Lives: The Politics and History of Family Violence, Boston 1880–1960.* London: Virago.

Graham, J. (1996) 'The Organisation and Functioning of Juvenile Justice.' In S. Asquith (ed) *Children and Young People in Conflict with the Law,* Research Highlights in Social Work 30. London: Jessica Kingsley.

Grimshaw, R. with Berridge, D. (1994) *Educating Disruptive Children.* London: National Children's Bureau.

Hagell, A. and Newburn, T. (1994) *Persistent Young Offenders.* London: Policy Studies Institute.

Hall, P., Land, H., Parker, R. and Webb, A. (1975) *Change, Choice and Conflict in Social Policy.* London: Heinemann.

Hamilton, C. (1997) 'Physical Restraint of Children: A New Sanction for Schools.' *Childright, 138,* 14–6.

Harding, S. (1987) 'Is there a Feminist Method?' In S. Harding (ed) *Feminism and Methodology.* Milton Keynes: Open University Press.

Harold, G. (1997) 'Children's Perceptions of Marital Conflict have Lasting Effects on their Development.' *Childright, 139,* 8–9

Harrington, R. and Dyer, E. (1993) 'Suicide and attempted suicide in adolescence', *Current Opinion in Psychiatry, 6,* 467–9.

Harris, R. and Timms, N. (1993) *Secure Accommodation in Child Care: Between Hospital and Prison or Thereabouts?* London: Routledge.

Harris, R. and Timms, N. (1993a) 'Children in Secure Accommodation.' *British Journal of Social Work, 23*, 597–612.

Hart, R. (1992) *Children's Participation: From Tokenism to Citizenship.* Innocenti Essays. Florence: UNICEF International Child Development Centre.

Harter, S. (1985) *The Self-Perception Profile for Children.* University of Denver.

Harter, S. (1987) 'The Determinants and Mediational Role of Global Self-Worth in Children.' In N. Eisenberg (ed) *Contemporary Topics in Developmental Psychology.* Chichester: John Wiley.

Harter, S. (1988) *The Self-Perception Profile for Adolescents.* University of Denver.

Hartmann, H. (1981) 'The family as the locus of gender, class and political struggle.' *Signs, 6*, 366–94.

Hartsock, N. (1983) 'The Feminist Standpoint: Developing the Ground for a Specifically Feminist Historical Materialism.' In S. Harding and M. Hintikka (eds) *Discovering Reality: Feminist Perspectives on Epistemology, Metaphysics, Methodology and Philosophy of Science.* Dordrecht: Reidel.

Hawton, K. (1993) 'Factors associated with suicide after parasuicide in young people.' *British Medical Journal, 306*, 6893, 1641–4.

Hearn, J. (1990) 'Child Abuse and Men's Violence.' In *Taking Child Abuse Seriously.* The Violence Against Children Study Group, London: Unwin Hyman.

Heidensohn, F. (1996) *Women and Crime.* London: Macmillan Press.

Hester, M. Kelly, L. and Radford, J. (1996) (eds) *Women, Violence and Male Power.* Buckingham: Open University Press.

Hester, M., Pearson, C. and Harwin, N. (2000) *Making an Impact – Children and Domestic Violence.* London: Jessica Kingsley Publishers.

Hewitt, P. (1986) Foreword in B. Franklin (ed) *The Rights of Children.* Oxford: Basil Blackwell.

Hill, M. and Tisdall, K. (1997) *Children and Society* London: Longman.

Hills, D., Child, C., Hills, J., Blackburn, V. and Tavistock Institute (1998) *Evaluating Residential Care Training: Towards qualified leadership.* London: John Wiley.

Hodgkin, R. (1993) 'Policy Review: Young Offenders.' *Children and Society, 7*, 3, 304–7.

Hodgson, D. (1996) *Young People's participation in Social Work Planning: A Resource Pack.* London: National Children's Bureau.

Hoghughi, M. (1978) *Troubled and Troublesome: Coping with Severely Disordered Children.* London: Burnett Books.

Holt, J. (1975) *Escape from Childhood.* Harmondsworth: Penguin.

Home Office (1959) *Report of the enquiry into the disturbances at Carlton School in August 1959.* Cmd 937.

Home Office (1960a) *Report of the Home Office Working Party on closed and other special facilities in Approved Schools.*

Home Office (1960b) *Report of the Home Office Working Party on Approved Schools. HH1014/60R.*

Home Office (1960c) *Report of the Committee on Children and Young Persons (Ingleby Committee).* Cmd 1191.

Home Office (1967) *Special Units in Approved Schools.* Home Office SU9.

Home Office (1968) *Report of a working party on severely disturbed children and young people in approved schools.* Home Office SDC 16.

Home Office (1970) *Revised report on Special Units in Approved Schools.* Home Office SU9.

Home Office, Department of Health, Department of Education and Science, Welsh Office (1991) *Working Together under the Children Act 1989.* London: HMSO.

Home Office (1997) *Tackling Youth Crime. A Consultation Paper.* London: Home Office.

Home Office (1999) *Guides to the Crime and Disorder Act.* Circular 9/99.

Hooper, C.A. (1992) *Mothers Surviving Child Sexual Abuse.* London: Routledge.

House of Commons Expenditure Committee (1975) *Report on the 1969 Children and Young Persons Act* London: HMSO.

Howard League (1995) *Banged Up, Beaten Up, Cutting Up: Report of the Howard League Commission of Inquiry into Violence in Penal Institutions for Young People.* London: Howard League.

Howard League (1997) *Lost Inside – the imprisonment of teenage girls.* London: Howard League.

Howard League (1998a) 'Imprisoning Children.' *HLM, 16,* 3, 5.

Howard League (1998b) 'Prisons within Prisons', *HLM, 16,* 4, 3.

Hudson, A. (1989) 'Troublesome Girls.' In M. Cain (ed) *Growing Up Good.* London: Sage.

Hudson, B. (1984) 'Adolescence and Femininity.' In A. McRobbie and M. Nava (eds) *Gender and Generation.* London: Macmillan.

Hudson, B. (1989) 'Justice or Welfare.' In M. Cain (ed) *Growing Up Good.* London: Sage.

Human Rights Act 1998. London: HMSO.

Hurrelman, K. (1989) 'The social world of adolescents: A sociological perspective.' In K. Hurrelman and U. Engel (eds) *The social world of adolescents: International perspectives.* New York: Walter de Gruyter.

Jaffa, T. and Deszery, A. (1989) 'Reasons for admission to an adolescent unit.' *Journal of Adolescence, 12,* 187–95.

Jaffe, P., Wolfe, D. and Wilson, S.K. (1990) *Children of Battered Women.* London: Sage.

James, W. (1968) 'The Self.' In C. Gordon and K. Gergen (eds) *The Self in Social Interaction, Vol 1: Classic and Contemporary Perspectives.* London: John Wiley.

James, A. and Prout, A. (1990) (eds) *Constructing and Reconstructing Childhood.* London: Falmer Press.

Jansz, J. (1995) 'Self-Narratives as Personal Structures of Meaning.' In A. Oosterwegel and R. Wicklund (eds) *The Self in European and North American Culture: Development and Processes.* Dordrect: Kluwer Academic Publishers.

Janus, M., McCormack, A., Wolbert-Burgess, A. and Hartman, C. (1987) *Adolescent Runaways: Causes and Consequences.* Lexington MA.: Lexington Books.

Jarvis, G. (1996) 'Provision of Secure Accommodation.' Paper given at NAGALRO Conference, *Secure Accommodation – Providing a Service for Children, 13 May 1996.*

Jesson, J. (1991) *Young Women in Care, The Social Services Care System and Juvenile Prostitution.* Birmingham: Birmingham Social Services Department.

Jesson, J. (1993) 'Understanding Adolescent Female Prostitution: A Literature Review.' *British Journal of Social Work, 23,* 517–30.

Jones, J. (1993) 'Child Abuse: Developing a Framework for Understanding Power Relationships in Practice.' In H. Ferguson, R. Gilligan and R. Torode (eds) *Surviving Childhood Adversity.* Dublin: Social Studies Press.

Jones, J. and Myers, J. (1997) 'The Future Detection and Prevention of Institutional Abuse: Giving Children a Chance to Participate in Research.' *Early Child Development and Care, 133,* 115–25.

Kahan, B. (1994) *Growing Up in Groups.* London: HMSO.

Katz, A. (1995) 'The Keys are on the Couch.' *The Guardian,* 29 November 1995, 7.

Kaufman, J. and Zigler, E. (1987) 'Do abused children become abusive parents?' *American Journal of Orthopsychiatry, 57*, 2, 186–92.

Kellmer Pringle, M. (1980) *The Needs of Children.* London: Hutchinson.

Kelly, B. (1992) *Children Inside: Rhetoric and Practice in a Locked Institution for Children.* London: Routledge.

Kelly, L. (1988) *Surviving Sexual Violence.* Cambridge: Polity Press.

Kelly, L. (1994) 'The Interconnectedness of Domestic Violence and Child Abuse: Challenges for Research, Policy and Practice.' In A. Mullender and R. Morley (eds) *Children Living with Domestic Violence.* London: Whiting and Birch.

Kelly, L. (1996) 'When Does the Speaking Profit Us? Reflections on the challenges of developing feminist perspectives on abuse and violence by women.' In M. Hester *et al.* (eds) *Women Violence and Male Power.* Buckingham: Open University Press.

Kelly, L., Burton, S. and Regan, L. (1994) 'Researching Women's Lives or Studying Women's Oppression? Reflections on What Constitutes Feminist Research.' In M. Maynard and J. Purvis (eds) *Researching Women's Lives from a Feminist Perspective.* London: Taylor and Francis.

Kelly, L., Regan, L. and Burton, S. (1991) *An Exploratory Study of the Prevalence of Sexual Abuse in a Sample of 16–21 Year Olds.* Child Abuse Studies Unit, North London Polytechnic.

Kemp, S. and Squires, J. (1997) (eds) *Feminisms.* Oxford: Oxford University Press.

Kennedy, H. (1995) Preface in *Banged Up, Beaten Up, Cutting Up.* London: Howard League.

Kerfoot, M. (1988) 'Deliberate self-poisoning in childhood and early adolescence.' *Journal of Child Psychology and Psychiatry, 29*, 335–43.

Kerfoot, M., Harrington, R. and Dyer, E. (1995) 'Brief home-based intervention with young suicide attempters and their families.' *Journal of Adolescence, 18*, 557–68.

Kerfoot, M. (1996) 'Suicide and Deliberate Self-harm in Children and Adolescents: A Research Update.' *Children and Society, 10*, 236–41.

King, R., Raynes, N. and Tizard, J. (1971) *Patterns of Residential Care.* London: Routledge and Kegan Paul.

Kirkwood, A. (1993) *The Leicestershire Inquiry.* Leicester: Leicestershire County Council.

Kitzinger, S. (1988) 'Defending Innocence: Ideologies of Childhood.' *Feminist Review 28*, 277–87.

Kohlberg, L. (1981) *The Philosophy of Moral Development.* San Francisco: Harper and Row.

Kurtz, Z., Thornes, R. and Wolkind, S. (1994) *Services for the Mental Health of Children and Young People in England: A National Review. London: Maudsley Hospital and South Thames (West) Regional Health Authority.*

Labour Party (1996) *Tackling Youth Crime: Reforming Youth Justice.* London.

Labov, W. (1982) 'Speech actions and reactions in personal narrative.' in D. Tannen (ed) *Analyzing Discourse: Text and Talk.* Washington DC: Georgetown University Press.

Lagree, J. and Lew Fai, P. (1989) 'Girls in street gangs in the suburbs of Paris.' In M. Cain (ed) *Growing Up Good: Policing the Behaviour of Girls in Europe.* London: Sage.

Land, H. (1978) 'Who cares for the family?' *Journal of Social Policy, 7*, 3, 257–84.

Lane, D.A. (1989) 'Violent histories: Bullying and Criminality.' In D.P. Tattum and D.A. Lane (eds) *Bullying in Schools.* Stoke on Trent: Trentham Books.

Lane, D.A. and Tattum, D.P. (1989) *Supporting the Child in School.* Milton Keynes: Open University Press.

Lansdown, G. (1995) 'Children's rights to participation: a critique.' In C. Cloke and M. Davies (eds) *Participation and Empowerment in Child Protection.* London: Pitman Publishing.

Lea, J. and Young, J. (1984) *What is to be done about Law and Order?* Harmondsworth: Penguin.

Lee, R. (1993) *Doing Research on Sensitive Topics.* London: Sage.

Lee, M. and O'Brien, R. (1995) *The Game's Up: Redefining Child Prostitution.* London: The Children's Society.

Lees, S. (1986) *Losing Out: Sexuality and Adolescent Girls.* London: Hutchinson.

Lees, S. (1989) 'Learning to Love.' In M. Cain (ed) *Growing Up Good.* London: Sage.

Lees, S. and Mellor, J. (1986) 'Girls' Rights.' In B. Franklin (ed) *The Rights of Children.* Oxford: Basil Blackwell.

Lemert, E. (1967) *Human Deviance, Social Problems and Social Control.* New York: Prentice Hall.

Levinson, D. (1989) *Family Violence in Cross-Cultural Perspective.* Newbury Park, California: Sage.

Levy, A. and Kahan, B. (1991) *The Pindown Experience and the Protection of Children.* Stafford: Staffordshire County Council.

Lindsay, M. (1991) 'Giving Children a Future.' Paper presented at The National Summit for Children, International Maritime Organisation, 30 January 1991.

Little, M. (1990) *Young Men in Prison.* Aldershot: Dartmouth.

Littlechild, B. (1997) 'Young offenders, punitive policies and the rights of children.' *Critical Social Policy, 17,* 4, 73–92.

Littlewood, P. (1987) *Care Appropriate to their Needs? Summary of a Sociological Study of a Secure Unit for Children in Scotland (1982–86).* Scottish Office Central Research Unit Papers, Social Work Services Group, Scottish Education Department, Edinburgh: Scottish Office.

Littlewood, P. (1996) 'Secure Units.' In Asquith, S. (ed) *Children and Young People in Conflict with the Law.* Research Highlights in Social Work 30. London: Jessica Kingsley.

Lloyd-Smith, M. and Davies, J. D. (1995) 'Issues in the Educational Careers of "Problem" Pupils.' In M. Lloyd-Smith and J. D. Davies (eds) *On the Margins: The Educational Experience of 'Problem' Pupils.* Stoke on Trent: Trentham Books.

Lunt, I. and Evans, J. (1994) 'Dilemmas in Special Educational Needs: some effects of local management of schools.' In S. Riddell and S. Brown (eds) *Special Educational Needs Policy in the 1990s: Warnock in the Market Place.* London: Routledge.

Lyon, T. (1996) *The Years of Decision 10–25: The Legal Framework.* Paper presented at the Centre for the Study of the Child, the Family and the Law, University of Liverpool, 10 December 1996.

Lyon, T. and Parton, N. (1995) 'Children's Rights and the Children Act 1989.' In B. Franklin (ed) *The Handbook of Children's Rights.* London: Routledge.

MacKinnon, C. (1987) 'Feminism, Marxism, Method and the State: Toward Feminist Jurisprudence.' In S. Harding (ed) *Feminism and Methodology.* Milton Keynes: Open University Press.

Madge, B. (1994) *Children in Residential Care in Europe.* London: National Children's Bureau.

Malek, M. (1991) *Psychiatric Admissions.* London: The Children's Society.

Malek, M. (1993) *Passing the Buck: Institutional responses to controlling children with difficult behaviour.* London: The Children's Society.

Martin, F. (1995) *Tales of Transition. Self Narrative and Direct Scribing in Exploring Care Leaving.* Unpublished Paper, University of Bristol.

Maslow, A. (1970) *Motivation and Personality.* New York: Harper and Row.

Masson, J. (1991) 'Adolescent Crises and Parental Power.' *Family Law 21,* 528–31.

Maynard, M. (1994) 'Methods, Practice and Epistemology: The Debate about Feminism and Research.' In M. Maynard and J. Purvis (eds) *Researching Women's Lives from a Feminist Perspective.* London: Taylor and Francis.

McCarthy, B. and Hagan, J. (1992) 'Mean Streets: the theoretical significance of situational delinquency among homeless youths.' *American Journal of Sociology, 98,* 597–627.

McClelland, D. (1975) *Power: The Inner Experience.* New York: Irvington.

McNay, M. (1992) 'Social Work and Power Relations: Towards a Framework for an Integrated Practice.' In M. Langan and L. Day (eds) *Women, Oppression and Social Work.* London: Routledge.

Miller, J.B. (1976) *Toward a New Psychology of Women.* Boston: Beacon Press.

Millett, K. (1971) *The prostitution papers: A candid dialogue.* New York: Avon.

Millham, S., Bullock, R. and Hosie, K. (1978) *Locking Up Children: Secure Provisions within the Child Care System.* Farnborough: Saxon House.

Millham, S., Bullock, R., Hosie, K. and Haak, M. (1986) *Lost in Care.* Aldershot: Gower Publications.

Minister, K. (1991) 'A Feminist Frame for the Oral History Interview.' In S. Gluck and D. Patai (eds) *Women's Words: The Feminist Practice of Oral History.* London: Routledge.

Mishler, E. (1986) 'The Analysis of Interview-Narratives.' In T. Sarbin (ed) *Narrative Psychology: The Storied Nature of Human Conduct.* London: Praeger.

Moore, S. (1993) 'Not Angels, Not Devils, Just Kids.' *The Guardian,* 26 March, p.11.

Morley, R. and Mullender, A. (1994) 'Domestic Violence and Children: What do we know from research?' In A. Mullender and R. Morley (eds) *Children Living with Domestic Violence.* London: Whiting & Birch.

Morris, A. (1976) *Crime, Criminology and Social Policy: Essays in Honour of Sir Leon Radzinowitz.* London: Heinemann.

Morris, A. and Giller, H. (1983) *Providing Criminal Justice for Children.* London: Edward Arnold.

Morris, A., Giller, H., Szwed, E. and Geach, H. (1980) *Justice for Children.* London: Macmillan Press.

Morrison, B. (1994) 'Little Angels, Little Devils.' *Without Walls,* Channel 4, 10 May 1994.

Morrison, T. (1990) 'The Emotional Effects of Child Protection Work on the Worker.' *Practice, 4,* 4, 253–71.

Mullender, A. and Morley, R. (eds) (1994) *Children Living with Domestic Violence: Putting Men's Abuse of Women on the Child Care Agenda.* London: Whiting and Birch.

Mullender, A. (1995) *Domestic Violence and Social Care: A report on two conferences held by the Social Services Inspectorate.* London: SSI/DOH.

NACRO (1992) *Young Black People in Custody: A Review of Home Office Prison Statistics.* London: NACRO.

Nasjleti, M. (1980) 'Suffering in Silence: the male incest victim.' *Child Welfare, 59,* 269–75.

National Children's Bureau (1995) *Safe to Let Out? The current and future use of secure accommodation for children and young people.* London: National Children's Bureau.

National Children's Bureau (1998) *Locked Up or Looked After.* Conference 9 June 1998.

Nava, M. (1984) 'Youth Service Provision, Social Order and the Question of Girls.' In A. McRobbie and M. Nava (eds) *Gender and Generation.* London: Macmillan.

NCCL (1991) *A People's Charter: Liberty's Bill of Rights.* London: Liberty.

NCH Action for Children (1992) *The Report of the Committee of Enquiry into Children and Young People who Sexually Abuse other Children.* London: NCH.

NCH Action for Children (1994) *Messages from Children.* London: NCH.

Nelson, K. (1989) *Narratives from the crib.* Cambridge, MA: Harvard University Press.

Newell, P. (1991) *The UN Convention and Children's Rights in the UK.* National London: Children's Bureau.

Newell, P. (1995) 'Respecting Children's Right to Physical Integrity.' In B. Franklin (ed) *The Handbook of Children's Rights.* London: Routledge.

Newman, C. (1989) *Young Runaways: findings from Britain's first safe house.* London: The Children's Society.

NHS Advisory Service (1986) *Bridges Over Troubled Waters: A Report on Services for Disturbed Adolescents.* London: HMSO.

NHS Advisory Service (1995) *Child and Adolescent Mental Health Services: Together We Stand. The Commissioning, Role and Management of Child and Adolescent Mental Health Services.* London: HMSO.

Nunno, M. and Motz, J. (1988) 'The Development of an Effective Response to the Abuse of Children in out of Home Care.' *Child Abuse and Neglect, 12,* 521–28.

Ogden, J. (1991) 'Care or Control?' *Social Work Today,* July 1991, 9.

O'Hara, M. (1994) 'Child Deaths in Contexts of Domestic Violence: Implications for Professional Practice.' In A. Mullender and R. Morley (eds) *Children Living with Domestic Violence.* London: Whiting and Birch.

Ollendorff, R. (1972) 'The Rights of Adolescents.' In P. Adams *et al.* (eds) *Children's Rights.* London: Panther.

O'Malley, P. and Bachman, J. (1983) 'Self-esteem: Change and stability between ages 13 and 23.' *Developmental Psychology, 19,* 257–68.

O'Neill, M. (1996) 'Researching Prostitution and Violence: towards a feminist praxis.' In M. Hester *et al.* (eds) *Women, Violence and Male Power.* Buckingham: Open University Press.

O'Neill, M., Goode, N. and Hopkins, K. (1995) 'Juvenile Prostitution – the experience of young women in residential care.' *Childright, 113,* 14–6.

O'Neill, O. (1992) 'Children's Rights and Children's Lives.' *International Journal of Law and the Family, 6,* 24–42.

Packman, J., Randall, J. and Jacques, N. (1986) *Who Needs Care?* Oxford: Blackwell.

Packman, J. and Hall, C. (1995) *Draft Report on the Implementation of Section 20 of the Children Act 1989.* Report to the Department of Health.

Parker, R., Ward, H., Jackson, S. and Wedge, P. (eds) (1991) *Looking After Children. Assessing Outcomes in Child Care.* London: HMSO.

Parker, R. (1996) Conference Paper, *Focus on Teenagers,* 11 April 1996, York.

Parkin, W. and Green, L. (1997) 'Cultures of Abuse within Residential Child Care.' *Early Child Development and Care, 133,* 73–86.

Pearson, G. (1993) 'Youth Crime and Moral Decline: Permissiveness and tradition.' *The Magistrate,* December 1993.

Penal Affairs Consortium (1994) *The Case Against the Secure Training Centre.* London: Penal Affairs Consortium.

Personal Narratives Group (1989) *Interpreting Women's Lives: Feminist Theory and Personal Narratives.* Indianapolis: Indiana University Press.

Petrie, C. (1986) *The Nowhere Girls.* Aldershot: Gower Publications.

Piaget, J. (1932) *The Moral Judgement of the Child.* New York: The Free Press.

Pitts, J. (1988) *The Politics of Juvenile Crime.* London: Sage.

Pitts, J. (1990) *Working with Young Offenders.* London: Macmillan.

Platt, A. (1969) *The Child Savers.* Chicago: University of Chicago Press.

Pratt, J. (1985) 'Juvenile Justice, social work and social control: The need for positive thinking.' *British Journal of Social Work, 15,* 1–24.

Pritchard, C. (1995) *Suicide – The Ultimate Rejection?* Buckingham: Open University Press.

Punishment, Custody and the Community. Green Paper (1988). Parliamentary Paper, Cm 424. London: HMSO.

Pynoos, R. S. and Nader, K. (1993) 'Issues in the Treatment of Posttraumatic Stress in Children and Adolescents.' In J.P. Wilson and B. Raphael (eds) *International Handbook of Traumatic Stress Syndromes.* New York: Plenum Press.

Quinton, D. and Rutter, M. (1988) *Parenting Breakdown: The Making and Breaking of Inter-generational Links.* Aldershot: Avebury.

Qvortrup, J. (1994) 'Childhood Matters: An Introduction.' In J. Qvortrup, M. Bardy, G. Sgritta, H. Wintersberger (eds) *Childhood Matters.* Aldershot: Avebury.

Radford, L. (1995) 'How Does Domestic Violence Affect Families?' In *Domestic Violence and Social Care.* A Report on Two Conferences held by Social Services Inspectorate, London: Department of Health.

Radford, L. and Stanko, E. (1996) 'Violence against Women and Children: the contradictions of crime control under patriarchy.' In M. Hester *et al.* (eds) *Women, Violence and Male Power.* Buckingham, Open University Press.

Re R [1991] 4 A11 ER 177.

Re W [1992] 4 A11 ER 627.

Re K, W and H [1993] 1 FLR 854.

Re S [1993] 2 FLR 437.

Re M [1995] 1 FLR 418.

Reder, P., Lucey, C. and Fredman, G. (1991) 'The challenge of deliberate self-harm by young adolescents.' *Journal of Adolescence, 14,* 135–48.

Rees, G. (1993) *Hidden Truths: Young People's Experience of Running Away.* London: The Children's Society.

Richardson, L (1994) 'Writing: A Method of Inquiry.' In N. Denzin and Y. Lincoln (eds) *Handbook of Qualitative Research.* London: Sage.

Riessman, C. (1993) *Narrative Analysis.* London: Sage.

Riggs, S., Alario, A. J. and Mchorney, C. (1990) 'Health risk behaviours and attempted suicide in adolescents who report prior maltreatment.' *The Journal of Pediatrics, 116,* 815–21.

Ringwalt, C., Greene, J. and Robertson, M. (1998) 'Familial backgrounds and risk behaviours of youth with thrownaway experiences.' *Journal of Adolescence,* 21, 241–52.

Roberts, A. (1982) 'Adolescent Runaways in Suburbia – a new typology', *Adolescence, 17,* 6, 387–96.

Rosenbaum, M. and Newell, P. (1991) *Taking Children Seriously: A Proposal for a Children's Rights Commissioner.* London: Calouste Gulbenkian Foundation.

Rosenberg, M. (1979) *Conceiving the Self.* New York: Basic Books Inc.

Rosenwald, G. and Ochberg, R. (1992) (eds) 'Life Stories, Cultural Politics and Self-Understanding.' In *Storied Lives: The Cultural Politics of Self-Understanding.* New Haven: Yale University Press.

Rowe, J., Hundleby, M. and Garnett, L. (1989) *Child Care Now.* London: BAAF.

Royal College of Physicians of London: (1992) *Smoking and the Young. A report of a working party of the Royal College of Physicians.* London: Royal College of Physicians.

Russell, F. (1998) 'Crime and Disorder Bill – sentencing of young offenders.' *Criminal Justice, 16,* 1.

Rutherford, A. (1986) *Growing Out of Crime: Society and Young People in Trouble.* Harmondsworth: Penguin.

Rutherford, A. (1997) 'Labour's first sixty days.' *Criminal Justice, 15,* 3, 4–5.

Rutter, M. (1972) *Maternal Deprivation Reassessed.* Harmondsworth: Penguin.

Rutter, M. (1992) 'Adolescence as a Transition Period: Continuities and Discontinuities in Conduct Disorder.' *Journal of Adolescent Health, 13,* 451–60.

Rutter, M. (1993) 'Resilience: Some Conceptual Considerations.' *Journal of Adolescent Health, 14,* 626–31.

Rutter, M. and Giller, H. (1983) *Juvenile Delinquency.* Harmondsworth: Penguin.

Rutter, M. and Smith, D. (1995) 'Towards Causal Explanations of Time Trends.' In *Psychosocial Disorders in Young People: Time Trends and their Causes.* Chichester: John Wiley.

Sarbin, T. (1986) 'The Narrative as a Root Metaphor for Psychology.' In T. Sarbin (ed) *Narrative Psychology: The Storied Nature of Human Conduct.* New York: Praeger.

Scraton, P. (1997) 'Whose Childhood? What Crisis?' In P. Scraton (ed) *Childhood in Crisis.* London: UCL Press.

Seng, M. (1989) 'Child sexual abuse and adolescent prostitution: a comparative analysis.' *Adolescence, 24,* 665–75.

Sereny, G. (1984) *The Invisible Children.* London: Pan Books.

Shaw, I. and Butler, I. (1998) 'Understanding Young People and Prostitution: A Foundation for Practice?' *British Journal of Social Work, 28,* 177–96.

Sieber, J. and Stanley, B. (1988) 'Professional Dimensions of Socially Sensitive Research.' *American Psychologist, 43,* 49–55.

Simmons, R., Rosenberg, G. and Rosenberg, M. (1973) 'Disturbance in the Self-Image at Adolescence.' *American Sociological Review, 38,* 553–68.

Sinclair, R., Garnett, L. and Berridge, D. (1995) *Social Work and Assessments with Adolescents.* London: National Children's Bureau.

Sinclair, R. (1996) 'Children and Young People's Participation in Decision-Making: The Legal Framework in Social Services and Education.' In M. Hill and J. Aldgate (eds) *Child Welfare Services.* London: Jessica Kingsley Publishers.

Sinclair, I. and Gibbs, I. (1996) *Quality of Care in Children's Homes.* York: The University of York SWRDU.

Sinclair, I. and Gibbs, I. (1998) *Children's Homes: A Study in Diversity.* Chichester: John Wiley.

Skeggs, B. (1994) 'Situating the Production of Feminist Ethnography.' In M. Maynard and J. Purvis (eds) *Researching Women's Lives from a Feminist Perspective.* London: Taylor and Francis.

Smart, C. (1976) *Women, Crime and Criminology: A Feminist Critique.* London: Routledge and Kegan Paul.

Smith, C. and Gander, P. (1996) 'Secure accommodation under the Children Act 1989: legislative confusion and social ambivalence.' *Journal of Social Welfare and Family Law, 18,* 173–87.

Sone, K. (1994) 'The Forgotten Children.' *Community Care, 1014,* 22–3.

Spender, D. (1980) *Man Made Language.* London: Routledge.

SSI/OFSTED (1995) *The Education of Children who are being Looked After by Local Authorities.* London: HMSO.

Stainton-Rogers, R. and Stainton-Rogers, W. (1992) *Stories of Childhood.* London: Harvester Wheatsheaf.

Stanley, B. and Sieber, J. (1992) (eds) *Social Research on Children and Adolescents: Ethical Issues.* London: Sage.

Stanley, L. and Wise, S. (1993) *Breaking Out Again: Feminist Ontology and Epistemology.* London: Routledge.

Stark, E. and Flitcraft, A. (1985) 'Woman battering, child abuse and social heredity: what is the relationship?' In N. Johnson (ed) *Marital Violence.* London: Routledge and Kegan Paul.

Stark, E. and Flitcraft, A. (1988) 'Women and Children at risk: a feminist perspective on child abuse.' *International Journal of Health Services, 18,* 1, 97–118.

Stein, M. and Carey, K. (1986) *Leaving Care.* Oxford: Basil Blackwell.

Stein, M. (1993) 'The Uses and Abuses of Residential Care.' In H. Ferguson *et al.* (eds) *Surviving Childhood Adversity.* Dublin: Social Studies Press.

Stein, M., Rees, G. and Frost, N. (1994) *Running the Risk.* London: The Children's Society.

Steinberg, D. Galhenage, D. and Robinson, S. (1981) 'Two Years Referrals to a Regional Adolescent Unit: Some implications for psychiatric services.' *Social Science and Medicine, 15,* 113–22.

Stephens, M. and Hopper, B.(1992) *The New Role of the Guardian ad litem in Secure Accommodation Applications.* NAGALRO.

Stewart, G. and Tutt, N. (1987) *Children in Custody.* London: Avebury.

Stone, L. (1974) *The Massacre of the Innocents. New York.*

Street, D., Vinter, R. D. and Perrow, C. (1966) *Organisation for Treatment: A Comparative Study of Institutions for Delinquents.* New York: Free Press.

Sykes, W. and Hoinville, G. (1985) *Telephone Interviewing on a Survey of Social Attitudes: A comparison with Face-to-Face Procedures.* London: Social and Community Planning Research.

Taylor, L., Lacey, R. and Bracken, D. (1980) *In Whose Best Interests?* London: The Cobden Trust/MIND.

The Children (Secure Accommodation) Regulations 1991.

The Children's Society (1993) *A False Sense of Security: The case against locking up more children.* London: The Children's Society.

The Children's Society (1997) 'Child Prostitutes – Victims or Criminals?' In *Childright, 141,* 15–16.

Thoburn, J. (ed) (1992) *Participation in Practice – Involving Families in Child Protection.* Norwich: University of East Anglia.

Thorpe, D., Smith, D., Green, C. and Paley, J.(1980) *Out of Care.* London: Allen and Unwin.

Timms, J. (1995) *Children's Representation: A Practitioner's Guide.* London: Sweet & Maxwell.

Tong, L., Oates, K. and McDowell, M. (1987) 'Personality development following sexual abuse.' *Child Abuse and Neglect, 11*, 371–83.

Townley, M. (1992) 'Statutory Agency Responses to Anti-Social Behaviour in Adolescence.' Unpublished MA Thesis quoted in M. Malek (1991) *Passing the Buck.* London: The Children's Society.

Triseliotis, J., Borland, M., Hill, M. and Lambert, L. (1995) *Teenagers and the Social Work Services.* London: HMSO.

United Nations (1989) *United Nations Convention on the Rights of the Child.* New York: United Nations.

Utting, W. (1997) *People Like Us, The Report of the Review of the Safeguards for Children Living Away from Home.* London: HMSO.

van Welzenis, I. (1997) 'The self-concept of societally vulnerable and delinquent boys within the context of school and leisure activities.' *Journal of Adolescence, 20*, 695–705.

Wade, J., Biehal, N., Clayden, J. and Stein, M. (1998) *Going Missing: Young People Absent from Care.* Chichester: John Wiley.

Waldby, V. (1989) 'Theoretical Perspectives on Father–Daughter Incest.' In E. Driver and A. Droisen (eds) *Child Sexual Abuse: Feminist Perspectives.* London: Macmillan.

Walgrave, L. (1996) 'Restorative Juvenile Justice.' In Asquith, S. (ed) *Children and Young People in Conflict with the Law.* Research Highlights in Social Work 30. London: Jessica Kingsley.

Walton, R. (1976) 'The Best Interests of the Child.' *British Journal of Social Work, 6*, 4, 307–13.

Ward, H. (ed) (1995) *Looking After Children: Research into Practice.* London: HMSO.

Waterhouse (2000) *Lost in Care – The report of the tribunal of inquiry into the abuse of children in care in the former County Council Areas of Gwynedd and Clwyd since 1974.* London: DOH.

Weisberg, D. K. (1985) *Children of the Night: A Study of Adolescent Prostitution.* Lexington MA: Lexington Books.

Westcott, H. and Clement, M. (1992) *NSPCC Experience of Child Abuse in Residential Care and Educational Placements: Results of a Survey.* London: NSPCC.

Whitbeck, L. B. and Simons, R. L. (1990) 'Life on the streets – the victimisation of runaways and homeless adolescents.' *Youth and Society, 22*, 1, 108–25.

Widom, C. A. (1989) 'Does violence beget violence? A critical examination of the literature.' *Psychological Bulletin, 106*, 1, 3–28.

Wilson, J. P. and Raphael, B. (eds) (1993) *International Handbook of Traumatic Stress Syndromes.* New York, Plenum Press.

Wilson, P. (1994) quoted in K. Sone (1994) 'The Forgotten Children.' *Community Care, 1014*, 22–3.

Wolfe, D. A., Zak, L., Wilson, S. and Jaffe, P. (1986) 'Child witnesses to violence between parents: critical issues in behavioural and social adjustment.' *Journal of Abnormal Child Psychology, 14*, 1, 95–104.

Wylie, R. (1979) *The Self-Concept. Vol.2.* Lincoln: University of Nebraska Press.

Subject Index

Author Index